Decline of the New

Decline
of the
New

Irving Howe

HARCOURT, BRACE
& WORLD, INC.
NEW YORK

First edition

Library of Congress Catalog
Card Number: 78-95876

Printed in the United States of
America

The following chapters first appeared in *A World More Attractive,* copyright © 1963 by Irving Howe, and are reprinted by permission of the publisher, Horizon Press: "Céline: The Sod Beneath the Skin"; "The Fiction of Antiutopia"; "Edith Wharton: Convention and the Demons of Modernism"; "The Quest for Moral Style"; "Black Boys and Native Sons"; "Mass Society and Postmodern Fiction"; and "T. E. Lawrence: The Problem of Heroism." "Henry James and the American Scene" first appeared as an Introduction to *The American Scene* by Henry James, copyright © 1967, and is reprinted by permission of Horizon Press. "Silone: A Luminous Example" first appeared in *Politics and the Novel,* copyright © 1957, and is reprinted by permission of Horizon Press. "I. B. Singer: False Messiahs and Modern Sensibility" first appeared as the Introduction to *The Selected Short Stories of Isaac Bashevis Singer,* copyright © 1966 by Random House, Inc., and is reprinted by permission of the publisher. "Dreiser: The Springs of Desire" first appeared as an Afterword to Theodore Dreiser's *An American Tragedy,* copyright © 1964 by Irving Howe, and is reprinted by permission of New American Library. Some of the essays in this book first appeared in *Commentary, Denver Quarterly, Harper's,* and *New Republic.*

*For Arien
and Lisa
and Jonathan*

Preface

The essays in this book, composed over the last dozen or so years, keep returning to one complex of questions. They keep returning, first, to the idea that the literary culture of the last century has been dominated by a style of perception and composition—a style at once iconoclastic, difficult, and experimental —that we call modernist and, second, to the possibility that we are now living through the unsettling moral and intellectual consequences of the breakup of modernist culture, or the decline of the new. These essays have of course been written on various occasions and for a range of publications; but the unity I perceive in them, perhaps the only kind that matters, is that of a deep and recurrent interest, a steady return to a problem allowing one neither rest nor evasion nor easy answers.

Reading through this collection has persuaded me that I have been drawn to certain authors and topics not merely because of their interest—and one wants to insist that authors like T. E. Lawrence and Isaac Bashevis Singer must be read first of all for their intrinsic interest—but also because all of them touch upon this central problem of literary modernism. Some of the essays deal with it directly, some at a tangent, and one or two brush past it; but for good or bad it has been at the center of my critical work in recent years. That is why I would venture the claim that this book, while a collection of essays, each distinct and self-sufficient, is not simply a miscellany; it represents a series of approaches to the same problem.

To show as many facets as I can of this recurrent concern, I have included seven essays that first appeared in an earlier book, *A World More Attractive*. The remaining ten pieces, including the two central essays in the book, "The Culture of Modernism" and "The New York Intellectuals," appear here for the first time in book form, some of them enlarged and revised.

Finally, pleasure in giving thanks. First, to the Center for Advanced Studies in the Behavioral Sciences which in 1968–69 received me with characteristic generosity and enabled me to finish a book that may not exactly look like behavioral science. Second, to the City University of New York and especially to Provost Mina Rees, Dean Ruth Weintraub, and Professor Helaine Newstead, all of whom have been repeatedly helpful. Third, to Ben Raeburn for being a constant friend and ideal reader.

As for the persons mentioned in the dedication, they have made life interesting.

I.H.

Contents

PART IV

Part I

The Culture
of Modernism

In the past hundred years we have had a special kind of literature. We call it modern and distinguish it from the merely contemporary; for where the contemporary refers to time, the modern refers to sensibility and style, and where the contemporary is a term of neutral reference, the modern is a term of critical placement and judgment. Modernist literature seems now to be coming to an end, though we can by no means be certain and there are critics who would argue that, given the nature of our society, it cannot come to an end.

The kind of literature called modern is almost always difficult: that is a sign of its modernity. To the established guardians of culture, the modern writer seems willfully inaccessible. He works with unfamiliar forms; he chooses subjects that disturb the audience and threaten its most cherished sentiments; he provokes traditionalist critics to such epithets as "unwholesome," "coterie," and "decadent."

The modern must be defined in terms of what it is not, the embodiment of a tacit polemic, an inclusive negative. Modern writers find that they begin to work at a moment when the culture is marked by a prevalent style of perception and feeling; and their modernity consists in a revolt against this prevalent style, an unyielding rage against the official order. But modernism does not establish a prevalent style of its own; or if it does, it denies itself, thereby ceasing to be modern. This presents it

3

with a dilemma which in principle may be beyond solution but in practice leads to formal inventiveness and resourceful dialectic—*the dilemma that modernism must always struggle but never quite triumph, and then, after a time, must struggle in order not to triumph.* Modernism need never come to an end, or at least we do not really know, as yet, how it can or will reach its end. The history of previous literary periods is relevant but probably not decisive here, since modernism, despite the precursors one can find in the past, is, I think, a novelty in the development of Western culture. What we do know, however, is that modernism can fall upon days of exhaustion, when it appears to be marking time and waiting for new avenues of release.

At certain points in the development of a culture, usually points of dismay and restlessness, writers find themselves affronting their audience, and not from decision or whim but from some deep moral and psychological necessity. Such writers may not even be aware that they are challenging crucial assumptions of their day, yet their impact is revolutionary; and once this is recognized by sympathetic critics and a coterie audience, the avant-garde has begun to emerge as a self-conscious and combative group. Paul Goodman writes:

. . . there are these works that are indignantly rejected, and called not genuine art, but insult, outrage, *blague, fumiste,* willfully incomprehensible. . . . And what is puzzling is not that they are isolated pieces, but some artists persistently produce such pieces and there are schools of such "not genuine" artists. What are they doing? In this case, the feeling of the audience is sound—it is always sound—there *is* insult, willful incomprehensibility, experiment; and yet the judgment of the audience is wrong—it is often wrong—for this is a genuine art.

Why does this clash arise? Because the modern writer can no longer accept the claims of the world. If he tries to acquiesce in the norms of the audience, he finds himself depressed and outraged. The usual morality seems counterfeit; taste, a genteel indulgence; tradition, a wearisome fetter. It becomes a condition of being a writer that he rebel, not merely and sometimes not at all against received opinions, but against the received ways of doing the writer's work.

A modernist culture soon learns to respect, even to cherish, signs of its division. It sees doubt as a form of health. It hunts for ethical norms through underground journeys, experiments with sensation, and a mocking suspension of accredited values. Upon the passport of the Wisdom of The Ages, it stamps in bold red letters: *Not Transferable*. It cultivates, in Thomas Mann's phrase, "a sympathy for the abyss." It strips man of his systems of belief and his ideal claims, and then proposes the one uniquely modern style of salvation: a salvation by, of, and for the self. In modernist culture, the object perceived seems always on the verge of being swallowed up by the perceiving agent, and the act of perception in danger of being exalted to the substance of reality. *I see, therefore I am.*

Subjectivity becomes the typical condition of the modernist outlook. In its early stages, when it does not trouble to disguise its filial dependence on the Romantic poets, modernism declares itself as an inflation of the self, a transcendental and orgiastic aggrandizement of matter and event in behalf of personal vitality. In the middle stages, the self begins to recoil from externality and now devotes itself, almost as if it were the world's body, to a minute examination of its own inner dynamics: freedom, compulsion, caprice. In the late stages, there occurs an emptying-out of the self, a revulsion from the wearisomeness of both individuality and psychological gain. (Three writers as exemplars of these stages: Walt Whitman, Virginia Woolf, Samuel Beckett.) Modernism thereby keeps approaching—sometimes even penetrating—the limits of solipsism, the view expressed by the German poet Gottfried Benn when he writes that "there is no outer reality, there is only human consciousness, constantly building, modifying, rebuilding new worlds out of its own creativity."

Behind this extreme subjectivity lurks an equally extreme sense of historical impasse, the assumption that something about the experience of our age is unique, a catastrophe without precedent. The German novelist Herman Hesse speaks about "a whole generation caught . . . between two ages, two modes of life, with the consequence that it loses all power to understand itself and has no standards, no security, no simple acquiescence." Above all, no simple acquiescence.

Whether all of this is true matters not nearly so much as the fact that modernist writers, artists, and composers—Joyce, Kafka, Picasso, Schoenberg—have apparently worked on the tacit assumption that it is true. The modernist sensibility posits a blockage, if not an end, of history: an apocalyptic cul-de-sac in which both teleological ends and secular progress are called into question, perhaps become obsolete. Man is mired—take your choice—in the mass, in the machine, in the city, in his loss of faith, in the hopelessness of a life without anterior intention or terminal value. By this late date, these disasters seem in our imaginations to have merged into one.

"On or about December 1910 human nature changed." Through this vivid hyperbole Virginia Woolf meant to suggest that there is a frightening discontinuity between the traditional past and the shaken present; that the line of history has been bent, perhaps broken. Modernist literature goes on the tacit assumption that human nature has indeed changed, probably a few decades before the date given by Mrs. Woolf; or, as Stephen Spender remarks, the circumstances under which we live, forever being transformed by nature, have been so radically altered that people feel human nature to have changed and thereby behave as though it has. Commenting on this notion, Spender makes a keen distinction between the "Voltairean I" of earlier writers and the "I" of the moderns:

The "Voltairean I" of Shaw, Wells, and others acts upon events. The "modern I" of Rimbaud, Joyce, Proust, Eliot's *Prufrock* is acted upon by events. . . . The faith of the Voltairean egoists is that they will direct the powers of the surrounding world from evil into better courses through the exercise of the superior social or cultural intelligence of the creative genius, the writer-prophet. The faith of the moderns is that by allowing their sensibility to be acted upon by the modern experience as suffering, they will produce, partly as the result of unconscious processes, and partly through the exercise of critical consciousness, the idioms and forms of new art.

The consequences are extreme: a break-up of the traditional unity and continuity of Western culture, so that the decorums of its past no longer count for very much in determining its present, and a loosening of those ties which, in one or another way, had bound it to the institutions of society over the centuries. Not their enemies but art and literature themselves assault the *Gemütlichkeit* of autonomy, the classical balances and resolutions of the past. Culture now goes to war against itself, partly in order to salvage its purpose, and the result is that it can no longer present itself with a Goethean serenity and wholeness. At one extreme there is a violent disparagement of culture (the late Rimbaud) and at the other, a quasi-religion of culture (the late Joyce).

In much modernist literature one finds a bitter impatience with the whole apparatus of cognition and the limiting assumption of rationality. Mind comes to be seen as an enemy of vital human powers. Culture becomes disenchanted with itself, sick over its endless refinements. There is a hunger to break past the bourgeois proprieties and self-containment of culture, toward a form of absolute personal speech, a literature deprived of ceremony and stripped to revelation. In the work of Thomas Mann both what is rejected and what is desired are put forward with a high, ironic consciousness: the abandoned ceremony and the corrosive revelation.

But if a major impulse in modernist literature is a choking nausea before the idea of culture, there is another in which the writer takes upon himself the enormous ambition not to remake the world (by now seen as hopelessly recalcitrant and alien) but to reinvent the terms of reality. I have already quoted Benn's remark that "there is only human consciousness . . . rebuilding new worlds out of its own creativity." In a similar vein, the painter Klee once said that his wish was "not to reflect the visible, but to make visible." And Baudelaire: "The whole visible universe is but an array of images and signs to which the imagination gives a place and relative value. . . ." At first glance this sentence reads like something an English Romantic poet or even a good American transcendentalist might have said; but in the context of Baudelaire's experience as a poet—that experience which led him to say that "every man who refuses to accept the conditions of life sells his soul"—it comes to seem the report of a desire to create or perhaps re-create the very grounds of being, through a permanent revolution of sensibility and style, by means of which art could raise itself to the level of white or (more likely) black magic. Rationalistic psychoanalysts might regard this ambition as a substitute gratification of the most desperate kind, a grandiose mask for inner weakness; but for the great figures of literary modernism it is the very essence of their task.

We approach here another dilemma of modernism, which may also in principle be beyond solution but in practice leads to great inventiveness—that, as the Marxist critic Georg Lukacs has charged, *modernism despairs of human history, abandons the idea of a linear historical development, falls back upon notions of a universal* condition humaine *or a rhythm of eternal recurrence, yet within its own realm is committed to ceaseless change, turmoil, and re-creation.* The more history comes to be seen as static (in the Marxist idiom: a locomotive stalled in the inescapable present), the more art must take on relentless dynamism.

It is quite as if Hegel's "cunning of reason," so long a motor force of progress in history, were now expelled from its exalted place and locked into the exile of culture. E. H. Gombrich speaks of philosophies of historical progress as containing "a strong Aristotelian ingredient in so far as they look upon progress as an evolution of inherent potentialities which will follow a predictable course and must reach a predictable summit." Modernist versions of literature do assign to themselves "an evolution of inherent potentialities": there is always the hope for still another breakthrough, always the necessary and prepared-for dialectical leap into still another innovation, always an immanent if by no means gradual progress in the life of a form. But these do not follow "a predictable course" nor can they reach a predictable summit—since the very idea of "predictable" or the very goal of "summit" violates the modernist faith in surprise, its belief in an endless spiral of revolution in sensibility and style. And if history is indeed stalled in the sluggishness of the mass and the imperiousness of the machine, then culture must all the more serve as the agent of a life-enhancing turmoil. The figure chosen to embody and advance this turmoil, remarks Gombrich, is the Genius, an early individualistic precursor of the avant-garde creative hero. If there is then "a conflict between a genius and his public," declares Hegel in a sentence which thousands of critics, writers, and publicists will echo through the years, "it must be the public that is to blame . . . the only obligation the artist can have is to follow truth and his genius." Close to Romantic theory at this point, modernism soon ceases to believe in the availability of "truth" or the disclosures of "genius." The dynamism to which it then commits itself—and here it breaks sharply from the Romantics—becomes not merely an absolute without end but sometimes an absolute without discernible ends.

It is a dynamism of asking and of learning not to reply. The past was devoted to answers, the modern period confines itself to questions. And after a certain point, the essence of modernism reveals itself in the persuasion that the true question, the one alone worth asking, cannot and need not be answered; it need only be asked over and over again, forever in new ways. It is as if the very idea of a question were redefined: no longer an interrogation but now a mode of axiomatic description. We present ourselves, we establish our authenticity by the questions we allow to torment us. "All of Dostoevsky's heroes question themselves as to the meaning of life," writes Albert Camus. "In this they are modern: they do not fear ridicule. What distinguishes modern sensibility from classical sensibility is that the latter thrives on moral problems and the former on metaphysical problems."

A modernist culture is committed to the view that the human lot is inescapably problematic. Problems, to be sure, have been noticed at all times, but in a modernist culture the problematic as a style of existence and inquiry becomes imperious: men learn to find comfort in their wounds. Nietzsche says: "Truth has never yet hung on the arm of an absolute." The problematic is adhered to, not merely because we live in a time of uncertainty when traditional beliefs and absolute standards, having long disintegrated, give way to the makeshifts of relativism—that is by now an old, old story. The problematic is adhered to because it comes to be considered good, proper, and even beautiful that men should live in discomfort. Again Nietzsche:

Objection, evasion, joyous distrust, and love of irony are signs of health; everything absolute belongs to pathology.

One consequence of this devotion to the problematic, not always a happy consequence, is that in modernist literature there is a turn from truth to sincerity, from the search for objective law to a desire for authentic response. The first involves an effort to apprehend the nature of the universe, and can lead to metaphysics, suicide, revolution, and God; the second involves an effort to discover our demons within, and makes no claim upon the world other than the right to publicize the aggressions of candor. Sincerity becomes the last-ditch defense for men without belief, and in its name absolutes can be toppled, morality dispersed, and intellectual systems dissolved. But a special kind of sincerity: where for the Romantics it was often taken to be a rapid motion into truth, breaking past the cumbersomeness of intellect, now for the modernists it becomes a virtue in itself, regardless of whether it can lead to truth or whether truth can be found. Sincerity of feeling and exact faithfulness of language —which often means a language of fragments, violence, and exasperation—become a ruling passion. In the terrible freedom it allows the modernist writer, sincerity shatters the hypocrisies of bourgeois order; in the lawlessness of its abandonment, it can become a force of darkness and brutality.

Disdainful of certainties, disengaged from the eternal or any of its surrogates, fixated upon the minute particulars of subjective experience, the modernist writer regards settled assumptions as a mask of death, and literature as an agent of metaphysical revolt. Restlessness becomes the sign of sentience, anxiety the premise of responsibility, peace the flag of surrender—and the typewriter a Promethean rock. Nowhere is this mode of sensibility expressed with greater energy than in an essay by the Russian novelist of the 1920's, Eugene Zamiatin. "On Literature, Revolution and Entropy" is a decisive manifesto of the modernist outlook:

Revolution is everywhere and in all things: it is infinite, there is no final revolution, no end to the sequence of integers. Social revolution is only one in the infinite sequence of integers. The law of revolution is not a social law, it is immeasurably greater, it is a cosmic, universal law.

Red, fiery, death-dealing is the law of revolution; but that death is the birth of a new life, of a new star. And cold, blue as ice, as the icy interplanetary infinities is the law of entropy. The flame turns from fiery red to an even, warm pink, no longer death-dealing but comfort-producing; the sun ages and becomes a planet suitable for highways, shops, beds, prostitutes, prisons: that is a law. And in order to make the planet young again, we must set it afire, we must thrust it off the smooth highway of evolution: that is a law.

Explosions are not comfortable things. That is why the exploders, the heretics, are quite rightly annihilated by fire, by axes, and by words. Heretics are harmful to everybody today, to every evolution, to the difficult, slow, useful, so very useful, constructive process of coral reef building; imprudently and foolishly they leap into today from tomorrow. They are romantics. It was right and proper that in 1797

Babeuf had his head cut off; he had leaped into 1797, skipping one hundred fifty years. It is equally right and proper that heretical literature that is damaging to dogma, should also have its head cut off: such literature is harmful.

But harmful literature is more useful than useful literature: because it is antientropic, militates against calcification, sclerosis, encrustedness, moss, peace. It is utopian and ridiculous. Like Babeuf, in 1797, it is right one hundred and fifty years later . . .

The old, slow, soporific descriptions are no more. The order of the day is laconicism—but every word must be supercharged, high voltage. Into one second must be compressed what formerly went into a sixty-second minute. Syntax becomes elliptical, volatile; complicated pyramids of periods are dismantled and broken down into the single stones of independent clauses. In swift movement the canonical, the habitual eludes the eye: hence the unusual, often strange symbolism and choice of words. The image is sharp, synthetic, it contains only the one basic trait which one has time to seize upon from a moving automobile. . . . A new form is not intelligible to all; for many it is difficult. Maybe. The habitual, the banal is of course simpler, pleasanter, more comfortable. Euclid's world is very simple and Einstein's world is very difficult; nevertheless it is now impossible to return to Euclid's. No revolution, no heresy is comfortable and easy. Because it is a leap, it is a rupture, of the smooth evolutionary curve, and a rupture is a wound, a pain. But it is a necessary wound: most people suffer from hereditary sleeping sickness, and those who are sick with this ailment must not be allowed to sleep, or they will go to their last sleep, the sleep of death.

Zamiatin's rhetoric is unmistakably that of modernism, and to follow the thrust of his language is to notice that he provides tacit answers to major questions: To what extent can modernism be seen as a phenomenon arising autonomously, as the outcome of an inner logic, from the development of earlier, especially Romantic literature? And to what extent can it be located in terms of a need or drive toward formal experimentation?

Zamiatin suggests, rightly I think, that the seeds of modernism lie deep within the Romantic movement, but that revolutionary events in the outer world must occur before those seeds will sprout. The Romantic poets break loose from classical-Christian tradition, but they do not surrender the wish to discover in the universe a network of spiritual meaning which, however precariously, can enclose their selves. They anticipate the preoccupation with psychic inwardness, by means of which the self is transformed into a cosmic center and mover, as this will later become characteristic of certain modernist writers; but they still seek to relate this preoccupation to transcendent values, if not sources, in the external world. For them the universe is still alert, still the active transmitter of spiritual signs. Northrop Frye remarks that "the sense of identity with a larger power of creative energy meets us everywhere in Romantic culture," and Marius Bewley writes still more pointedly that "the desire to merge oneself with what is greater than oneself—to take one's place in a divine or transcendental continuum of some kind—is indeed the central fact for most of the Romantics." Now it seems to me impossible that anyone should use language of this sort in describing the work of Joyce or Kafka, Baudelaire or Brecht. For the modernist writer the universe is a speechless presence, neither hospitable nor hostile; and after a time he does not agonize, as did nineteenth-century writers like Hardy, over the dispossession of man in the cosmic scheme. He takes that dispossession for granted, and turns his anxieties inward, toward the dispossession of meaning from inner life. Whatever spiritual signs he hears come from within his own imaginative resources and are accepted pragmatically as psychic events. Romanticism is, among other things, an effort to maintain a transcendent perspective precisely as or because the transcendent objects of worship are being withdrawn; modernism follows upon the breakdown of this effort. To be sure, a writer like Yeats tries in his famous "system" to take his "place in a divine or transcendental continuum of some kind," but the attempt remains eccentric, willful and by no means organically related to his poetry. In his great lyrics Yeats shares in the premises and aftereffects of modernism.

To the second question posed in Zamiatin's manifesto he gives an answer that again seems correct. Formal experiment may frequently be a consequence or corollary of modernism, but its presence is not a sufficient condition for seeing a writer or a work as modernist. This view of the matter suggests that the crucial factor in the style of a literary movement or period is some sort of inspiriting "vision," a new way of looking upon the world and man's existence; and while such a "vision" will no doubt lead to radical innovations in form and language, there is by no means a direct or invariable correlation. In certain works of literature, such as Thomas Mann's stories, formal experiment is virtually absent, yet the spirit of modernism is extremely powerful, as a force of both liberation and mischief. Correspondingly, there are works in which the outer mannerisms and traits of the modern are faithfully echoed or mimicked but the animating spirit has disappeared—is that not a useful shorthand for describing much of the "advanced" writing of the years after World War II? A writer imbued with the spirit of modernism will be predisposed toward experiment, if only because he needs to make visibly dramatic his break from tradition; yet it is an error—and an error indulging the modernist desire to exempt itself from historical inquiry—to suppose that where one sees the tokens of experiment there must also be the vision of the modern.

At this point my essay will have to suffer from what Henry James called "a misplaced middle." For I should now speak at some length about the intellectual sources of modernism, especially those major figures in the nineteenth century who initiated the "psychology of exposure"—that corrosion of appearance in order to break into reality—by means of which old certainties were dislodged and new ones discouraged. I should speak about J. G. Frazer and his proclamation of archetypal rhythms in human life, above all, the rhythm of the birth and rebirth of the gods, and the role of myth as a means for re-establishing ties with primal sources of experience in a world deadened by "functional rationality." I should speak about Marx, who unmasked— they were all unmaskers, the great figures of the nineteenth century—Marx, who unmasked the fetishism of a commodity-producing society which "resolves personal worth into exchange value" and in which the worker's deed "becomes an alien power . . . forcing him to develop some specialized dexterity at the cost of a world of productive impulses." I should speak about Freud, who focuses upon the irremediable conflict between nature and culture, from which there followed the notorious "discontents of civilization," the damage done the life of instinct. I should speak, above all, about Nietzsche, a writer whose gnomic and paradoxical style embodies the very qualities of modernist sensibility. But there is no space, and perhaps by now these are familiar matters. Let me, therefore, turn to a few topics concerning the formal or distinctly literary attributes of modernism.

The historical development of a literature cannot, for any length of time, be hermetic. It has a history of its own, in which there occurs a constant transformation of forms, styles, and kinds of sensibility. At a given moment writers command an awareness of those past achievements which seem likely to serve them as models to draw upon or deviate from. That, surely, is part of what we mean by tradition: the shared assumptions among contemporaries as to which formal and thematic possibilities of the literary past are "available" to them. Tradition makes itself felt; tradition is steadily remade. Whether they know it or not, writers establish their personal line of vision through a tacit acceptance or rejection of preceding masters. In that sense, then, one can speak of a literary history that is autonomous, with its own continuities of decorum, its own dialectic of strife, its own interweaving of traditions.

Yet over an extended period this literary history must be affected by the larger history of which it is part, the history of mankind. About certain moments in the life of a literature—say, that of eighteenth-century English poetry—one can say that the power of internal tradition is so enormous that the historian's stress must properly be on the inner logic of form and style: Dryden through Pope, a line of masters whose innovations become tradition. About the eighteenth-century novel, by contrast, it would be impossible to speak intelligently without noticing the flanking pressures exerted by the society of the time.

In considering a major revolution in cultural style, it is very hard to know precisely how much causal weight to assign to accumulating modulations in the career of a literary form and how much to the thrust of external historical events as these bear down upon the writers employing that form. I would venture the hypothesis—not a very novel one—that while the internal evolution of a form can significantly affect its nature and dress, there must also occur some overwhelming historical changes for a major new cultural style to flourish. Retrospectively we can see that the shift from neo-Classicism to Romanticism was anticipated by certain late eighteenth-century poets, but I doubt that a serious literary historian would suppose that transition to be no more than the outcome of an immanent development of literary forms.

In any case, it is when the inner dynamics of a literature and the large-scale pressures of history cross that there follows a new cultural style, in this case modernism. The results are to be observed in at least three areas: modernist writers discard the formal procedures and decorums of their Romantic predecessors; they begin to feel that the very idea of literary tradition is a nuisance, even a tyranny, to be shaken off; and they question the Romantic faith in transcendence through individual ego or through its pantheistic merger with a God-filled universe, as well as the belief held by some Romantics that the poet should actively engage himself in behalf of a militant liberalism. And soon the new writing is signaled by a dramatic change in the social place and posture of the advanced writers.

Forming a permanent if unacknowledged and disorganized opposition, the modernist writers and artists constitute a special caste within or at the margin of society, an avant-garde marked by aggressive defensiveness, extreme self-consciousness, prophetic inclination, and the stigmata of alienation. "Bohemia," writes Gustave Flaubert, "is my fatherland," bohemia both as an enclave of protection within a hostile society and as a place from which to launch guerrilla raids upon the bourgeois establishment, frequently upsetting but never quite threatening its security. The avant-garde abandons the useful fiction of "the common reader"; it demands instead the devotions of a cult. The avant-garde abandons the usual pieties toward received aesthetic assumptions; "no good poetry," writes Ezra Pound in what is almost a caricature of modernist dogma, "is ever written in a manner twenty years old." The avant-garde scorns notions of "responsibility" toward the audience; it raises the question of whether the audience exists—or should exist. The avant-garde proclaims its faith in the self-sufficiency, the necessary irresponsibility, and thereby the ultimate salvation of art.

As a device of exposition I write in the present tense; but it seems greatly open to doubt whether by now, a few decades after World War II, there can still be located in the West a coherent and self-assured avant-garde. Perhaps in some of the arts, but probably not in literature. (Only in the Communist countries is there beyond question a combative and beleaguered avant-

garde, for there, as a rule, the state persecutes or seriously inconveniences modern writers and artists, so that it forces them
into a self-protective withdrawal, sometimes an "internal emigration.")

In the war between modernist culture and bourgeois society,
something has happened recently which no spokesman for the
avant-garde quite anticipated. Bracing enmity has given way to
wet embraces, the middle class has discovered that the fiercest
attacks upon its values can be transposed into pleasing entertainments, and the avant-garde writer or artist must confront the one
challenge for which he has not been prepared: the challenge
of success. Contemporary society is endlessly assimilative, even
if it vulgarizes what it has learned, sometimes foolishly, to praise.
The avant-garde is thereby no longer allowed the integrity of
opposition or the coziness of sectarianism; it must either watch
helplessly its gradual absorption into the surrounding culture or
try to preserve its distinctiveness by continually raising the ante
of sensation and shock—itself a course leading, perversely, to a
growing popularity with the bourgeois audience. There remains,
to be sure, the option for the serious writer that he go his own
way regardless of fashion or cult.

Still another reason should be noticed for the recent breakup
of the avant-garde. It is very difficult to sustain the stance of a
small, principled minority in opposition to established values
and modes of composition, for it requires the most remarkable
kind of heroism, the heroism of patience. Among the modernist
heroes in literature, only James Joyce, I would say, was able to
live by that heroism to the very end. For other writers, more
activist in temper or less firm in character, there was always the
temptation to veer off into one or another prophetic stance, often
connected with an authoritarian politics; and apart from its intrinsic disasters, this temptation meant that the writer would
sooner or later abandon the confinements of the avant-garde and
try, however delusionally, to re-enter the arena of history. Yeats
and Pound, on the right; Brecht, Malraux, and Gide, on the left:
all succumbed to the glamour of ideology or party machines,
invariably with painful results. Fruitful as avant-garde intransigence was for literature itself and inescapable as it may have
been historically, it did not encourage a rich play of humane
feelings. On the contrary, in every important literature except

the Yiddish, the modernist impulse was accompanied by a revulsion against traditional modes of nineteenth-century liberalism and by a repugnance for the commonplace materials of ordinary life (again with the exception of Joyce). Imperiousness of mind and impatience with flesh were attitudes shared by Yeats and Malraux, Eliot and Brecht. Disgust with urban trivialities and contempt for *l'homme moyen sensual* streak through a great many modernist poems and novels.

That modern literature apprehended with unrivaled power the decline of traditional liberalism, its lapse into a formalism ignoring both the possibilities of human grandeur and the needs of human survival, is not to be questioned. But especially in Europe, where democracy has never been a common premise of political life to the extent that it has in the United States, this awareness of the liberal collapse frequently led to authoritarian adventures: the haughty authoritarianism of Yeats, with his fantasies of the proud peasant, and the haughty authoritarianism of Malraux, with his visions of the heroic revolutionist. It is by no means possible to pass an unambiguous judgment on the literary consequences, since major writing can be released through the prodding of distasteful doctrine. But once such writers turned to daily politics and tried to connect themselves with insurgent movements, they were well on the way to abandoning the avant-garde position. In retrospect, even those of us committed—however uneasily—to the need for "commitment" will probably have to grant that it would have been much better for both literature and society if the modernist writers had kept themselves aloof from politics. Only Joyce, the greatest and most humane among them, remained pure in his devotion to a kind of literary monasticism; and Beckett, the most gifted and faithful of his disciples, has remained pure in that devotion to this very day.

For brief moments, the avant-garde mobilized into groups and communities: Paris, Moscow, Rome, during the early twenties. Most of the time, however, these groups broke up almost as fast as they were formed, victims of polemic and schism, vanity and temperament. The metaphor lodged in the term avant-garde can be seriously misleading if it suggests a structured phalanx or implies that the modernist writers, while momentarily cut off from society at large, were trying to lead great numbers of people into a new aesthetic or social dispensation. Not at all.

When we refer to the avant-garde we are really speaking of isolated figures who share the burdens of intransigence, estrangement, and dislocation; writers and artists who are ready to pay the costs of their choices. And as both cause and effect of their marginal status, they tend to see the *activity* of literature as self-contained, as the true and exalted life in contrast to the life of contingency and mobs. (When now and again they make a foray into political life, it is mainly out of a feeling that society has destroyed the possibility of a high culture and that to achieve such a culture it is necessary to cleanse or bleed society.) Joyce demanded a reader who will devote a lifetime to his work; Wallace Stevens composed poems endlessly about the composition of poetry. These are not mere excesses or indulgences; they are, at one extreme, programs for creating quasi-religious orders or cults of the aesthetic, and at the other extreme, ceremonies for the renewal and rediscovery of life—and then, in the boldest leap of all, for the improvisation of a realm of being which will simply dispense with the gross category of "life."

The crucial instance of the effort to make the literary work self-sufficient is Symbolist poetry. Symbolism moves toward an art severed from common life and experience—a goal perhaps unrealizable but valuable as a "limit" for striving and motion. The Symbolists, as Marcel Raymond remarks, "share with the Romantics a reliance upon the epiphany, the moment of intense revelation; but they differ sharply about its status in nature and its relation to art. Wordsworth's spiritual life is founded on moments of intense illumination, and his poetry describes these and relates them to the whole experience of an ordered lifetime." For the Symbolist poet—archetypal figure in modernism—there is no question, however, of *describing* such an experience; for him the moment of illumination occurs only through the action of the poem, only through its thrust and realization as a particular form. Nor is there any question of relating it to the experience of a lifetime, for it is unique, transient, available only in the matter—perhaps more important, only in the moment—of the poem. Not transmission but revelation is the poet's task. And thereby the Symbolist poet tends to become a Magus, calling his own reality into existence and making poetry into what Baudelaire called "suggestive magic."

Mallarmé, the Symbolist master, and Defoe, the specialist in verisimilitude, stand at opposite poles of the aesthetic spectrum, yet both share a desire to undo the premises and strategies of traditional art. Neither can bear the idea of the literary work as something distinct from, yet dependent upon, the external world. Defoe wishes to collapse his representation into the world, so that the reader will feel that the story of Moll Flanders *is* reality; Mallarmé wishes to purge his revelation of the contingent, so that the moment of union with his poem becomes the world. Both are enemies of Aristotle.

Stretched to its theoretic limit, Symbolism proposes to disintegrate the traditional duality between the world and its representation. It finds intolerable the connection between art and the flaws of experience; it finds intolerable the commonly accepted distance between subject and act of representation; it wishes to destroy the very program of representation, either as objective mimesis or subjective outcry. It is equally distant from realism and expressionism, faithfulness to the dimensions of the external and faithfulness to the distortions of the eye. Symbolism proposes to make the poem not merely autonomous but hermetic, and not merely hermetic but sometimes impenetrable. Freed from the dross of matter and time, poetry may then regain the aura, the power, of the mysterious. Passionately monistic, Symbolism wishes finally that *the symbol cease being symbolic* and become, instead, an act or object without "reference," sufficient in its own right. Like other extreme versions of modernism, Symbolism rebels against the preposition "about" in statements that begin "art is about. . . ." It yearns to shake off the burden of meaning, the alloy of idea, the tyranny and coarseness of opinion; it hopes for sacrament without faith. To fill up the spaces of boredom it would metamorphose itself into the purity of magic—and magic which, at its most pure, becomes a religion without costs.

In his brilliant book *From Baudelaire to Surrealism* Marcel Raymond writes about the Symbolist vision:

This state of happiness, "perfect and complete," ineffable as such, is also ephemeral. When it is gone, man is left with an even more acute awareness of his limitations and of the precariousness of his life. He will not rest until he has again forced the gates of Paradise, or if this is impossible, until he has profited from these revelations. . . . The soul engages in a kind of game, but aspires to an activity that is more elevated than any game—aspires to re-create its lost happiness by means of the *word*. And the function of these images, whose elements are borrowed from the dust of sensation, is not to describe external objects, but to prolong or revive the original ecstacy. "In this state of illusion," says Novalis, "it is less the subject who perceives the object than conversely, the objects which come to perceive themselves in the subject. . . ." Words are no longer signs; they participate in the objects, in the psychic realities they evoke.

If, then, the poet becomes for a moment a kind of God or surrogate God, he finds that after six days of creation he cannot rest on the seventh: his work has crumbled into "the dust of sensation" and he must start again, shuffling the materials of omnipotence and helplessness, and forced to recognize once again the world he had hoped to transcend—perhaps had even managed to transcend—through the power of the word.

Here the crucial instance is Rimbaud, breaking with the conception of language as a way of conveying rational thought, returning to its most primitive quality as a means for arousing emotions, incantatory, magical, and automatistic. Rimbaud praised Baudelaire in terms of his own artistic ends: "To inspect the invisible and hear things unheard [is] entirely different from gathering up the spirit of dead things. . . ."

Heroic as this effort may have been, the Symbolist aesthetic is inadequate in principle, a severe reduction of the scope and traditional claims of literature, and beyond sustaining in practice for more than a few moments. It cannot survive in daylight or the flatness of time. The fierce dualism it proposes cannot be maintained for long; soon the world contaminates the poem and the poem slides back into the world. Symbolism is a major element in modernist consciousness but more, I suspect, as a splendid drama to invoke than a fruitful discipline to follow.

As European civilization enters the period of social disorder and revolt that runs parallel to the life of literary modernism, there is really no possibility for maintaining a hermetic aestheticism. What follows from the impact of social crisis upon modernist literature is quite without that order and purity toward which Symbolism aspires—what follows is bewildering, plural, noisy. Into the vacuum of belief left by the collapse of Romanticism there race a number of competing world views, and these are beyond reconciling or even aligning. That is one reason it is quite impossible to sum up the central assumptions of modernism, as one can for Romanticism, by listing a sequence of beliefs and visions. Literary modernism is a battle of internal conflicts more than a coherent set of theories or values. It provides a vocabulary through which the most powerful imaginations of the time can act out a drama of doubt. Yet this commitment to the problematic is terribly hard to maintain, it requires nerves of iron; and even as the great figures of modernism sense that for them everything depends on keeping a firm grip on the idea of the problematic, many of them cannot resist completely the invading powers of ideology and system. It is at this point that there arises the famous, or but recently famous, problem of belief, perhaps the most discussed topic in the literary criticism of the past fifty years.

At a time when a number of competing world views impinge upon literature, each radically in conflict with one another, there arise severe difficulties in trying to relate the tacit assumptions of the writer to those of the reader. The bonds of premise between the two are broken, and must now become a matter of inquiry, effort, conflict. We read the late novels of D. H. Lawrence or the cantos of Ezra Pound, aware that these are works of enormously gifted writers yet steadily troubled by the outpouring of authoritarian and Fascist ideas. We read Bertolt Brecht's "To Posterity," in which he offers an incomparable evocation of the travail of Europe in the period between wars yet also weaves in a justification of the Stalin dictatorship. How are we to respond to all this? The question is crucial in our experience of modernist literature. We may say that the doctrine is irrelevant, as many critics do say, and that would lead us to the impossible position that the commanding thought of a poem need not be seriously considered in forming a judgment of its value. Or we may say that the doctrine, being obnoxious, destroys our pleasure in the poem, as some critics do say, and that would lead us to the impossible position that our judgment of the work is determined by our opinion concerning the author's ideology. There is, I think, no satisfactory solution in the abstract, and we must learn to accept the fact that modernist literature is often—not in this way alone!—"unacceptable." It forces us into distance and dissociation; it denies us wholeness of response; it alienates us from its own powers of statement even when we feel that it is imaginatively transcending the malaise of alienation.

The problem of belief appears with great force in the early phases of modernism and is then intensely discussed for some decades later, most notably in the criticism of T. S. Eliot and I. A. Richards. Later there arises a new impulse to dissolve the whole problem and to see literature as beyond opinion or belief, a performance or game of surfaces. Weariness sets in, and not merely with this or the other belief, but with the whole idea of belief. Through the brilliance and fervor of its straining, modernism begins to exhaust itself.

Yet no matter what impasse it encounters in its clashes with the external world, modernism is ceaselessly active within its own realm, endlessly inventive in destruction and improvisation. Its main enemy is, in one sense, the culture of the past, even though it bears within itself a marvelously full evidence of that culture. Literature now thrives on assaulting the traditional rules, modes, and limits of literature; the idea of aesthetic order is abandoned or radically modified.

To condemn modernist literature for a failure to conform to traditional criteria of unity, order, and coherence is, however, quite to miss the point, since, to begin with, it either rejects these criteria or proposes radical new ways of embodying them. When the critic Yvor Winters attacks the "fallacy of imitative form" (e.g., literary works dealing with the chaos of modern life themselves take on the appearance and sometimes the substance of chaos), he is in effect attacking modernist writing as such, since much of it cannot dispense with this "fallacy." In its assumption that the sense of the real has been lost in conventional realism, modern writing yields to an imperative of distortion. A "law" could be advanced here: *modernist literature replaces the traditional criteria of aesthetic unity with the new criterion of aesthetic expressiveness, or perhaps more accurately, it downgrades the value of aesthetic unity in behalf of even a jagged and fragmented expressiveness.*

The expectation of formal unity implies an intellectual and emotional, indeed a philosophic composure; it assumes that the artist stands above his material, controlling it and aware of an impending resolution; it assumes that the artist has answers to his questions or that answers can be had. But for the modern writer none of these assumptions holds, or at least none of them can simply be taken for granted. He presents dilemmas; he cannot and soon does not wish to resolve them; he offers his *struggle* with them as the substance of his testimony; and whatever unity his work possesses, often not very much, comes from the emotional rhythm, the thrust toward completion, of that struggle. After Kafka it becomes hard to believe not only in answers but even in endings.

In modernist literature nature ceases to be a central subject and symbol. Beginning partly with Wordsworth, nature is transformed from an organic setting into a summoned or remembered *idea*, sometimes into a mere term of contrast. We remark upon the river Liffey, or the Mississippi woods, or the big two-hearted river, or the Abruzzi countryside, but mostly as tokens of deprivation and sometimes as mere willed signs of nostalgia. These places are elsewhere, not our home; nature ceases to be natural.

Perversity—which is to say: surprise, excitement, shock, terror, affront—becomes a dominant motif. I borrow from G. S. Fraser a charming contrast between a traditional poet:

> *Love to Love calleth,*
> *Love unto Love replieth—*
> *From the ends of the earth, drawn by invisible bands,*
> *Over the dawning and darkening lands*
> *Love cometh to Love.*
> *To the heart by courage and might*
> *Escaped from hell,*
> *From the torment of raging fire,*
> *From the signs of the drowning main,*
> *From the shipwreck of fear and pain*
> *From the terror of night.*

and a modern poet:

> *I hate and love*
> *You ask, how can that be?*
> *I do not know, but know it tortures me.*

The traditional poet is Robert Bridges, who lived as far back as the early twentieth century; the modern poet, our twin, is Catullus.

The modernist writer strives for sensations, in the serious sense of the term; his epigones, in the frivolous sense. The modernist writer thinks of subject matter not as something to be rehearsed or recaptured but rather to be conquered and enlarged. He has little use for wisdom; or if he does, he conceives of it not as something to be dug out of the mines of tradition, but to be won for himself through an exercise in self-penetration, sometimes self-disintegration. He becomes entranced with depths—whichever you choose: the depths of the city, or the self, or the underground, or the slums, or the extremes of sensation induced by sex, liquor, drugs; or the shadowed half-people crawling through the interstices of society: *Lumpen*, criminals, hipsters; or the drives at the base of consciousness. Only Joyce, among the modernist writers, negotiates the full journey into and through these depths while yet emerging into the commonplace streets of the city and its ongoing commonplace life: which is, I think, one reason he is the greatest of the modernist writers, as also perhaps the one who points a way beyond the liberation of modernism.

The traditional values of decorum, both in the general ethical sense and the strictly literary sense, are overturned. Everything must now be explored to its outer and inner limits; but more, there are to be no limits. And then, since learning seems often to be followed by ignorance, there come the demi-prophets who scorn the very thought of limits; so that they drive themselves into the corner of wishing always to go beyond while refusing to acknowledge a line beyond which to go.

A plenitude of sophistication narrowing into decadence—this means that primitivism will soon follow. The search for meaning through extreme states of being reveals a yearning for the primal: for surely man cannot have been bored even at the moment of his creation! I have already spoken of the disgust with culture, the rage against cultivation, that is so important a part of modernism: the turning-in upon one's primary characteristics, the hatred of one's gifts, the contempt for intelligence, which cuts through the work of men so different as Rimbaud, Dostoevsky, and Hart Crane. For the modern sensibility is always haunted by

the problem of succession: what, after such turnings and dis-
tensions of sensibility, can come next? One of the seemingly
hopeful possibilities is a primitivism bringing a vision of new
manliness, health, blood consciousness, a relief from enervating
rationality. A central text is D. H. Lawrence's story, "The Woman
Who Rode Away"—that realistic fable, at once so impressive and
ridiculous—in which a white woman seeks out an Indian tribe
to surrender her "quivering nervous consciousness" to its stricken
sun god and thereby "accomplish the sacrifice and achieve the
power." But within the ambience of modernism there is another,
more ambiguous and perhaps sinister kind of primitivism: the
kind that draws us with the prospect not of health but of decay,
the primitive as atavistic, an abandonment of civilization and
thereby, perhaps, of its discontents. The central fiction expressing
this theme is Joseph Conrad's *Heart of Darkness*, in which Mar-
low the narrator and *raisonneur* does not hesitate to acknowledge that the pull of the jungle for Kurtz and also, more am-
biguously, for himself is not that it seems to him (I am quoting
Lionel Trilling) "noble or charming or even free but . . . base
and sordid—and for *that* reason compelling: he himself feels
quite overtly its dreadful attraction." In this version of primitivism, which is perhaps inseparable from the ennui of decadence,
the overwhelming desire is to shake off the burdens of social re-
straint, the disabling and wearisome moralities of civilized in-
hibition. The Greek poet C. P. Cavafy has written a brilliant
poem in which the inhabitants of a modern city wait for a
threatened invasion by barbarians and then, at the end, suffer
the exasperating disappointment that the barbarians may, after
all, not come. The people of the city will have to continue living
as in the past, and who can bear it?

> *Why should this uneasiness begin all of a*
> *sudden,*
> *And confusion? How serious people's faces have*
> *become.*
> *Why are all the streets and squares emptying*
> *out so quickly,*
> *And everyone turning home again so full of*
> *thought?*
> *Because night has fallen and the Barbarians*
> *have not come,*

> *And some people have arrived from the*
> *frontier,*
> *They said there are no Barbarians any more.*
> *And now what will become of us without*
> *Barbarians?*
> *These people were some sort of solution.*

If technical experiment and thematic surprise characterize modernist poetry, there are equivalent changes in the novel: a whole new sense of character, structure, and the role of its protagonist or hero. The problematic nature of experience tends to replace the experience of human nature as the dominant subject of the modern novel. Abandoning the assumption of a life that is knowable, the novelist turns to the problem of establishing a bridgehead into knowability as the precondition for portraying any life at all. His task becomes not so much depiction as the hypothesizing of a set of *as-if* terms, by means of which he may lend a temporary validation to his material.

Characters in a novel can no longer be assumed, as in the past, to be fixed and synthetic entities, with a set of traits available through notations of conduct and reports of psychic condition. The famous remark of D. H. Lawrence—that he had lost interest in creating the "old stable ego of character," but wished to posit "another ego, according to whose action the individual is unrecognizable, and passes through, as it were, allotropic states which it needs a deeper sense than any we've been used to exercise, to discover are states of the same radically unchanged element"—this is not merely a statement of what he would try to do in *The Rainbow* and *Women in Love*; it also reflects a general intention among modern novelists. Character, for modernists like Joyce, Virginia Woolf, and William Faulkner, is regarded not as a coherent, definable, and well-structured entity, but as a psychic battlefield, or an insoluble puzzle, or the occasion for a flow of perceptions and sensations. This tendency to dissolve character into a stream of atomized experiences, a kind of novelistic *pointillisme*, gives way, perhaps through extreme reaction, to an opposite tendency (yet one equally opposed to traditional concepts of novelistic character) in which character is severed from psychology and confined to a sequence of severely objective events.

Similar radical changes occur in the modernist treatment of

plot. The traditional eighteenth or nineteenth century novel depends upon a plot which reveals a major destiny, such as Henchard's in Hardy's *The Mayor of Casterbridge.* A plot consists here of an action purposefully carved out of time, that is, provided with a beginning, sequence of development, and climax, so that it will create the impression of completeness. Often this impression comes from the sense that the action of a novel, as given shape by the plot, has exhausted its possibilities of significant extension; the problems and premises with which it began have reached an appropriate terminus. Thus, we can say that in the traditional kind of novel it is usually the plot which carries or releases a body of meanings: these can be profound or trivial, comic or tragic. *The Mayor of Casterbridge* contains a plot which fulfills the potential for self-destruction in the character of Henchard—but it is important to notice that in *this* kind of novel we would have no knowledge of that potential except insofar as we can observe its effects through an action. Plot here comes to seem inseparable from meaning, and meaning to inhere in plot.

When a writer works out a plot, he tacitly assumes that there is a rational structure in human conduct, that this structure can be ascertained, and that doing so he is enabled to provide his work with a sequence of order. But in modernist literature these assumptions come into question. In a work written on the premise that there is no secure meaning in the portrayed action, or that while the action can hold our attention and rouse our feelings, we cannot be certain, indeed must remain uncertain, as to the possibilities of meaning—in such a characteristically modern work what matters is not so much the plot but a series of *situations,* some of which can be portrayed statically, through tableaux, set-pieces, depth psychology, and others dynamically, through linked episodes, stream of consciousness, and so on. Kafka's fiction, Joyce's novels, some of Faulkner's—these all contain situations rather than plot.

Still more striking are the enormous changes which the modern novel brings about in its treatment of the fictional hero.

The modern world has lost the belief in a collective destiny. Hence, the hero finds it hard to be certain that he possesses—or that anyone can possess—the kind of powers that might transform human existence. Men no longer feel themselves bound in a sacred or even, often enough, in a temporal kinship. Hence, the hero finds it hard to believe in himself as a chosen figure acting in behalf of a divine commandment or national will.

Since the beginnings of the bourgeois era, a central problem for reflective men has been the relation of the individual to the collectivity. In modern fiction this problem often appears as a clash between a figure of consciousness who embodies the potential of the human and a society moving in an impersonal rhythm that is hostile or, what is perhaps worse, indifferent to that potential. One likes to feel, by way of contrast, that in certain kinds of ancient or traditional heroes there was a union of value and power, the sense of the good and the capacity to act it out. But in modern literature, value and power are taken to be radically dissociated. In Ernest Hemingway's novels the price of honor is often a refusal of the world. In André Malraux's novels the necessity for action is crossed by a conviction of its absurdity. In Ignazio Silone's novels the condition of humaneness is a readiness to wait. Between the apprehension and the deed falls a shadow of uncertainty.

D. H. Lawrence, not only a great novelist but himself a major hero of modern literature, embodies this duality. At one point he says: "Insofar as I am I, and only I am I, and I am only I, insofar as I am inevitably and eternally alone, it is my last blessedness to know it, and to accept it, and to live with this as the core of my self-knowledge." It is the self-knowledge of the Lawrentian hero, strong in pride, sick in strength. But there is another D. H. Lawrence: "What ails me is the absolute frustration of my primeval societal instinct. . . . I think societal instinct much deeper than sex instinct—and societal repression much more devastating. . . . I am weary even of my individuality, and simply nauseated by other people's." It is the yearning of the Lawrentian hero, eager for disciples, driven to repel those who approach him. This is a conflict which, in our time, cannot be resolved. The Lawrentian hero remains a man divided between the absolutism of his individuality and the frustration of his societal instinct.

Let me push ahead a bit farther, and list several traits of "the modern hero," though not in the delusion that any fictional character fulfills all or even most of them:

The modern hero is a man who believes in the necessity of action; he wishes, in the words of Malraux, to put "a scar on the map." Yet the moral impulsions that lead him to believe in action, also render him unfit for action. He becomes dubious about the value of inflicting scars and is not sure he can even locate the map.

He knows that traditionally the hero is required to act out the part of bravery, but he discovers that his predicament requires courage. Bravery signifies a mode of action, courage a mode of being. And since he finds it difficult to reconcile the needs of action with those of being, he must learn that to summon courage he will have to abandon bravery. His sense of the burden he must carry brings him close to the situation described by William James: "Heroism is always on a precipitous edge, and only keeps alive by running. Every moment is an escape."

He knows that the hero can act with full power only if he commands, for his followers and himself, an implicit belief in the meaningfulness of the human scheme. But the more he commits himself to the gestures of heroism, the more he is persuaded of the absurdity of existence. Gods do not speak to him, prophets do not buoy him, nor doctrines assuage him.

The classical hero moved in a world charged with a sense of purpose. In the early bourgeois era, the belief in purpose gave way to a belief in progress. This the hero managed to survive, if only because he often saw through the joke of progress. But now his problem is to live in a world that has moved beyond the idea of progress; and that is hard.

The modern hero often begins with the expectation of changing the world. But after a time his central question becomes: Can I change myself?

If the modern hero decides the world is beyond changing, he may try, as in the novels of Hemingway, to create a hermetic world of his own in which an unhappy few live by a self-willed code that makes possible—they tell themselves—struggle, renewal, and honorable defeat.

Still, the modern hero often continues to believe in the quest, and sometimes in the grail, too; only he is no longer persuaded that quest is necessarily undertaken through public action and he is unsure as to where the grail can be found. If he happens to be an American named Jay Gatsby, he may even look for it on the shores of Long Island. There is reason to believe that this is a mistake.

The modern hero moves from the heroic deed to the heroism of consciousness, a heroism often available only in defeat. He comes as a conqueror and stays as a pilgrim. And in consciousness he seeks those moral ends which the hero is traditionally said to have found through the deed. He learns, in the words of Kyo Gisors in Malraux's *Man's Fate*, that "a man resembles his suffering."

The modern hero discovers that he cannot be a hero. Yet only through his readiness to face the consequences of this discovery can he salvage a portion of the heroic.

In its multiplicity and brilliant confusion, its commitment to an aesthetic of endless renewal—in its improvisation of "the tradition of the new," a paradox envisaging the limit of *limitlessness*—modernism is endlessly open to portraiture and analysis. For just as some of its greatest works strain toward a form freed from beginning or end, so modernism strains toward a life without fixity or conclusion. If, nevertheless, there is in literary modernism a dominant preoccupation which the writer must either subdue or by which he will surely be destroyed, that is the specter of nihilism.

Nihilism is a term not only wide-ranging in reference but heavily charged with historical emotion. It signifies at least some of the following:

A specific doctrine, positivist in stress, of an all-embracing rebellion against traditional authority which appeared in mid-nineteenth-century Russia;

A consciously affirmed and accepted loss of belief in transcendent imperatives and secular values as guides to moral conduct, together with a feeling that there is no meaning resident—or, at least, further resident—in human existence;

A loss of those tacit impulses toward an active and striving existence which we do not even know to be at work in our consciousness until we have become aware of their decline.

In Western literature nihilism is first and most powerfully foreshadowed by Dostoevsky: there is nothing to believe in but the senses and the senses soon exhaust themselves. God is impossible but all is impossible without him. Dostoevsky is maliciously witty, maliciously inventive in his perception of the faces of nihilism. He sees it, first, as a social disorder without boundary or shame: Pyotr Verhovensky in an orgy of undoing, mocking the very idea of purpose, transforming the ethic of modernist experiment into an appeal for collective suicide, seizing upon the most exalted words in order to hollow them out through burlesque. "If there's no God, how can I be a captain then," asks an old army officer in *The Possessed*, and in the derision that follows one fancies that Dostoevsky joins, in half-contempt, half-enchantment. Nihilism appears in moral guise through the figures of Kirillov and Ivan Karamazov, the first a man of purity and the second a man of seriousness; that both are good men saves them not at all, for the demon of emptiness, says Dostoevsky, lodges most comfortably in the hearts of the disinterested. And in Stavrogin, that "subtle serpent" stricken with metaphysical despair and haunted by "the demon of irony," nihilism achieves an ultimate of representation: nothingness in flesh, flesh that would be nothing. "We are all nihilists," says Dostoevsky in the very course of his struggle to make himself into something else. His great achievement is to sense, as Nietzsche will state, the intrinsic connection between nihilism as doctrine and nihilism as experience of loss. Just as Jane Austen saw how trivial lapses in conduct can lead to moral disaster, so Dostoevsky insisted that casual concessions to boredom can drive men straight into the void.

Flaubert, though not concerned with the problem abstractly, writes: "Life is so horrible that one can only bear it by avoiding it. And that can be done by living in the world of Art." The idea of Art as a sanctuary from the emptying-out of life is intrinsic to modernism: it is an idea strong in Nietzsche, for whom the death of God is neither novelty nor scandal but simply a given fact. The resulting disvaluation of values and the sense of bleakness which follows, Nietzsche calls nihilism. He sees it as connected with the assertion that God exists, which robs the world of ultimate significance, and with the assertion that God does not exist, which robs everything of significance.

Nihilism, then, comes to imply a loss of connection with the sources of life, so that both in experience and in literature it is always related to, while analytically distinguishable from, the blight of boredom.

Recognizing all this, Dostoevsky tries to frighten the atheist both within himself and within his contemporaries by saying that once God is denied, everything—everything terrible—has become possible. Nietzsche gives the opposite answer, declaring that from the moment man believes neither in God nor immortality, "he becomes responsible for everything alive, for everything that, born of suffering, is condemned to suffer from life." And thus for Nietzsche, as later for the existentialists, a confrontation with the nihilist void becomes the major premise of human recovery.

With remarkable powers of invention and variation, this theme makes its way through all of modernist literature. In Kafka's work negation and faith stand forever balanced on the tip of a question mark; there are no answers, there are no endings, and whether justice can be found at the trial, or truth in the castle, we never know for certain. The angel with whom Kafka wrestles heroically and without letup is the angel of nothingness. Proust constructs a social world marvelously thick and rich in texture, yet a shadow, too, which a mere wind blows away; and the only hope we have that some meaning may be salvaged is through the power of art, that thin cloak between men and the beyond which nevertheless carries "the true last judgment." This very power of art is seen by Mann as a demon of nihilism trailing both himself and his surrogate figures from novel to novel, as a portent of disease in *Death in Venice* and as a creator-destroyer in *Doctor Faustus* who disintegrates everything through parody. Brecht leers at the familiar strumpet of city nihilism, vomits with disgust when she approaches too closely, and then kidnaps her for a marriage with the authoritarian idea: the result endears him to the contemporary world. But it is Joyce who engages in the most profound modern exploration of nihilism, for he sees it everywhere, in the newspaper office and the church, on the street and in bed, through the exalted and the routine. Exposing his characters to every version of nausea and self-disgust, bringing Stephen Dedalus to his outcry of "*Nothung*" in the brothel, Joyce emerges, as William Troy remarks, with "an energetic and still uncorrupted affirmation of life that is implicit in every movement of his writing." As for those who follow these masters, they seem to have relaxed in the death-struggle with the shapeless demon and some, among the more fashionable of the moment, even strike a pleasant truce with him. But the

power of example remains a great one and if a writer like
Norman Mailer does not choose to wrestle with the angel Kafka
encountered, there are moments when he is prepared to challenge it to a bit of amiable hand-wrestling.

Nihilism lies at the center of all that we mean by modernist
literature, both as subject and symptom, a demon overcome and
a demon victorious. For the terror which haunts the modern
mind is that of a meaningless and eternal death. The death of
the gods would not trouble us if we, in discovering that they
have died, did not have to die alongside them. Heroically the
modern sensibility struggles with its passion for eternal renewal,
even as it keeps searching for ways to secure its own end.

But no, it will not die, neither heroically nor quietly, in struggle or triumph. It will live on, beyond age, through vulgar re-
incarnation and parodic mimesis. The lean youth has grown
heavy; he chokes with the approval of the world he had dismissed; he cannot find the pure air of neglect. Not the hostility
of those who came before but the patronage of those who come
later—that is the torment of modernism.

How, come to think of it, do great cultural movements reach
their end? It is a problem our literary historians have not sufficiently examined, perhaps because they find beginnings more
glamorous, and a problem that is now especially difficult because there has never been, I think, a cultural period in Western
history quite like the one we call modern. But signs of a denouement begin to appear. A lonely gifted survivor, Beckett, remains
to remind us of the glories modernism once brought. Meanwhile,
the decor of yesterday is appropriated and slicked up; the noise
of revolt, magnified in a frolic of emptiness; and what little remains of modernism, denied so much as the dignity of opposition.

How enviable death must be to those who no longer have
reason to live yet are unable to make themselves die! Modernism
will not come to an end; its war chants will be repeated through
the decades. For what seems to await it is a more painful and
certainly less dignified conclusion than that of earlier cultural
movements: what awaits it is publicity and sensation, the kind
of savage parody which may indeed be the only fate worse than
death.

~~§
Beliefs
of the
Masters

In the fifties, perhaps even the early sixties, John Harrison's study of the politics of the great modern writers * would have raised a storm of debate among our younger English instructors and those students concerned with literary criticism. Writers like Eliot, Yeats, and Lawrence were accredited culture-heroes of the literary young, and attacks upon or even analyses of their political views were likely to be dismissed as gross, Marxistic or, most damning of all, "unliterary." When evidence was marshaled to show that these writers had flirted with authoritarian outlooks and movements, there would usually be two kinds of reply: first, that it didn't really matter since the political views of the great modernist writers were of small importance (an estimate not shared by these writers themselves), and second, that the political statements of poets and novelists had to be accorded a special reading, one that avoids the sin of the literal and in which the usual criteria for judging an argument are relaxed in behalf of "the imagination." In the literary discussions of the 1950's, "the imagination" was allotted an absolute sovereignty, beyond check or challenge and sometimes beyond specification.

By now, all this has changed. Young people interested in literature have, so far as I can tell, no special concern for Eliot, Yeats, and Pound, though a few still celebrate Lawrence. They tend to look upon the literary "modernism" of the last seventy-five

* John Harrison, *The Reactionaries* (New York, Schocken Books, 1967).

or one hundred years as a period tucked away in a dim past. Feeling no particular kinship with the masters of literary modernism, they experience little distress at learning that Pound was a propagandist for Fascism, Yeats harbored authoritarian visions, and Eliot several times verged on or crossed into anti-Semitism.

For readers of my generation, however, such facts were extremely painful. We looked upon "The Waste Land" as the voice of our age: it was more than a poem, more even than a great poem; it spoke for us in a profoundly intimate and authoritative way. How then could we reconcile ourselves to Eliot's nastiness about "Bleistein with a cigar" or his proclaimed admiration for Charles Maurras, the French theorist of authoritarianism? Dilemmas of this kind forced many critics into convolutions and ingenuities concerning "the problem of belief"—by which was meant, among other things, the problem of maintaining a separation, in analysis if not always in response, between the literary work itself and offensive doctrines that might animate or course through it.

For middle-aged readers, Mr. Harrison's book comes, therefore, as a sharp reminder of unfinished business. The "problem of belief," like most intellectual difficulties, was never really resolved, nor could it be; what happened was that both writers and readers grew weary of it. Yet such questions have a way of lodging themselves in a corner of one's mind and breaking out again with renewed force. No sooner did *The Reactionaries* appear than several distinguished literary men—Philip Rahv, Stephen Spender, Denis Donoghue—wrote extended reviews in which they turned back to the politics of the modern masters. And reading Mr. Harrison's book has also brought me back to the passions of a decade or two ago.

What Mr. Harrison has done is to bring together material more or less familiar, material drawn from both the literary works and public statements of Eliot, Yeats, Lawrence, Pound, and Wyndham Lewis, and then to offer speculations as to what drove writers of such eminence to opinions so appalling and inhumane. *The Reactionaries* is a civilized book, not a rant or a philippic; but finally it is not the book it ought to be. Mr. Harrison writes in that bluff and low-keyed manner which has recently been affected by English writers who consider themselves admirers of George Orwell, enemies of establishment gentility, and stalwarts of hygienic provincialism. Since, however, Mr. Harrison has chosen to tackle a subject that is extremely complicated and often beyond the reach of red-brick common sense, the result is a book inadequate to the problems it casts out. Nevertheless I am glad to have it, if only because it does raise questions which both the formalist critics of yesterday and the literary swingers of today prefer to avoid.

Yeats yearned for an aristocracy of spirit and perhaps blood, which would return Ireland to the dignity he associated with an age (not clearly located) of nobles and peasants united in mutual responsibility. He hated the commercial spirit:

> A levelling, rancorous, rational sort of mind
> That never looked out of the eyes of a saint
> Or out of a drunkard's eye.
>   All's Whiggery now,
> But we old men are massed against the world.

Yeats was never at ease with common humanity and his peasants were mostly creatures of fantasy. What stirred him was contempt for the petty egotism of the middle class, its calculations and lack of heroic temper. He was impatient with the patience of humanity, and like many other European intellectuals, he had no use for the sluggishness of flesh. For the creaky apparatus of the modern state he snapped out his distate:

> A statesman is an easy man,
> He tells his lies by rote;
> A journalist makes up his lies
> And takes you by the throat;
> So stay at home and drink your beer
> And let the neighbors vote.

Yeats mourned the loss of "the old religion of the Irish with its magical view of nature, its unbounded sorrow at the universal victory of old age and decay, the ultimate rejection of nature by the lonely spirit of man." Hoping for an ordered hierarchical state that would be ruled by a natural aristocracy, he turned in 1932-33, not in action but sentiment, to the Blueshirts of O'Duffy, the leader of Irish Fascism. "A fascist opposition is forming behind the scenes," he wrote. "There is so little in our stocking that we are ready at any moment to turn it inside out, and how can we not feel emulous when we see Hitler juggling with his sausage of stocking. Our chosen color is blue, and blue shirts are marching about all over the country."

The case of Eliot is more complicated. Possessed of a literary culture both more learned and more deracinated than that of Yeats, Eliot could not satisfy himself with the particularities, or the eccentricities, of a national tradition. In his most serious intellectual phase, Eliot wanted a return to the classical culture of Christian Europe; but he also understood, at least as well as his secular critics, that such a return was highly improbable. He was not nearly so ideological as Pound and he clung to fewer historical fantasies than Yeats; a more contemplative man than either, he had no interest in organized movements, with or without shirts. Yet his despair over the quality of the civilization in which he lived, his conviction that without religion all modern cultures must end in sterility and nihilism, and his own difficulties in establishing a firm grip upon the faith to which he aspired—all these led to outbreaks of what might be called apocalyptic irritation, as for example in the disgraceful passage about the Jews in *After Strange Gods*. Whatever his other virtues—and they were notable—Eliot found it hard to ease his soul into Christian charity toward the slobs, sensualists, and slack-minded agnostics he saw populating the modern world.

Intellectually, however, Eliot was far more serious than the self-deluded Yeats or the hapless Pound, a midwestern provincial let loose in the inferno of Europe. Eliot had a better sense of the historical dynamics of mass society; he understood that the aspects of modern industrialism and urbanism he detested were probably irrevocable; and he therefore thought in terms not of mass movements or anointed leaders but of a saving remnant, a devoted semimonastic minority which would hold fast to the Christian word through the oncoming dark ages. Given the desperation of this project, it is hardly any wonder that Eliot lapsed into rhetorical excesses and occasional nastiness.

The other writers discussed by Mr. Harrison are, politically, less interesting. Pound was free of the snobbism and aristocratic pretensions of Eliot and Yeats, but except in regard to some literary matters, he simply could not think. And Lawrence is also somewhat special: not really political at all. Much of what he cried forth—his blood cult, his bullying contempt for the weak, his painful effort to establish himself as a prophetic hero—seems to me intolerable and vicious. But while all this has its obvious political implications, Lawrence was so idiosyncratic a figure, and as a writer often so vibrantly attuned to human needs and depths, that it will not do simply to pin him with a political label.

What was it that drove many writers in the modernist era toward one or another form of authoritarianism? Mr. Harrison provides a clue when he suggests that they "were really interested in society only in so far as it would allow the arts to flourish." Eliot would largely have to be exempted from this charge, but in the main Mr. Harrison seems right. The "reactionaries" hoped that an authoritarian state would restore an earlier cultural grandeur, real or imaginary; they yearned for style in life and art, distinction in bearing, honor in relationships, decorum in conduct—all the versions of order modern society conspicuously lacks. They knew little about what Fascism would mean, any more than most of the left-wing writers knew what Stalinism would mean; and with the exception of Pound they neither supported nor were actively involved with Fascism once it came to power. To that extent, their records are somewhat better than those of certain writers who continued to defend Stalinism long after its criminal brutality had become obvious.

What can, however, be charged against the "reactionaries" is intellectual dilettantism, arrogance, and irresponsibility. Yeats would never have dared talk about metrics with the ignorance he showed in talking about politics, nor Pound about diction with the ignorance he showed about economics. They assumed that because they were eminent writers they had special qualifications for speaking on social topics. They said things that would have been laughed away by the intellectual public if coming from anyone but famous writers. They arrogated to themselves an authority they had not earned. They played with fire and did not even know it. The detachment of a Joyce, even in the years when political choices were desperately needed, seems by comparison a stance of honor and humaneness. Years earlier Yeats had written:

> I think it better that in times like these
> A poet's mouth be silent, for in truth
> We have no gift to set a statesman right

But he did not remember or heed his own words.

Still, this is by no means the whole story: the defense is still to be heard. In a formidable attack on Mr. Harrison's book (*Commentary*, August 1967) Denis Donoghue writes:

> Mr. Harrison cannot conceive of a profound case that might be directed against the kind of mass society which we have today, or the kind of democracy which determined English life between the wars. He does not understand the sense in which liberal democratic life is, as Pound called it, "a mess of mush." Or the forces which drove Yeats to write "Lapis Lazuli," or anyone at all to conceive "a sympathy with the abyss."

Fair enough. Mr. Harrison does not sufficiently grasp, and having been born in 1937 perhaps he cannot grasp the justified revulsion which almost all the writers of the modernist generation felt toward bourgeois Europe. Surely this was a major source of their imaginative energy: Eliot's nightmare of the wasteland, Lawrence's horror before the English mining town, Yeats's contempt for an age that must "engender in the ditch."

These were the shared perceptions of the time: shared by writers of both left and right, by writers without politics, and even by such old-fashioned liberals as E. M. Forster. Insofar as the reaction of the modernist writers took a cultural form, it was extremely valuable for their criticism of bourgeois civilization. They enjoyed the vantage point of criticism from the rear, in the name of tried verities and proven glories; they had at their command the tokens and sediments of tradition; and they spoke for a sense of community which, no matter how illusory it may now seem, enabled them to dramatize the moral shoddiness of Europe. All of this hardly constitutes an adequate politics, and could easily lead, as in fact it did, to political delusion and adventurism, most notably through the assumption that the categories of the literary imagination could readily be transferred to political analysis. But for the "reactionary" writers simply as writers, the stance they took often brought critical strength and sharpness of perspective.

Still more can be said in their behalf. Mr. Harrison operates mostly with abstract ideas or details of a literary text; and he is ingenious enough to claim that he can demonstrate "the relationship between the 'tendency' of these five writers and their literary style, also their literary principles." Were he in fact able to do this, he would become at one stroke the greatest critic of our time; but of course he cannot. Style is at once too impersonal, the consequence of a received tradition, and too personal, the signature of a unique individual, to permit any decisive correlation with political "tendency." There is, however, in the work of novelists and poets an intermediary area, between overarching ideology and local style, which has to do with their deepest sense of human existence: their biases, insights, emotions, barely articulated values. In trying to locate this area we speak, awkwardly but perhaps unavoidably, of a writer's vision, that quality of his work for the description of which ideological pattern is too gross and *stylistic* detail too fine. Precisely here did Eliot, Yeats, and Lawrence manifest their greatness as writers, in the sense of human dilemma and possibility that is embodied in their best work. What emerges in their poems and novels is often in conflict with their abstract statements, and almost always to the benefit of the poems and novels.

Having gone this far with Mr. Donoghue, I want to go a step farther and turn his argument against him. In the decade between the Paris Commune and World War II both right- and left-wing intellectuals were gravely mistaken—and I would add, morally at fault—in their easy and contemptuous dismissal of liberalism. That the society which they saw as the tangible embodiment of bourgeois liberalism required the most scathing criticism and attack, I do not for a moment question. But they failed utterly to estimate the limits of what was historically possible or relevant in their time, as they failed, even more importantly, to consider what the consequences might be of their intemperate attacks upon liberalism. These attacks could never restore ancient glories, but they might help usher in modern barbarism. It was all very well to denounce bourgeois liberalism as a "mess of mush," for so it often was, and worse, too; but to assault the vulnerable foundations of democracy meant to bring into play social forces repressive in a way the writers could not—or at least did not—foresee. There were, as it turned out, far worse things in the world than a "mess of mush."

Nor am I indulging in mere retrospective wisdom. Writers so vastly different as E. M. Forster and Bertrand Russell (in his *Theory and Practice of Bolshevism*) warned of the frightful consequences of that apocalyptic nihilism—that brutal haste to destroy democratic institutions and values but recently created and inherently precarious—which was shared by writers of both the far right and far left. (One weakness of Mr. Harrison's book is the absence—if only as an analytic "control"—of the Stalinist intellectuals, quite as deadly enemies of democracy as the "reactionaries" and often a good deal more active in this enmity.)

The society of bourgeois Europe, as everyone sensed, was overripe for deep-going social change. But the assumptions that such change required a trampling on liberal values in the name of hierarchical order or proletarian dictatorship and that liberal values were inseparable from cultural decadence and capitalist economy—these proved a disaster beyond reckoning. Beyond reckoning! In the joy and brutality of their verbal violence, the intellectuals did not realize how profound a stake they had in preserving the norms of liberalism. They felt free to sneer at liberalism because, in a sense, they remained within its psychological orbit: they could not really imagine its destruction and took for granted that they would continue to enjoy its shelter. Even the most authoritarian among them, on both right and left, could not foresee a situation in which *their* freedom as writers would be destroyed. Dreaming of natural aristocrats, they helped pave the way for maniac *Lumpen*. They had inherited and then grotesquely magnified the critique of liberalism which had been a major intellectual activity of the nineteenth century; they joined to it a hostility toward "the mob," a disdain for the masses stifling and bored in the cities; but they failed utterly to consider that the assault upon liberalism in which they joined so voraciously might lead to unwished-for consequences, as this assault would sweep away both scruples and hopes in the tide of totalitarianism. There are times when the price of fecklessness runs high.

But is it not too much to ask that in an age of chaos and

disintegration, writers honor the kind of distinctions I have here suggested? No, it is not too much. For if writers are not intransigent in defense of liberty, who then will be?

Precisely their extreme awareness of the depths of crisis to which liberal bourgeois society had sunk should have led the "reactionaries"—and the radicals also—to see the absolute value of liberal norms and procedures, those norms and procedures which transcend and should survive any particular form of society. And in fact there were writers who remained true to the heritage of Western humanism, while they strove for a re-creation of Western society. Even so nonpolitical a man as Joyce grasped intuitively the need to reject the smelly little orthodoxies of authoritarianism; he had no use for all those bullying leaders and movements. He remarked sardonically in 1934, "I am afraid poor Mr. Hitler will soon have few friends in Europe apart from my nephews, Masters W. Lewis and E. Pound"; and throughout his career he never lost his connection, however complicated and ironic, with ordinary human existence. That is why, among all the modernist writers, he now seems the most humane and the most durable. Carrying experiment further than anyone, he could also break past the rigid liberations of experiment. Wyndham Lewis, that snarling authoritarian, attacked *Ulysses* for "plainmanism" and few words of praise count as much as this one of damnation.

I know that what I have been saying in these last few paragraphs goes against the dominant notions of the fifties and sixties, the new conservatism and the new leftism, both of which—for opposite but symmetrical reasons—refuse to make the essential distinction between transient bourgeois institutions and abiding values of liberal freedom. But I do not claim that what I have said is novel or exciting; I claim only that it is true.

✌️
Martin du Gard:
The Novelty
of Goodness

I first came across Roger Martin du Gard's *The Thibaults* in 1944 while lying about, idle and depressed, in an army camp waiting to be shipped overseas. A gash upon the western Pennsylvania countryside, this camp seemed an ultimate denial of human life, a way station to those zones of combat and death we kept nervously discussing in the barracks. In this place of half-spoken fears and emotional sterility, I began to read *The Thibaults*, one of those gigantic family chronicles that had been so popular in Europe at the turn of the century and which up-to-date literary people would dismiss as hopelessly old-fashioned during the postwar years when "everyone" was reading Faulkner and Kafka.

Old-fashioned *The Thibaults* may well seem. In a fine appreciation that recently appeared in the Italian journal *Tempo Presente*, Nicola Chiaramonte has called it "the last great novel in the classical nineteenth-century manner." The book moves with the measured pace of the nineteenth-century novel, as if to register a world at ease with its own norms, rational in its apprehension of time and causality, secure in its expectation that the decades of a man's life will follow and fulfill one another with a stately rightness. I lost myself, with mounting gratitude, in the French bourgeois world of the years between 1890 and World War I, the world of Oscar Thibault, an overpowering Catholic "public man," and his two sons, Jacques and Antoine: Jacques, neurotic, fevered, and destined to become a left-wing socialist who destroys himself in a hopeless pacifist adventure during the war, and Antoine, healthy, balanced, destined to end his life gassed in the war and at the moment of his expiration to keep a remarkable journal of his psychological and physiological reactions.

I say that I felt a mounting gratitude while reading this sequence of novels—in their sum about the length of Proust's *Remembrance of Things Past*—but actually that is a pallid understatement. For Martin du Gard's book brought a sense of life's renewal, regained for me a connection with the immediacies and delights of experience. As never before, I understood what D. H. Lawrence meant when he praised the novel as the greatest of literary genres, the book of life from which we best gain the illusion of transparency and identification.

At the outset, *The Thibaults* seems a little like Thomas Mann's *Buddenbrooks*, the story of a solid, representative family. Jacques Thibault, an inflamed boy who loves and hates his insufferable father, runs away with a Protestant friend (the ghastliness of it, an infidel Protestant!) and wanders off through the streets of Marseilles, only to be caught, chained again into the prison life of the French *bourgeoisie*, and then sent off to a reform school sponsored by his father. Juxtaposed to him is the older brother, Antoine, whose life moves—for a time—as a harmonious development, a gradual slide into manhood and the liberating disciplines he finds in his work as a physician. But as the book proceeds, one comes to see that the comparison to be made is not merely with Mann's *Buddenbrooks* but also with *The Magic Mountain,* a novel that ends with its protagonist, Hans Castorp, caught in World War I.

Reading further and further into *The Thibaults*, one becomes aware that Martin du Gard (1881–1958) was not a nineteenth-century writer at all. He was really "one of us," a modern man troubled by our skepticisms and anxieties. Somewhat like Boris Pasternak in *Doctor Zhivago*, Martin du Gard employed a traditional literary form, but not out of a mindless wish to mimic the past; his purpose was to gain an oblique or roundabout perspective on modern life. Traditional in technique, he was radical in sensibility. Martin du Gard was one of those rare twentieth-century novelists alert to the corrosions of bourgeois Europe,

such as would lead a few decades later to the crisis literature of
Sartre and Camus, yet still able to appropriate, without anach-
ronism or slackness of mind, the Tolstoyan novel. The Tolstoyan
novel in all its plenitude of representation, the novel of a seemingly stable world with its rich "gallery of characters" and interplay of incidents—precisely this "outmoded" form became for
Martin du Gard a way of registering the death throes of the nineteenth century, the suicide of the traditional culture of Europe.

Why then did *The Thibaults* never win a large American
audience? I can only speculate. Written in the years between
1920 and 1940, it must already have come to seem too ordered
and rational, too leisurely and dispassionate, for our anguished
decades. Every once in a while I would meet a person or read a
book that spoke with admiration of Martin du Gard—most recently H. Stuart Hughes's fine study of contemporary French
thought, *The Obstructed Path*. But perhaps because he was a
writer without fanaticism or ideology, Martin du Gard never
became the object of a cult. It was just as well.

Martin du Gard began his novel with the customary expectation—customary for premodernist writers—that he would chart
the destinies of linked individuals within the spectrum of roles
allowed them by family and society. As he later remarked, he
proposed to show

two beings with temperaments as different, as divergent, as possible,
but fundamentally marked by the obscure similarities which are created, between two people of the same blood, by a very powerful
common atavism. Such a subject offered me the possibility of simultaneously expressing two contradictory tendencies in my nature: the
instinct of independence, of evasion, of revolt, the refusal of all conformity; and that instinct for order, for measure, that refusal of extremes, which I owe to my heredity.*

The passage is notable for what it reveals about the making of
a novel—and not merely Martin du Gard's novel. He starts with
the assumption that a stable social background will permit the

---

* This quotation, as well as one or two later, is taken from a useful study,
Roger Martin du Gard: The Novelist and History, by David L. Schalk
(Ithaca: Cornell University Press, 1967). Professor Schalk's powers as a
literary critic are limited, but he writes well on the complex relationship
between Martin du Gard's creative life and the development of modern
European history.

etching of fine nuances of character in the foreground. That traditional bourgeois France can be assumed to be "there," solid and unmovable; that the elder Thibault in his own bulky person forms a barrier of will and prejudice, incarnating the conservatism of Catholic France, against which his sons must thrust themselves to achieve a degree of definition; that the fixity of social norms and manners allows the novelist to chart moral formation through seemingly trivial incidents of family life—all these are among the deepest foundations of the nineteenth-century novel. At the start, but only at the start, Martin du Gard turns to them almost instinctively. The revolt of Jacques Thibault begins as a friendship, slightly tinged by eroticism, with a Protestant schoolboy; he then enters the home of his friend's family and finds among the Fontanins a purity of moral life and an openness of feeling—but also a libertinism in the handsome, wandering father—he has not known in his own family. This juxtaposition of family environments and, indirectly, religious styles, creates a strong immediate effect: it helps prepare the way for Jacques's lifelong rebellion. But while Martin du Gard is himself a thorough skeptic, he understands that the novelist must always strengthen those forces within his book which resist his own sentiments and predispositions; so that many pages later the tables are turned and the seeming anti-Catholic bias is complicated. As Antoine Thibault leaves the funeral of his father, he engages in a sustained dialogue with a sensitive Catholic priest in which the latter has the last and perhaps the best word. In the world of the great novelists, no debate is ever done.

The single overriding theme of the European novel has been the conflict between rigid social arrangements and a protagonist straining for personal freedom—a conflict seen not as resolved but as continuous, and thereby open to changes wrought by the will and intelligence of the characters. It is in these terms that *The Thibaults* begins. The older Thibault, barricaded behind his moralism and righteousness, is an unattractive man, but also the most passionate and vigorous in the book; he looms as the archetypal father, an Abraham to be feared and loved as the principle of authority made flesh. Jacques rebels against individual and idea, but his rebellion takes on its fiercely dramatic quality because he remains enthralled by both Oscar Thibault the man and the paternal power he represents. There follows a prolonged struggle of wills, first as an unavoidable encounter of generations, hot blood against cold, and then as a confrontation of two world views, secular denial against religious authority. The conflict becomes internalized within Jacques, as a division between his need for self-assertion and his yearning for parental affection. And it is here that the felt presence of a stable society, even an unjust or authoritarian one, is for the novelist an enormous advantage. If Jacques were able simply to discard the bonds of family life, if he could simply decide that the old man is a tyrant or a bore who need no longer be listened to, the result might be socially pleasing or psychologically enabling; but it would damage the entire structure of relationships and meanings Martin du Gard has created. The incidents multiply: Jacques brought home contrite and sullen; Jacques at the reform school almost, as we would say, brainwashed and unable, in the swamp of his humiliation, to tell his brother how unhappy he is; Jacques later passing his examinations brilliantly but still beyond reconciliation with his father. In all these bits of narrative, what establishes the tension is the fact that the emotional tie Jacques feels to his father is more powerful and enduring than the social or intellectual values the father represents; that life has a dynamism and thrust beyond any beliefs we may have about it. Jacques can declare himself a revolutionary, but when the time comes to return for the old man's death he still trembles like a frightened little boy.

Which other modern novelist, by contrast, has been able to employ the family as a binding and defining unit in his work? Faulkner, I suppose. But he sees the Southern family as a collapsing institution, so that in his greatest novel, *The Sound and the Fury*, there is an extremely poignant sense of how much has been lost through the collapse of the Compsons but little evidence that the family still shapes and disciplines the lives of its members. And in our own moment it is almost impossible to imagine a novel in which youthful rebellion finds a force of resistance among the older generation sufficient to allow for sustained drama.

Martin du Gard's stress upon the settled traits of Jacques and Antoine Thibault creates for the reader the fascinating possibility of "choosing" between the two characters—and choosing is here more than a game, it is a kind of moral signature. The two brothers are strongly drawn and highly intelligent men, each with his own claim on our sympathies. Jacques reminds one a little of Stendhal's Fabrice in *The Charterhouse of Parma*, that curious mixture of rebellion against the world and a dreamy abstracted removal from it, almost as if the character were musing away his own existence. Antoine is given a whole book in which a day in his life as a doctor is depicted with enormous detail, and the result is a *tour de force* in the dramatization of commonplace life and the vindication of work as the rationale for our existence.

Albert Camus observes: "In art, the more prosaic the reality chosen as one's subject matter, the more difficult it is to transfigure." And he feels that it is Antoine who emerges as the true protagonist of the novel, for he argues brilliantly that Jacques is a kind of Dostoevskian echo, "the terrorist" as foreshadowed in *The Possessed*, one of those men "who want to change life in order to change themselves," and who "leave life untouched . . . sterile and disturbing witnesses for everything in man that refuses and always will refuse to live." A telling point; yet even as one sees its truth for the novel and its truth for our times, one is inclined to ask: does not the entire momentum of twentieth-century history, which in turn becomes the momentum of Martin du Gard's novel, force a wrenching from private life to a life engulfed by historical consciousness? And does this not provide a justification of sorts for Jacques—the kind of dangerous justification Bertholt Brecht employs in his great poem, "To Posterity," where he asks later generations to understand why twentieth-century men had to become so brutal: "we changed our countries more often than our shoes"? I say, a dangerous justification, because it could be used, as Brecht did, to rationalize the ghastliness of totalitarian society; yet who, turning away in disgust from Brecht, could simply accept the private life of an Antoine Thibault? In any case, that was the dilemma which Martin du Gard dramatized with a sympathetic detachment few modern writers have equaled.

Martin du Gard's stress upon the seemingly fixed differences in character between Jacques and Antoine Thibault is but one instance of the ruling psychology of the book. It is a pre-Freudian psychology, rationalistic and empirical, which assumes that character is marked by contained and knowable traits and that our conduct is explainable through categories of thought. We are inclined, at this moment in the twentieth century, to discount this sort of psychology: it does not make sufficient allowance for the irrational; it blots out the chaos of the unconscious, it overestimates the coherence and accessibility of the psyche. No doubt. But an advance in knowledge, if that is what the various depth psychologies really constitute, is not necessarily an advantage for literature. Even as we recognize the theoretic limitations of Martin du Gard's psychology, we must also acknowledge its creative uses. Because the characters, *as a preliminary step*, can easily be assigned to familiar psychological categories, Martin du Gard is then free to draw upon a superb repertoire of variation and nuance. Just as tradition, for the writer, can yield possibilities for freedom and innovation, so the relatively conventional psychology of *The Thibaults* makes possible novelty and surprise.

I want to develop this point a little further. If character consists in a given potential of traits, as a rationalistic psychology tends to assume, then we are going to see the growth of a character as the realization or fulfillment of that potential. In the abstract this may seem very mechanistic; but in Martin du Gard's novel itself, since we can never really know what the full potentiality of a Jacques or Antoine may be, our gradual discovery of their characters comes, in fact, as a series of small surprises. In the traditional novel, that is, *surprise comes from the fact that the characters act according to their true natures*, which we know in general but never completely.

At first Antoine Thibault seems the essence of the normal. Then, during an emergency operation, he meets a vivid and mysterious woman named Rachel, and in the glowing romance that follows his life is transformed—but transformed through fulfillment, a release of the capacities for sexual pleasure and love we have already sensed him to possess. Here the writing becomes more intense and lyrical, the tone of realism gives way for a time to a tone of romanticism, as if the quickening of life means a quickening of language. Martin du Gard the novelist-healer becomes Martin du Gard the novelist-romancer. And while his psychology may be rationalistic, that does not keep him from recognizing the powers of the sub- and irrational, the thrust of desire, the autonomous demands of the body, the imperiousness of ego.

Martin du Gard offers almost no description of the physical love-making of Antoine and Rachel, yet the pages in which they come together are among the most erotically stimulating I have ever read, infinitely more suggestive—to say nothing of romantic! —than those contemporary novels which chart a full course of sexual calisthenics. Martin du Gard understands, for he is a writer with an enormous sense of *experience*, that sexuality itself can rarely be made interesting in a serious novel; what can be made interesting is the force of desire which leads to sexuality, the complications of feeling that surround it, the aftermath of loss which is perhaps inevitable.

Through his immersion in sensual pleasure, soon brought to an end by Rachel's departure, Antoine suffers and grows. Later, dying from poison gas, he will think back: "It was a sorry adventure, but that sorry adventure is, despite all, the best that there is in my sorry life."

Equally impressive as a depiction of that continuous physical life which commands us even in the most firmly structured of societies, is Martin du Gard's lengthy depiction of the elder Thibault's deathbed agonies. I think Martin du Gard must be the greatest master in fiction of the death struggle, realistic, detailed, yet never sensational in effect: the death struggle as it becomes a kind of impersonal *agon* leaving character and social definition behind it. Toward the end of the whole chronicle there will be another great death scene, the one in which Antoine watches himself dying with the detachment of a physician. Oscar Thibault struggles with animal-like ferocity against death, Antoine Thibault accepts it with that loss of energy which seems inseparable from the stoical imagination.

To read *The Thibaults* is sooner or later to ask oneself, why and in which ways is Martin du Gard inferior as a novelist to Tolstoy? Even to put the question is, of course, to pay Martin du Gard an enormous compliment.

The difference between the two writers is not merely, perhaps not even mainly, a difference in the magnitude of their talents. There are, to be sure, things that Tolstoy can do and Martin du

Gard cannot: massive scenes of warfare in which whole groups of characters become the protagonists of the action, intervals of religious elevation in which a saintly figure finds himself in communion with the godhead, excursions into primitivist simplicity which serve Tolstoy as equivalents to his early-Christian faith. Camus develops this contrast beautifully:

Martin du Gard shares with Tolstoy a liking for human beings, the art of depicting them in the mystery of their flesh, and a knowledge of forgiveness—virtues outdated today. The world Tolstoy described nevertheless formed a whole, a single organism animated by the same faith; his characters meet in the supreme adventure of eternity. One by one, visibly or not, they all, at some point in their stories, end up on their knees.

Martin du Gard lacks the faith—and to go a step beyond Camus, he thereby lacks the *animation*—of Tolstoy's world. Composed in the twentieth century, his work, as Camus says, "is one of doubts, of disappointed and persevering reason, of ignorance acknowledged, and of a wager that man has no other future than his own." *The Thibaults* presents a world in a twilight gray, even if sometimes streaked with a brilliant flare of color. As Jacques and Antoine move into the war, no one knows any longer why their world exists, what it means, or why it kills. And the result finally is not merely a difference in tone between Tolstoy and Martin du Gard, but a loss of creative energy, a greatness in the French writer but a diminished greatness.

A further crucial difference between the two writers: Where Tolstoy integrated, indeed could not even conceive as long separate, the two main strands of his narrative, that dealing with individual lives and that dealing with historical events, Martin du Gard could not manage this. The logic of his narrative leads to an abandonment of personal life, even though in its early parts personal life is treated as self-sufficient, even sacred. One of his French critics, Pierre-Henri Simon, writes that in the early years of the twentieth century Western man "lost the experience and the sense of history. . . . It took, to reawaken him [to history], the tocsin and the cannon of August 1914." This is certainly a description of a major theme in *The Thibaults*; but I think it must also be added that Martin du Gard is one of those writers for whom this "reawakening" had the quality of nightmare: he believes in the absolute value of personal experience, and toward the end of his life remarks in a letter: ". . . you are completely correct in emphasizing how many of my qualities are due to my bourgeois origins. . . . All my life I have *struggled against*, and at the same time, *made my peace with*, these elements."

The shift to historical narrative which occurs in the later parts of *The Thibaults* is one that its author, like his characters, negotiates reluctantly, under the blows of circumstance; and when he comes to the war and the socialist movement in *Summer 1914* (the concluding portion of the whole sequence), his writing becomes a little uncertain and abstract. A lifelong pacifist and man of the left, Martin du Gard is still in his innermost being a private man, the historian of individual fate rather than the individual who chronicles the fate of history.

"The final word that can be said about this work," says Camus, "remains the one that it has been difficult to use about a writer since the death of Tolstoy: goodness. . . . What we are concerned with here is a particularly lucid virtue, which absolves the good man because of his weaknesses, the evil man because of his generous impulses, and both of them together because of their passionate membership in a human race that hopes and suffers."

I should like to add to "goodness" one other word, "acceptance." Unavoidably the writers of this century have been driven to play the role of visionary or prophet. Much has thereby been gained for literature, but something also lost. The visionary or prophet tends to impose himself on his work, to twist and wrench his characters in behalf of his presuppositions, to stamp his personality on each phrase and word. Martin du Gard is another kind of novelist entirely. We do gain from his work the sense of a man profoundly humane and stoical, at once passionate and withdrawn, though forever sympathetic to all those who risk themselves in the human enterprise. But we feel that this writer does not want to fix his imagined creatures into the mold of his own theories, he wants instead to give them a full range of freedom to live out their own destinies. He does not wish to tyrannize over his world, but rather to accept human life as it is, with all its faults and weaknesses. He understands Jacques and shares in his aspirations; but in the end it is Antoine's spirit which encloses the book.

the emotions of Romanticism. Especially important here is the comparison with Dostoevsky, for it suggests how radically the underground man has experienced a change of character. Dostoevsky's underground man trembles in fright and despair before the possibility of nihilism; Céline's no longer regards a valueless existence as anything but a commonplace fact of life.

Just as the hero of his novels is utterly unheroic ("I wasn't very wise myself but I'd grown sensible enough to be definitely a coward forever"), so is the style of these novels the opposite of literary and academic conventions. Fierce, sputtering, brawling, sometimes on the verge of hysteria, it is an "antistyle," a deliberate nose-thumbing at classical decorum. "To resensitize the language," Céline has written, "so that it pulses more than it reasons—that was my goal." As a statement of intention this is far less original than he supposes, but in its very familiarity it fits perfectly with the general impulse of modern literature. Like most modern writers Céline does not hesitate to sacrifice composure to vividness, unity of effect to ferocity of expression. He neither cares about a fixed literary tradition nor worries about such tiresome souvenirs as formal tidiness. His aim is to burst out, to launch the diatribe of a Parisian who is at one and the same time a miserable sod and an outraged man. Psychological refinements, introspective turns of self-analysis, romantic agonies—Céline will have none of these. The underground man who moves through his novels is beyond the Promethean gesture; he looks upon modern society as a blend of asylum and abattoir; so it is, so it must be; and meanwhile, with a jovial toughness, he acts out the slogan of the declassed and disabused: *Je m'en fiche.*

The "I" of the novel is something of a louse, quite indifferent to the cautions of morality, yet a man who can lay claim to one virtue: he dislikes lying to himself. Not that he is infatuated with notions about the sacredness of truth. It is simply that in weighing his own feelings he wants an honest measure: he intends to be sincere with himself, even if with no one else. In one of his infrequent moments of contemplativeness, he tells himself:

The greatest defeat, in anything, is to forget, and above all to forget what it is that has smashed you, and to let yourself be smashed without ever realizing how thoroughly devilish men can be. When our time is up, we people mustn't bear malice, but neither must we forget. . . .

The dominant motif of the book is undirected flight. From its opening pages, in which the narrator casually volunteers for the army (why not?), he is constantly running from the terrors and apparitions of his world. Céline, or, as he now calls himself in the novel, Bardamu, is trapped in World War I and unable to think about it; he refuses to take it seriously, even to the point of opposition. The pages describing the wartime experiences of Bardamu, in their reduction of official glory to nihilist farce, are among the most scathing ever composed on this theme. Bardamu prepares to go off to war; Poincaré, President of the Republic, prepares "to open a show of lapdogs"; *Vive la France!* Bardamu learns, soon enough, that bullets whistle and he must run. For a while he serves as runner to a senile, delicate, and rose-loving general, and his reward—Bardamu's, not the general's—is that his feet smell. Running for the general, Bardamu comes to a major decision: if he is to survive he will have to stop running for generals and begin running from them. Heroism is for Sundays; meanwhile, the Bardamus must exploit the resources of their cowardice.

And so he runs: from the army to the rear; from one hospital to another; from France to a fantastic trading post in a rotting African jungle; from the African jungle to the industrial jungle of America, first as a bum and then as a worker on the Detroit assembly lines; from America back to France, where, still running up and down stairs to earn a few francs, he becomes an indigent doctor. The one peaceful spot he finds is a post in an insane asylum. For "when people are well, there is no way of getting away from it, they're rather frightening. . . . When they can stand up, they're thinking of killing you. Whereas when they're ill, there's no doubt about it, they're less dangerous."

Throughout the book Bardamu keeps looking for a strange character named Robinson, his down-at-the-heels and laconic double. Go to the edge of hopelessness and there you will find Robinson: in the front lines, where he proposes a scheme for desertion; in Africa, where he is getting ready to run off with the company's funds; in Detroit, where he provides tips on brothels. Repeated through the book as mock ritual, these meetings between underground man and shameless alter ego lead to nothing, for here all quests are futile, even one so modest as Bardamu's for Robinson. When Robinson dies there is nothing

more to look for, and the concluding words of the book, a manifesto of disgust, are: "Let's hear no more of all of this."

Images of death streak the novel. The African episode is a
journey to the death of archaic tribalism, the American a journey
to the death of industrial civilization. Backward or forward, it's
all the same, "a great heap of worm-eaten sods like me, bleary,
shivering and lousy." Céline is obsessed not merely with the
inexorability of death but even more with the vision of putre-
faction: ". . . three feet below ground I . . . will be streaming
with maggots, stinking more horribly than a heap of bank-holiday
dung, all my disillusioned flesh absurdly rotting."

The algebra of our century: flight from death equals flight to
death. But is there in this wild and rasping novel perhaps something more, perhaps a flicker of positive vision? Doesn't the
enormity of Céline's hatred indicate some hidden yearning for the
good which he himself can hardly express? In principle it is hard
to deny such a possibility. Céline, too, has his humanities, and
can be lavish with bottom-dog compassion; some yearning for
the good, one might suppose, is indispensable if he is to summon
the energy needed for so vindictive an outburst against "man's
viciousness." But the particular truth about this novel is less
ennobling, less assuaging. As a force within the book, this pre-
sumptive yearning for good is hard to discover, perhaps because
it is buried beneath the debris of disillusion. Beneath that debris
there may well be a misshapen core of moral sentiment, but it
can seldom compete for attention with Céline's rich provisioning
of symptoms of disorder and sensations of disgust.

In *Death on the Installment Plan* (*Mort à Crédit*) Céline
returned to his childhood and adolescence in order to complete
the record of his experience. An even grizzlier testimony than
Journey to the End of the Night, Céline's second novel is written
in a fitful and exuberant prose, and its tone is one of joyous loath-
ing at having to turn back in memory to the miasma of youth.
The misanthropy of the earlier novel ripens into outright para-
noia: but with such bubbling energy, such a bilious and sizzling
rhetoric, such a manic insistence upon dredging up the last recollection of filth! *Death on the Installment Plan* is a prolonged
recital of cheating, venality, and betrayal: the child as victim of
the world. Still a boy, he learns to hate the whole social order:
"It made me choke to think of it . . . of all the treachery of things!

. . . all the swinishness! . . . the whole collection of ordures! Yes, God Almighty, I'd had my bellyful."

Two linked motifs control the book: the richest account of retching in modern literature and a profound yearning for solitude. Both are sequels to the running motif in *Journey*: one runs from the filth and hopes to find a corner of quiet and a bit of peace. When Céline describes retching, he is an absolute virtuoso: "She brings up the lot . . . right into the wind . . . and I get it full in my face, the whole stinking stew that's been gurgling in her throat . . . I, who haven't so much as a crumb to bring up! Ah, now, yes, I find I have, after all . . . my stomach gives one more turn. . . ." Vomit links with Céline's fruitless effort to disgorge the whole of his experience, as he runs through the darkness of the night. If only he could start afresh, with nothing on his stomach, and be rid of the rubbish of the past . . . but it cannot be done, there is always one more crumb of recollection.

The yearning for solitude is poignantly developed in *Death on the Installment Plan*. All a paranoid ever wants is "to be let alone," a wish that, to be satisfied on his terms, would require nothing less than a reconstruction of the universe. In one section of the novel, a set piece displaying Céline's gifts at their best, he describes a stay in an English country school, where he finds a happiness of sorts through taking long walks with a little idiot boy and an unobtrusive woman teacher, neither of whom troubles him by attempts at conversation. With the dumb and gentle he finds a paradise of muteness; here defenses can be lowered and nerves unraveled. And in this solitude it is also possible to enjoy the modest pleasures of masturbation. The adolescent hero of *Death on the Installment Plan* masturbates systematically, not with the excited curiosity of a youth but with the tameness of an old man. Pleasure can come only from himself, and only when alone with himself. And who knows, perhaps for the underground man as secret sharer of his potency, this is a kind of good faith, an act of sincerity.

There are writers in whose work a literary theme can barely be kept apart from a personal obsession, and psychological illness, through some perverse dynamic, becomes the source of a boundless creative energy. Céline is one of these.

The Nose and the Mound. Céline depicts a severed universe:

on one side, he himself, the big nose, and on the other, the world at large, an enormous mound of *merde*. Maestro of bad smells, Céline learns that his nose is the one organ he can trust implicitly: it is the organ that remains sincere, and by it one can know women, cities, nations, destinies. "It's by smells that people, places and things come to their end. A whiff up one's nostrils is all that remains of past experience." His journey to America is a prolonged exploit in olfactory revulsion, climaxed by a visit to an underground urinal in New York, where he is simply awe-stricken—Cortez before the Pacific!—by "its joyous communion of filth."

Forever exposing himself to the multiplicity of *merde*, Céline reacts not merely to the hideousness of our social arrangements but even more, to the very conditions of existence itself, which dictate the stupidity of death, intolerable enough, and the prolonged stench of dying, still more intolerable. In *Journey* he declares himself "appalled by my realization of biological ignominy," the last two words of this clause breaking forth as the very source of Céline's inspiration. He flinches before the sensual attributes of the least offensive body, and every time he sees a man engaging in the physiological functions he seethes with rage. Lusting after Lola, the sweet American nurse with piquant buttocks, he shudders in his lust: worms will reign over that flesh, too. Had Céline lived in the early Christian era, he would have found himself a Manichean sect and spat upon sensual appetite as the taste of the devil. Being a twentieth-century Parisian, he submits to the most humiliating debaucheries precisely from his fury at being unable to avoid decay. Sartre and Camus may be students in the metaphysic of nausea, but what, by comparison with Céline, do they know about its actual qualities? In the art of nausea they are mere theoretic specialists, while Céline is an empiric master.

Perhaps we can now understand somewhat better the running motif of *Journey to the End of the Night*. Céline is running not merely from society but from the sight of every living creature, and running, he trips over the knowledge that it is from himself he would flee, the self that is alone inescapable. In *Death on the Installment Plan* he often befouls himself as a child, an act which at first seems the physical equivalent of his readiness to abandon self-respect as a luxury too dangerous for this world, but which after a time comes also to signify a recognition that even he is hopelessly implicated in the physicality against which he rages. One thinks of Swift, whose balked sense of purity melts into a fascination with filth, but there is a notable difference: Swift's writings almost always chart a descent from idea to matter, there is a wracking struggle of opposed life principles, while in Céline rot is sovereign and flesh serves as argument for a gargantuan cosmic deception.

The Cheat of Language. Where finally can the compulsion to sincerity, to the last shameless self-revelation, lead but to silence? Céline writes: "I grow foul as soon as anyone talks to me; I hate it when they prattle." Or again: "The very idea made me howl with terror. Having to talk again—oh, Gawd." Anything beyond the reach of the nose is to be distrusted; all talk about human life is mere drivel unless it begins and ends with the breviary: "I am . . . thou art . . . all of us are despoilers, cheats, slobs." But once that has been said and said again and again, once Céline has spent the virtuosity of his rhetoric upon the denunciation of language, what then remains?

Comedy and Nausea. Cut away from its context in the novels, Céline's outlook upon life is narrow-spirited and tiresome. What saves him as a writer is that he so enjoys roaring his invective from the sewers, he makes his nausea into something deeply comic. In *Journey*, talking about the war, he solemnly observes that "horses are lucky. They go through the war, like us, but they're not asked to . . . seem to believe in it. In this business they are unfortunate but free." During his visit to Africa, after suffering the afflictions of the jungle, he remarks that he is especially misfortunate because, as it happens, he "does not like the country." In *Death on the Installment Plan* his boss, a bogus scientist, launches a typical Célinesque diatribe after having failed in a piece of chicanery: "I'll get them right this time . . . Their bellies, Ferdinand! Not their heads, but their bellies. Their digestions shall be my customers . . . I'm through with the spirit for keeps! We're onto the bowels now, Ferdinand, the grand alimentary canal."

It is this comic nausea that accounts for the vividness of Céline's novels. His hatred and fear of abstraction lead him to stake everything on the specific incident. With noisy verbs and cascades of adjectives, he assaults nose, ear, eye, creating a carnival of sensations. But precisely this vividness soon reveals Céline's limitation as a writer, for it tends to be monolithic and exhausting. Céline is not a satirist in the sense that Swift was, despite the remarkable energy of disgust the two writers share; Céline is neither intelligent nor discriminating enough to be a true satirist. His métier is a kind of savage burlesque. The nausea that makes him recoil from experience is linked to the comedy that makes him relish the experience of recoil—beyond that he cannot go.

Philistine and Genius. Halfway, both of Céline's novels begin to lag, for they are really more like a vaudeville, a grab bag of skits, than coherently developed fictions. In terms of sheer *performance* they contain pages rivaling Dickens, yet once the climax of a skit is known there is seldom much point in waiting for either its conclusion or repetition. By its very nature, the skit cannot be sustained over a long period of time: it is essentially a virtuoso device and virtuosity holds one's attention largely through initial shock or brilliance. This is a technical difficulty, but as always, the technical difficulty reflects a deeper problem in literary intelligence. The opening of a Céline novel is so seductively vigorous in manner and conclusive in meaning that little remains for further development. A mere accumulation of misfortunes, even when rendered with comic genius, becomes enervating unless the misfortunes are controlled by some principle of selection, some idea of greater scope than the probability of further misfortune.

One comes at times to suspect that Céline writes from a total emptiness, that his show of energy hides a void, that he is really without any genuine attitude or values. At such points his novels seem like charades in which the gestures of life are enacted but the content has been lost. Driven by his simplistic ethics and his raging indiscriminateness of feeling to always greater assertions of cynicism, he falls, predictably, into the opposite error of sentimentalism. When he falls in love, it is with an embarrassing callowness. Let a Detroit prostitute show him an ounce of kindness or an inch of thigh, and he moons like a schoolboy.

The ultimate limitation in Céline's work is a limitation of intelligence. He does not know what to do with his outpourings, except to multiply them; he cannot surmount his brilliant monomania. He is unable to distinguish among the kinds and degrees of loathsomeness, between a speck of dust and a mound of filth. Irritation and outrage, triviality and betrayal grate on his nerves with equal force. Except on grounds of radical incompleteness, it would be difficult to quarrel with Céline's description of twentieth-century experience; but there is something exasperating, at times even stupid, about a writer who roars with the same passion against nuisance and disaster. So overwhelmed is he by his demon of dirt, so infatuated with the invective he sends hurtling through his pages, he seems unable to think—and in the kind of novels he wrote, thought can be postponed but not dismissed. For all his authentic sense of affliction and all his gift for comedy, Céline remains something of a philistine, a philistine blessed with genius but a philistine nonetheless.

Shortly after the appearance of *Journey to the End of the Night* there appeared a striking critical essay by Leon Trotsky praising the novel—"Céline walked into great literature as other men walk into their own homes"—and predicting that Céline "will not write a second book with such an aversion for the lie and such a disbelief in the truth. The dissonance must resolve itself. Either the artist will make his peace with the darkness or he will perceive the dawn."

Trotsky's timing was a little off, and what he meant by "the dawn" need not concern us here. Céline did manage to write a second novel with the same attitudes as those in *Journey,* but essentially the prediction of Trotsky was correct. In 1936 Céline took a trip to Russia and shortly thereafter wrote a little book called *Mea Culpa* in which, together with some shrewd observations about the Stalin dictatorship, he indulged himself in a wild harangue against the inherent bestiality of mankind. Apart from the humor and inventiveness of his novels, Céline's reflections served only to reveal the radical limitations of the kind of modern novelist who presents his intellectual incapacity as a principled anti-intellectualism.

There now begins a visible disintegration of Céline as both writer and person. In 1938 he published a book entitled *Trifles for a Massacre (Bagatelles pour un Massacre),* a dreary tract in which he blamed the Jews for everything from the defeat of Napoleon to the rise of surrealism, the corruption of the French language and the Sino-Japanese war. Gide, reviewing the book, took it to be a satire on the assumption that it was impossible that a writer of Céline's gifts could mean what he said; but now it seems obvious that Céline did in fact mean what he said.

During World War II Céline played a dishonorable role, living at peace with the Nazi occupation forces and expressing admiration for the Vichy collaborators. (See the preface to *Guignol's Band*, a late fiction that has almost no literary value but some pathological interest.) After the war the French government accused Céline of having been a collaborator and he, self-exiled to Denmark, offered the sad reply that he had merely been an "abstentionist." Tried by the French authorities *in absentia*, he was convicted, sentenced, but not required to serve his time in prison. During the last decade of his life—he died in 1961— Céline was allowed to return to France, where he lived in semi-retirement, an embittered man. Young readers who have come to admire Samuel Beckett, Jean Genet, and William Burroughs seem hardly to know that behind these writers, both as predecessor and possible influence, stands the disheveled but formidable figure of Louis-Ferdinand Céline.

His career, like that of Ezra Pound, is a classical instance of how a writer suffers in his purely literary work when his powers of mind are unequal to his powers of imagination. From the depths of the underground man's soul Céline brought forth all its effluvia, so that the world could see what was simmering there. His first two novels, in their brilliant imperfection, seem likely to survive the sickness of their inspiration. But at the end, unable to transcend the foulness which was his authentic and entirely legitimate subject, he made "his peace with the darkness." And not he alone.

✍

The Fiction
of Antiutopia

"I feel sometimes as though the whole modern world of capitalism and Communism and all were rushing toward some enormous efficient machine-made doom of the true values of life."

This sentence was written in 1922 by Max Eastman, then a prominent intellectual defender of the Russian Revolution. It contains the crux of what would later fill volumes of disenchantment; and the need to speak it constitutes one reason why the intellectual experience of our time has been so full of self-distrust and self-assault. For some decades there had already been present a tradition in which conservative thinkers assaulted the idea of utopia as an impious denial of the limitations of the human lot, or a symptom of political naïveté, or a fantasy both trivial and boring—this last view finding a curious echo in Wallace Stevens' dismissal of the utopia called heaven: "Does ripe fruit never fall?" But the kind of fiction I have in mind and propose to call antiutopian does not stem from the conservative tradition, even when wryly borrowing from it.

Eastman's sentence would not seem remarkable if spoken by G. K. Chesterton or Hillaire Belloc; its continuing power to shock depends upon our knowledge that it came from a man of the left. And antiutopian fiction, as it seeks to embody the sentiments expressed by Eastman, also comes primarily from men of the left. Eugene Zamiatin (*We*) is a dissident from Communism; George Orwell (*1984*) a heterodox socialist; Aldous Huxley

(Brave New World) a scion of liberalism. The peculiar intensity of such fiction derives from the writer's discovery that in facing the prospect of a future he had been trained to desire, he finds himself struck with horror. The work of these writers is a systematic release of trauma, a painful turning upon their own presuppositions. It is a fiction of urgent yet reluctant testimony, forced by profoundly serious men from their own resistance to fears they cannot evade.

What they fear is not, as liberals and radicals always have, that history will suffer a miscarriage; what they fear is that the long-awaited birth will prove to be a monster. Not many Americans are able to grasp this experience: few of us ever having cultivated the taste for utopia, fewer still have suffered the bitter aftertaste of antiutopia. For Europeans, however, it all comes with the ferocity of shock. Behind the antiutopian novel lies not merely the frightful vision of a totalitarian world, but something that seems still more alarming. To minds raised on the assumptions, whether liberal or Marxist, of nineteenth-century philosophies of history—assumptions that the human enterprise has a purposive direction, or *telos,* and an upward rhythm, or progress —there is also the fear that history itself has proved to be a cheat. And a cheat not because it has turned away from our expectations, but because it betrays our hopes precisely through an inverted fulfillment of those expectations. Not progress denied but progress realized, is the nightmare haunting the antiutopian novel. And behind this nightmare lies a crisis of thought quite as intense as that suffered by serious nineteenth-century minds when they discovered that far more painful than doubting the existence of God was questioning the validity of his creation.

Whether to distinguish literary genres or subgenres through purely formal characteristics or to insist upon the crucial relevance of subject, theme, and intellectual content, is something of a problem for theorists of criticism. It is all the more so in regard to fiction, which is less a genre than a menagerie of genres. I am inclined to think that in regard to prose fiction strictly formal characteristics will never suffice, even while remaining necessary, for proper description; and so I shall note here some of the main intellectual premises shaping antiutopian fiction and then a few of those formal properties by which it may be distinguished from the familiar kinds of novel.

The first of the intellectual premises I have already remarked upon: what might be called the disenchantment with history—history both as experience and as idea. The second is closely related. It is the vision of a world foreseen by a character in Dostoevsky's *The Possessed*, who declares his wish for a mode of existence in which "only the necessary is necessary." Zamiatin's *We*, the first and best of the antiutopian novels, portrays a "glass paradise" in which all men live in principled unprivacy, without a self to hide or a mood to indulge. Zamiatin thus reflects, as Orwell later would in his "telescreen" and Charlie Chaplin in a sequence of *Modern Times*, the fear that the historical process, at breakneck speed and regardless of our will, is taking us toward a *transparent universe* in which all categories are fixed, the problematic has been banished, unhappiness is treason and the gratuitous act beyond imagining. In *Brave New World* docile human creatures are produced in a hatchery: the ideal of man's self-determination, so important to Western liberalism, becomes a mocking rationale for procreation by norm. One of the "disturbed" characters in *We* remarks to one of the well-adjusted: "You want to encircle the infinite with a wall" and, shifting from the metaphysical to the psychological, adds: "We are the happy arithmetical mean. As you would put it, the integration from zero to infinity, from imbeciles to Shakespeare."

This world of total integration is deprived of accident, contingency, and myth; it permits no shelter for surprise, no margin for novelty, no hope for adventure. The rational raised to an irrational power becomes its god. Reality, writes Orwell in *1984*, "is not external. Reality exists in the human mind and nowhere else . . . whatever the Party holds to be truth *is* truth." Reality is not an objective fact to be acknowledged or transformed or resisted; it is the culminating fabrication produced by the *hubris* of rationalism.

But a certain kind of rationalism, since none of the antiutopian novelists, at least in their novels, has anything to do with invoked mysticism. The sociologist Karl Mannheim distinguishes between two kinds of rationality, "substantial" and "functional." Substantial rationality is "an act of thought which reveals intelligent insight into the interrelations of events in a given situation." Functional rationality consists of

. . . a series of actions . . . organized in such a way that it leads to a previously defined goal, every element in this series of actions receiving a functional position and role. . . . It is by no means characteristic, however, of functional organization that . . . the goal itself be considered rational. . . . One may strive to attain an irrational eschatological goal, such as salvation, by so organizing one's ascetic behavior that it will lead to this goal. . . .

And Mannheim remarks:

The violent shocks of crises and revolutions have uncovered a tendency which has hitherto been working under the surface, namely the paralyzing effect of functional rationalization on the capacity for rational judgment.

In his abstract way Mannheim hits upon the nightmare vision of the antiutopian novelists: that what men do and what they are become unrelated; that a world is appearing in which technique and value have been split apart, so that technique spins forward with a mad fecundity while value becomes debased to a mere slogan of the state. This kind of "technicism," Spengler has remarked, is frequently visible in a society that has lost its self-assurance. And in his preface to *Brave New World* Huxley shows a keen awareness of the distinction between "substantial" and "functional rationality" when he remarks that "The people who govern the Brave New World may not be sane . . . but they are not madmen, and their aim is not anarchy but social stability." They live, that is, by the strict requirements of functional rationality.

All three of our writers have a lively appreciation of the need felt by modern men to drop the burden of freedom, that need crystallized in the remark of the nineteenth-century anarchist Michael Bakunin, "I do not want to be I, I want to be We." The schema of the antiutopian novel requires that in one or two forlorn figures, sports from the perfection of adjustment, there arise once more a spontaneous appetite for individuality. In *Brave New World* it takes the form of historical nostalgia; in *1984* a yearning for a personal relationship that will have no end other than its own fulfillment; and in *We,* a series of brilliant forays into self-consciousness. The narrator of *We* discloses the ethos of his world when he remarks that the half-forgotten Christians "knew that resignation is virtue and pride a vice; [and almost as if echoing Bakunin] that 'We' is from 'God,' and 'I' from the devil." But as a deviant from the deadening health of his society, he engages in a discovery of selfhood through a realization of how strange, how thoroughly artificial, the very notion of selfhood is:

Evening . . . the sky is covered with a milky-golden tissue, and one cannot see what is there, beyond, on the heights. The ancients "knew" that the greatest, bored skeptic—their god—lived there. We know that crystalline, blue, naked, indecent Nothing is there. . . . I had firm faith in myself; I believed that I knew all about myself. But then . . . I look in the mirror. And for the first time in my life, yes, for the first time in my life, I see clearly, precisely, consciously and with surprise, I see myself as some "him!" I am "he." . . . And I know surely that "he" with his straight brows is a stranger. . . .

The idea of the personal self, which for us has become an indispensable assumption of existence, is seen by Zamiatin, Orwell, and Huxley as a *cultural* idea. It is a product of the liberal era, and because it is susceptible to historical growth and decline, it may also be susceptible to historical destruction. All three of our antiutopian novels are dominated by an overwhelming question: can human nature be manufactured? Not transformed or manipulated or debased, since these it obviously can be; but manufactured by will and decision.

When speaking about the historical determinants of human nature, one tacitly assumes that there *is* a human nature, and that for all of its plasticity it retains some indestructible core. If Zamiatin, Orwell, and Huxley wrote simply from the premise of psychological relativism, they would deprive themselves of whatever possibilities for drama their theme allows, for then the very idea of a limit to the malleability of human nature would be hard to maintain. They must assume that there are strivings in men toward candor, freedom, truth, and love which cannot be suppressed indefinitely; yet they have no choice but to recognize that at any particular historical moment these strivings can be suppressed effectively, surviving for men of intelligence less as realities to be counted on than as potentialities to be nurtured. Furthermore, in modern technology there appears a whole new apparatus for violating human nature: brainwashing and torture in *1984*, artificial biological selection in *Brave New World*, and an operation similar to a lobotomy in *We*. And not only can desire be suppressed and impulse denied; they can be transformed into their very opposites, so that people sincerely take slavery to be freedom and learn, in *Brave New World*, that "the secret of happiness and virtue is liking what you've got to like."

Ultimately the antiutopian novel keeps returning to the choice posed by Dostoevsky's legend of the Grand Inquisitor in *The Brothers Karamazov:* the misery of the human being who must bear his burden of independence against the contentment of the human creature at rest in his obedience. But what now gives this counterposition of freedom and happiness a particularly sharp edge is the fact that through the refinements of technology Dostoevsky's speculation can be realized in social practice. In a number of intellectual and literary respects *Brave New World* is inferior to *1984* and *We*, but in confronting this central question it is bolder and keener, for Huxley sees that the problem first raised by Dostoevsky—will the satisfaction of material wants quench the appetite for freedom?—relates not only to totalitarian dictatorships but to the whole of industrial society. Like so many other manifestations of our culture, the antiutopian novel keeps rehearsing the problems of the nineteenth century: in this instance, not merely Dostoevsky's prophetic speculation but also the quieter fear of Alexis de Tocqueville that "a kind of virtuous materialism may ultimately be established in the world which would not corrupt but enervate the soul, and noiselessly unbend its springs of action."

The main literary problem regarding antiutopian fiction is to learn to read it according to its own premises and limits, which is to say, in ways somewhat different from those by which we read ordinary novels.

Strictly speaking, antiutopian fictions are not novels at all. Northrop Frye has usefully distinguished among kinds of fiction in order to remind us that we have lost in critical niceness by our habit of lumping all prose fiction under the heading of the novel. He is right, of course, but I suspect that for common usage the effort to revive such distinctions is a lost cause, and that it may be better to teach readers to discriminate among

kinds of novels. If we do for the moment accept Frye's categories it becomes clear that books like *We, 1984,* and *Brave New
World* are not really novels portraying a familiar social world
but are Menippean satire, a kind of fiction that

> . . . deals less with people as such than with mental attitudes. . . .
> The Menippean satire thus resembles the confession in its ability to
> handle abstract ideas and theories, and differs from the novel in its
> characterization, which is stylized rather than naturalistic, and presents
> people as mouthpieces of the ideas they represent. . . . At its most
> concentrated the Menippean satire presents us with a vision of the
> world in terms of a single intellectual pattern.

Accept this description and the usual complaints about the antiutopian novel come to seem irrelevant. By its very nature the
antiutopian novel cannot satisfy the expectations we hold, often
unreflectively, about the ordinary novel: expectations that are
the heritage of nineteenth-century Romanticism with its stress
upon individual consciousness, psychological analysis, and the
scrutiny of intimate relations. When the English critic Raymond
Williams complains that the antiutopian novel lacks "a substantial society and correspondingly substantial persons," he is offering a description but intends it as a depreciation, quite as if a
critic complained that a sonnet lacks a complex dramatic plot.
For the very premise of antiutopian fiction is that it projects a
world in which such elements—"substantial society . . . substantial persons"—have largely been suppressed and must now be
painfully recovered, if recovered at all.

One might even speculate that it would be a mistake for the
author of an antiutopian novel to provide the usual complement
of three-dimensional characters such as we expect in ordinary
fiction, or to venture an extended amount of psychological specification. For these books try to present a world in which individuality has become obsolete and personality a sign of sub-
version. The major figures of such books are necessarily
grotesques: they resemble persons who have lost the power of
speech and must struggle to regain it; Winston Smith and Julia
in *1984* are finally engaged in an effort to salvage the idea of the
human *as an idea,* which means to experiment with the possibilities of solitude and the risks of contemplation. The human relations which the ordinary novel takes as its premise, become

the possibilities toward which the antiutopian novel strains. What in the ordinary novel appears as the tacit assumption of the opening page is now, in the antiutopian novel, a wistful hope usually unrealized by the concluding page. That the writer of antiutopian fiction must deal with a world in which man has been absorbed by his function and society by the state, surely places upon him a considerable quota of difficulties. But this is the task he sets himself, and there can be no point in complaining that he fails to do what in the nature of things he cannot do.

The antiutopian novel lacks almost all the usual advantages of fiction: it must confine itself to a rudimentary kind of characterization, it cannot provide much in the way of psychological nuance, it hardly pretends to a large accumulation of suspense. Yet, as we can all testify, the antiutopian novel achieves its impact, and this it does through a variety of formal means:

1) *It posits a "flaw" in the perfection of the perfect.* This "flaw," the weakness of the remembered or yearned-for human, functions dramatically in the antiutopian novel quite as the assumption of original sin or a socially induced tendency toward evil does in the ordinary novel. The "flaw" provides the possibility and particulars of the conflict, while it simultaneously insures that the outcome will be catastrophic. Since the ending of the antiutopian novel is predictable and contained, so to say, within its very beginning, the tension it creates depends less on a developed plot than on an overpowering conception. And so—

2) *It must be in the grip of an idea at once dramatically simple and historically complex: an idea that has become a commanding passion.* This idea consists, finally, in a catastrophic transmutation of values, a stoppage of history at the expense of its actors. In reading the antiutopian novel we respond less to the world it projects than to the urgency of the projection. And since this involves the dangers of both monotony and monomania—

3) *It must be clever in the management of its substantiating detail.* Knowing all too well the inevitable direction of things, we can be surprised only by the ingenuity of local particulars. And here arises a possible basis for comparative valuations among antiutopian novels. Orwell's book is impressive for its motivating passion, less so for its local composition. Huxley's is notably clever, but too rationalistic and self-contained: he does

not write like a man who feels himself imperiled by his own vision. Zamiatin is both passionate and brilliant, clever and driven. His style, an astonishing mosaic of violent imagery, sustains his vision throughout the book in a way that a mere linear unfolding of his fable never could. But since the antiutopian novel must satisfy the conflicting requirements of both a highly charged central idea and cleverness in the management of detail, it becomes involved with special problems of verisimilitude. That is—

4) *It must strain our sense of the probable while not violating our attachment to the plausible.* To stay too close to the probable means, for the antiutopian novel, to lose the very reason for its existence; to appear merely implausible means to surrender its power to shock. Our writers meet this difficulty by employing what I would call the dramatic strategy and the narrative psychology of "one more step." Their projected total state is one step beyond our known reality—not so much a picture of modern totalitarian society as an extension, by just one and no more than one step, of the essential pattern of the total state.

5) *In presenting the nightmare of history undone, it must depend on the ability of its readers to engage in an act of historical recollection.* This means, above all, to remember the power that the idea of utopia has had in Western society. "The Golden Age," wrote Dostoevsky, "is the most unlikely of all the dreams that have been, but for it men have given up their life and all their strength. . . . Without it the people will not live and cannot die." Still dependent on this vision of the Golden Age, the antiutopian novel shares an essential quality of all modern literature: it can realize its values only through images of their violation. The enchanted dream has become a nightmare, but a nightmare projected with such power as to validate the remembered urgency of the dream.

~~❧~~

I. B. Singer:
False Messiahs and
Modern Sensibility

Interviewers: Would it be fair to say that you are actually writing in a somewhat artificial or illusory context, as if none of the terrible things that have happened to the Jewish people during the last two decades really did occur?

Singer: Yes, very fair. There was a famous philosopher, Vaihinger, who wrote a book called *The Philosophy of "As If,"* in which he showed that we all behave "as if." The "as if" is so much a part of our life that it really isn't artificial. . . . Every man assumes he will go on living. He behaves *as if* he will never die. So I wouldn't call my attitude artificial. It's very natural and healthy. We have to go on living and writing.

Interviewers: But do you agree that at the heart of your attitude there is an illusion which is consciously sustained?

Singer: Yes.*

No other living writer has yielded himself so completely and recklessly as has Isaac Bashevis Singer to the claims of the human imagination. Singer writes in Yiddish, a language that no amount of energy and affection seems likely to save from extinction. He writes about a world that is gone, destroyed with a brutality beyond historical comparison. He writes within a culture, the remnant of Yiddish in the Western world, that is more than a little dubious about his purpose and stress. He seems to

* This and the following direct statements by Isaac Bashevis Singer are from an interview that appeared in *Commentary,* November 1963.

75

take entirely for granted his role as a traditional storyteller speaking to an audience attuned to his every hint and nuance, an audience that values storytelling both in its own right and as a binding communal action—but also, as it happens, an audience that keeps fading week by week, shrinking day by day. And he does all this without a sigh or an apology, without so much as a Jewish groan. It strikes one as a kind of inspired madness: here is a man living in New York City, a sophisticated and clever writer, who composes stories about Frampol, Bilgoray, Kreshev *as if they were still there.* His work is shot through with the bravado of a performer who enjoys making his listeners gasp, weep, laugh, and yearn for more. Above and beyond everything else he is a great performer, in ways that remind one of Twain, Dickens, Sholom Aleichem.

Singer writes Yiddish prose with a verbal and rhythmic brilliance that, to my knowledge, can hardly be matched. When Eliezer Greenberg and I were working on our *Treasury of Yiddish Stories,* he said to me: "Singer has to be heard, to be believed." Behind the prose there is always a spoken voice, tense, ironic, complex in tonalities, leaping past connectives. Greenberg then read to me, with a fluency and pith I could never capture in my own reading of Yiddish, Singer's masterpiece, "Gimpel the Fool," and I knew at once—it took no great powers of judgment —that here was the work of a master. The story came as a stroke of revelation, like a fiction by Babel or Kleist encountered for the first time.

Singer's stories claim attention through their vivacity and strangeness of surface. He is devoted to the grotesque, the demonic, the erotic, the quasi-mystical. He populates his alien subworld with imps, devils, whores, fanatics, charlatans, spirits in seizure, disciples of false messiahs. A young girl is captured by the spirit of a dead woman and goes to live with the mourning husband as if she were actually his wife; a town is courted and then shattered by a lavish stranger who turns out to be the devil; an ancient Jew suffering unspeakable deprivations during World War I, crawls back to his village of Bilgoray and fathers a son whom, with marvelous aplomb, he names Isaac. Sometimes the action in Singer's stories follows the moral curve of traditional folk tales, with a charming, lightly phrased "lesson" at the end; sometimes, the spiral of a quizzical modern awareness; at best, the complicated motions of the old and the contemporary yoked together, a kind of narrative double-stop.

Orgiastic lapses from the moral order, pacts with the devil, ascetic self-punishment, distraught sexuality occupy the foreground of Singer's stories. Yet behind this expressionist clamor there is glimpsed the world of the *shtetl*, or East European Jewish village, as it stumbled and slept through the last few centuries. Though Singer seldom portrays it fullface, one must always keep this world in mind while reading his stories: it forms the base from which he wanders, the norm from which he deviates but which controls his deviation. And truly to hear these stories one must have at least a splinter of knowledge about the culture from which Singer comes, the world he continues to evoke as if it were still radiantly alive: the Hasidim still dancing, the rabbis still pondering, the children still studying, the poor still hungering, as if it had not all ended in ashes and death. Isaac Bashevis Singer was born in Radzymin, Poland, in 1904. Both his father and grandfather were rabbis, in the tradition of Hasidism, a kind of ecstatic pietism, though on his mother's side the *misnagid* or rationalist strain of Jewish belief was the stronger. "My father," recalls Singer, "always used to say that if you don't believe in the *zadikim* [the "wonder-rabbis" of Hasidism] today, tomorrow you won't believe in God. My mother would say, it's one thing to believe in God and another to believe in man. My mother's point of view is also my point of view."

Raised in a poor neighborhood of Warsaw, on Krochmalna Street, Singer received a strictly traditional Jewish education. He studied in a rabbinical seminary which "was a kind of college" providing secular as well as religious studies. During his adolescence he spent three or four years in his grandfather's *shtetl*, Bilgoray, which would later show itself as a strong influence upon his work. Bilgoray

was very old-fashioned. Not much had changed there in many generations. In this town the traditions of hundreds of years ago still lived. There was no railroad nearby. It was stuck in the forest and it was pretty much as it must have been during the time of Chmielnicki. . . . I could have written *The Family Moskat* [a novel set in Warsaw] without having lived in Bilgoray, but I could never have written *Satan in Goray* [a novelette dealing with seventeenth-century false messianism] or some of my short stories without having been there.

A decisive example was set by Singer's older brother, Israel Joshua, who began to write in his youth and would become a leading Yiddish novelist, author of *The Brothers Ashkenazi* and *Yashe Kolb*. Throughout a distinguished career, I. J. Singer would remain pretty much within the main lines of the Yiddish tradition, as to both moral and social attitudes, even though he was strongly influenced by contemporary Western writing, especially the kind of large-scale family novel popular in Europe at the turn of the century. Controlling the older Singer's fiction is the Jewish community, both as social framework and source of values; his style, fluent, relaxed, and smooth, can be taken as a model for cultivated modern Yiddish. The older brother represents that which I. B. Singer learned from, struggled with, and then mostly left behind. In the Jewish world of Warsaw during the time Singer was growing up, a decision to become a secular writer meant a painful conflict with family and culture, a symbolic break from the paths of tradition:

It was a great shock to [my parents]. They considered all the secular [Yiddish] writers to be heretics, all unbelievers—they really were too, most of them. To become a *literat* was to them almost as bad as becoming a *meshumed*, one who forsakes the faith. My father used to say that secular writers like Peretz were leading the Jews to heresy. He said everything they wrote was against God. Even though Peretz wrote in a religious vein, my father called his writing "sweetened poison," but poison nevertheless. And from his point of view, he was right. Everybody who read such books sooner or later became a worldly man and forsook the traditions. In my family, of course, my brother had gone first, and I went after him. For my parents this was a tragedy.

In these early years of the century Warsaw was a lively if troubled city, the main center of Jewish cultural life. The binding tradition of Yiddish literature had already been set by the pioneer generation of writers: Mendele Mocher Sforim, Sholom Aleichem, I. L. Peretz. It was a literature strongly devoted to problems of communal destiny and survival; characterized by a high, sometimes consuming ethical intent; closely tied to folk sources; drawing profoundly upon, even as it kept moving away from, religious tradition; resting upon a culture that might still be described as "organic" and certainly as coherent; and yet displaying many signs of the influence of European, especially

Russian, writing. In Warsaw the major social and cultural movements of East European Jewish life found their most sophisticated versions: Yiddishism, the effort to create an autonomous secular culture based on the language of *galut;* Bundism, the organization of a distinctively Jewish socialism; and Zionism, potentially of great importance but at this point still weak. Peretz's home became the gathering place for young writers fresh from the provinces where the majority of Jews still lived; here, in this cosmopolitan haven, they could begin planning their novels and stories about the overwhelming memory of the *shtetl.* And the religious community, though challenged from several directions and past the high point of its power, remained a major force within the world of the East European Jews.

As he grew up in this feverish but immensely stimulating atmosphere, the young Singer carved out a path of his own. He was not drawn to any of the Jewish movements: indeed, he has always been skeptical of the political messianism which, as a partial offshoot of the earlier religious messianism, runs through twentieth-century Jewish life. He edged away from formal piety, yet remained close to the Jewish religious tradition, especially its more esoteric and cabalistic elements. And while a master of the Yiddish language—he is second only to Sholom Aleichem in his command of its idiom—Singer was neither a programmatic Yiddishist nor notably at ease in the world of Yiddish culture, which has in the main been secular and rationalist in stress.

As a youth Singer began to read in forbidden tongues, discovering E. T. A. Hoffmann and Edgar Allan Poe in the libraries of Warsaw. The exotic romanticism of these writers stirred his imagination rather more than did the work of most Yiddish writers, who were then in a realistic or even naturalistic phase, and with whose materials he felt all too familiar. An even stronger alien influence was that of Knut Hamsun, the Norwegian novelist who enjoyed an international vogue during the years before World War II. Hamsun's novels, especially *Pan,* impressed upon the younger Singer the claims of the irrational in human existence, the power of the perverse within seemingly normal behavior. Now, several decades later, it is hard to see much evidence of Hamsun in Singer's work; perhaps it was the kind of influence that does not leave a visible stamp but instead liberates a writer to go his own way.

A still more alien influence—for a young Jewish writer fresh from the yeshiva, an influence downright bizarre—was that curious body of writings known as spiritualism or "psychic research," which Singer somehow came upon in Warsaw and would continue to follow throughout his life. Could anything be more distant from the tradition of Yiddish literature or, for that matter, from the whole body of Jewish religious thought? Fortunately for his career as a writer, Singer has preserved a keen Jewish skepticism—in that department he is entirely traditional!—toward this branch of "knowledge," taking the sophisticated view that belief in the reality of spirits provides his fiction with a kind of compositional shorthand, a "spiritual stenography." As he remarks: "The demons and Satan represent to me, in a sense, the ways of the world. Instead of saying this is the way things happen, I will say, this is the way demons behave." Which is precisely what any cultivated skeptic, totally unconcerned with "psychic research," would also say.

In 1935, convinced that "it was inevitable after Hitler came to power that the Germans would invade Poland," Singer emigrated to the United States. He joined the staff of the *Jewish Daily Forward*, a Yiddish newspaper, in which he printed serious fiction under his own name and a large quantity of journalism under the pen name of Warshofsky. His first major work, the novella *Satan in Goray*, appeared in Yiddish in 1935. Since then he has written full-scale novels, one of which, *The Family Moskat*, was published in an English translation in 1949, as well as a number of short novels (English titles: *The Magician of Lublin* and *The Slave*) and several collections of stories. His best work has been done in short forms, the novella and the story— exciting bursts and flares of the imagination.

Isaac Bashevis Singer is the only living Yiddish writer whose translated work has caught the imagination of the American literary public. Though the settings of his stories are frequently strange, the contemporary reader—for whom the determination not to be shocked has become a point of honor—is likely to feel closer to Singer than to most other Yiddish writers. Offhand this may be surprising, for Singer's subjects are decidedly remote and exotic: in *Satan in Goray* the orgiastic consequences of the false messianism of seventeenth-century East European Jewish life;

in *The Magician of Lublin* a portrait of a Jewish magician—Don Juan in late nineteenth-century Poland who exhausts himself with sensuality and ends as a penitent ascetic; in his stories a range of demonic, apocalyptic and perversely sacred moments of *shtetl* life. Yet one feels that, unlike many of the Yiddish writers who treat more familiar and up-to-date subjects, Singer commands a distinctly "modern" sensibility.

Now this is partly true—in that Singer has cut himself off from some of the traditional styles and assumptions of Yiddish writing. But it is also not true—in that any effort to assimilate Singer to literary "modernism" without fully registering his involvement with Jewish faith and history, is almost certain to distort his meanings.

Those meanings, one might as well admit, are often enigmatic and hard to come by. It must be a common experience among Singer's readers to find a quick pleasure in the caustic surfaces of his prose, the nervous tokens of his virtuosity, but then to acknowledge themselves baffled as to his point and purpose. That his fiction does have an insistent point and stringent purpose no one can doubt: Singer is too ruthlessly single-minded a writer to content himself with mere slices of representation or displays of the bizarre. His grotesquerie must be taken seriously, perhaps as a recoil from his perception of how ugly—how irremediably and gratuitously ugly—human life can be. He is a writer completely absorbed by the demands of his vision, a vision gnomic and compulsive but with moments of high exaltation; so that while reading his stories one feels as if one were overhearing bits and snatches of monologue, the impact of which is both notable and disturbing, but the meaning withheld.

Now these are precisely the qualities that the sophisticated reader, trained to docility before the exactions of "modernism," has come to applaud. Singer's stories work, or prey, upon the nerves. They leave one unsettled and anxious, the way a rationalist might feel if, waking at night in the woods, he suddenly found himself surrounded by a swarm of bats. Unlike most Yiddish fiction, Singer's stories neither round out the cycle of their intentions nor posit a coherent and ordered universe. They can be seen as paradigms of the arbitrariness, the grating injustice, at the heart of life. They offer instances of pointless suffering, dead-end exhaustion, inexplicable grace. And sometimes, as in

Singer's masterpiece, "Gimpel the Fool," they turn about, refusing to rest with the familiar discomforts of the problematic,
and drive toward a prospect of salvation on the other side of
despair, beyond soiling by error or will. This prospect does not
depend on any belief in the comeliness or lawfulness of the universe; whether God is there or not, He is surely no protector.
("He had worked out his own religion," writes Singer about one
of his characters. "There was a Creator, but He revealed Himself
to no one, gave no indications of what was permitted or forbidden.") Things happen, the probable bad and improbable
good, both of them subject to the whim of the fortuitous—and
the sacred fools like Gimpel, perhaps they alone, find the value
of their life in a total passivity and credulousness, a complete
openness to suffering.

Singer's stories trace the characteristic motions of human destiny: a heavy climb upward ("The Old Man"), a rapid tumble
downward ("The Fast"). Life forms a journeying to heaven and
hell, mostly hell. What determines the direction a man will
take? Sometimes the delicate maneuvers between his will and
desire, sometimes the heat of his vanity, sometimes the blessing
of innocence. But more often than not, it is all a mystery which
Singer chooses to present rather than explain. As his figures
move upward and downward, aflame with the passion of their
ineluctable destiny, they stop for a moment in the *shtetl* world.
Singer is not content with the limitations of materiality, yet not
at all indifferent to the charms and powers of the phenomenal
universe. In his calculus of destiny, however, the world is a
resting place and what happens within it, even within the social
enclave of the Jews, is not of lasting significance. Thick, substantial, and attractive as it comes to seem in Singer's representation,
the world is finally but the lure and appearance, a locale between
heaven and hell, the shadow of larger possibilities.

In most Yiddish fiction the stress is quite different. There the
central "character" is the collective destiny of the Jews in *galut*,
or exile; the central theme, the survival of a nation deprived of
nationhood; the central ethic, the humane education of men
stripped of worldly power yet sustained by the memory of
chosenness and the promise of redemption. In Singer the norm of
collective life is still present, but mostly in the background, as

a tacit assumption; his central actions break away from the limits of the *shtetl* ethic, what has come to be known as *Yiddish-keit*, and then move either backward to the abandon of false messianism or forward to the doubt of modern sensibility. (There is an interesting exception, the story called "Short Friday," which in its stress upon family affection, ritual proprieties, and collective faith, approaches rather closely the tones of traditional Yiddish fiction.)

The historical settings of East European Jewish life are richly presented in Singer's stories, often not as orderly sequences in time but as simultaneous perceptions jumbled together in the consciousness of figures for whom Abraham's sacrifice, Chmielnicki's pogroms, the rise and fall of Hasidism, and the stirrings of the modern world are all felt with equal force. Yet Singer's ultimate concern is not with the collective experience of a martyred people but with the enigmas of personal fate. Given the slant of his vision, this leads him to place a heavy reliance upon the grotesque as a mode of narration, even as an avenue toward knowledge. But the grotesque carries with it a number of literary and moral dangers, not the least being the temptation for Singer to make it into an end in itself, which is to say, something facile and sensationalistic. In his second-rank stories, he falls back a little too comfortably upon the devices of which he is absolute master, like a magician supremely confident his tricks will continue to work. But mainly the grotesque succeeds in Singer's stories because it comes to symbolize meaningful digressions from a cultural norm. An uninstructed reader may absorb Singer's grotesquerie somewhat too easily into the assumptions of modern literature; the reader who grasps the ambivalence of Singer's relation to Yiddish literature will see the grotesquerie as a cultural sign by means of which Singer defines himself against his own past.

It is hardly a secret that in the Yiddish literary world Singer is regarded with a certain suspicion. His powers of evocation, his resources as a stylist are acknowledged, yet many Yiddish literary people, including the serious ones, seem uneasy about him. One reason is that "modernism"—which, as these people regard Singer, signifies a heavy stress upon sexuality, a concern for the irrational, expressionist distortions of character, and a seeming indifference to the humane ethic of Yiddishism—has never won so strong a hold in Jewish culture as it has in the cultures of most Western countries. For Yiddish writers, "modernism" has been at best an adornment of manner upon a subject inescapably traditional.

The truly "modern" writer, however, is not quite trustworthy in relation to his culture. He is a shifty character by choice and need, unable to settle into that solid representativeness which would allow him to act as a cultural "spokesman." And to the extent that Singer does share in the modernist outlook he must be regarded with distrust by Yiddish readers brought up on such literary "spokesmen" as Peretz, Abraham Reisen, and H. Leivick. There is no lack of admiration among Yiddish readers for Singer's work: anyone with half an ear for the cadence and idiom of that marvelous language must respond to his prose. Still, it is a qualified, a troubled admiration. Singer's moral outlook, which seems to move with equal readiness toward the sensational and the ascetic, is hardly calculated to put Yiddish readers at their ease. So they continue to read him, with pleasure and anxiety.

And, as it seems to me, they are not altogether wrong. Their admiring resistance to Singer's work may constitute a more attentive and serious response to his iconoclasm than the gleeful applause of those who read him in English translation and take him to be another writer of "black comedy," or, heaven help us, a mid-twentieth-century "swinger."

"The death of Satan was a tragedy for the imagination."

Anyone with even a smattering of Yiddish should try to read Singer's stories in the original. By and large he has been fortunate in his translators, but no translation, not even Saul Bellow's magnificent rendering of "Gimpel the Fool," could possibly suggest the full idiomatic richness and syntactical verve of Singer's Yiddish. Singer has left behind him the oratorical sententiousness to which Yiddish literature is prone, has abandoned its leisurely meandering pace, what might be called the *shtetl* rhythm, and has developed a style that is both swift and dense, nervous and thick. His sentences are short and abrupt; his rhythms coiled, intense, short-breathed. The impression his prose creates is not of a smooth and equable flow of language but rather a series of staccato advances and withdrawals, with sharp breaks between sentences. Singer seldom qualifies, wanders, or circles back; his method is to keep darting forward, impression upon impression, through a series of jabbing declarative sentences. His prose is free of "literary" effects, a frequent weakness among Yiddish writers who wish to display their elegance and cultivation. And at the base of his prose is the oral idiom of Yiddish, seeded with ironic proverbs and apothegms ("Shoulders are from God, and burdens too"); but a speech that has been clipped, wrenched, syncopated.

What is most remarkable about Singer's prose is his ability to combine rich detail with fiercely compressed rhythms. For the translator this presents the almost insuperable problem of how to capture both his texture and his pace, his density of specification and his vibrating quickness. More often than not, even the most accomplished translator must choose between one effect and the other, if only because the enormous difficulty of rendering Yiddish idiom into another language forces him either to fill out or slow down Singer's sentences.

Pace cannot be illustrated, but the richness of Singer's detail can. As in this characteristic passage from "The Old Man":

His son had died long before, and Reb Moshe Ber said the memorial prayer, *kaddish,* for him. Now alone in the apartment, he had to feed his stove with paper and wood shavings from garbage cans. In the ashes he baked rotten potatoes, which he carried in his scarf, and in an iron pot, he brewed chicory. He kept house, made his own candles by kneading bits of wax and suet around wicks, laundered his shirt beneath the kitchen faucet, and hung it to dry on a piece of string. He set the mousetraps each night and drowned the mice each morning. When he went out he never forgot to fasten the heavy padlock on the door. No one had to pay rent in Warsaw at that time. . . .

The winter was difficult. There was no coal, and since several tiles were missing from the stove, the apartment was filled with thick black smoke each time the old man made a fire. A crust of blue ice and snow covered the window panes by November, making the rooms constantly dark or dusky. Overnight, the water on his night table froze in the pot. No matter how many clothes he piled over him in bed, he never felt warm; his feet remained stiff, and as soon as he began to doze, the entire pile of clothes would fall off, and he would have to climb out naked to make his bed once more. There was no kerosene; even matches were at a premium. Although he recited chapter upon chapter of the Psalms, he could not fall asleep. The wind, freely roaming about the rooms, banged the doors; even the mice left.

Or, in a more colorful vein, from "The Last Demon":

I [the last demon] came here from Lublin. Tishevitz is a God-forsaken village: Adam didn't even stop to pee there. It's so small that a wagon goes through town and the horse is in the market place just as the rear wheels reach the toll gate. There is mud in Tishevitz from Succoth until Tishe b'Ov. The goats of the town don't need to lift their beards to chew at the thatched roofs of the cottages. Hens roost in the middle of the streets. Birds build nests in the women's bonnets. In the tailors' synagogue a billy goat is the tenth in the quorum.

Or, grotesquely, from "Blood":

Frequently she sang for hours in Yiddish and in Polish. Her voice was harsh and cracked and she invented the songs as she went along, repeating meaningless phrases, uttering sounds that resembled the cackling of fowl, the grunting of pigs, the death-rattles of oxen. . . . At night in her dreams, phantoms tormented her: bulls gored her with their horns; pigs shoved their snouts into her face and bit her; roosters cut her flesh to ribbons with their spurs.

Or, tenderly, from "Gimpel the Fool":

I was an orphan. My grandfather who brought me up was already bent toward the grave. So they turned me over to a baker, and what a time they gave me there! Every woman or girl who came to bake a batch of noodles had to fool me at least once. "Gimpel, there's a fair in heaven; Gimpel, the rabbi gave birth to a calf in the seventh month; Gimpel, a cow flew over the roof and laid brass eggs." A student from the yeshiva came once to buy a roll, and he said, "You, Gimpel, while you stand here scraping with your baker's shovel the Messiah has come. The dead have arisen." "What do you mean?" I said. "I heard no one blowing the ram's horn!" He said, "Are you deaf?" And all began to cry, "We heard it, we heard! . . ."

To tell the truth, I knew very well that nothing of the sort had happened, but all the same, as folks were talking, I threw on my wool vest and went out. Maybe something had happened. What did I stand to lose by looking? Well, what a cat music went up! And then I took a vow to believe nothing more. But that was no go either. They confused me so that I didn't know the big end from the small.

Those of Singer's stories which speed downward into hell are often told by devils and imps, sometimes by Satan himself, marveling at the vanity and paltriness of the human creatures. Singer's arch-devil is a figure not so much of evil as of skepticism, a thoroughly modern voice to whose corrosive questions Singer imparts notable force in "A Tale of Two Liars":

Are you stupid enough to still believe in the power of prayer? Remember how the Jews prayed during the Black Plague, and nevertheless, how they perished like flies? And what about the thousands the Cossacks butchered? There was enough prayer, wasn't there, when Chmielnicki came? How were those prayers answered? Children were buried alive, chaste wives raped—and later their bellies ripped open and cats sewed inside. Why should God bother with your prayers? He neither hears nor sees. There is no judge. There is no judgment.

Using demons and imps as narrators proves to be a wonderful device for structural economy: they replace the need to enter the "inner life" of the characters, the whole plaguing business of the psychology of motives, for they serve as symbolic equivalents and co-ordinates to human conduct, what Singer calls a "spiritual stenography." In those stories, however, where Singer celebrates the power of human endurance, as in "The Little Shoemakers" and "The Old Man," he uses third person narrative in the closest he comes to a "high style," so that the rhetorical elevation will help to create an effect of "epical" sweep.

Within his limits Singer is a genius. He has total command of his imagined world; he is original in his use both of traditional Jewish materials and in his modernist attitude toward them; he provides a serious if enigmatic moral perspective; and he is a master of Yiddish prose. Yet there are times when Singer seems to be mired in his own originality, stories in which he displays a weakness for self-imitation that is disconcerting. Second-rate writers imitate others, first-rate writers themselves, and it is not always clear which is the more dangerous.

Having gone this far, we must now turn again. If Singer's work can be grasped only on the assumption that he is crucially a "modernist" writer, one must add that in other ways he remains profoundly subject to the Jewish tradition. And if the Yiddish reader is inclined to slight the "modernist" side of his work, the American reader is likely to underestimate the traditional side.

One of the elements in the Jewish past that has most fascinated Singer is the recurrent tendency to break loose from the burden of the Mosaic law and, through the urging of will and ecstasy, declare an end to the *galut*. Historically, this has taken the form of a series of messianic movements, one led in the seventeenth century by Sabbatai Zevi and another in the eighteenth by Jacob Frank. The movement of Sabbatai Zevi appeared after the East European Jewish community had been shattered by the rebellion-pogrom of the Cossack chieftain, Chmielnicki. Many of the survivors, caught up in a strange ecstasy that derived all too clearly from their total desperation, began to summon apocalyptic fantasies and to indulge themselves in long-repressed religious emotions which, perversely, were stimulated by the pressures of cabalistic asceticism. As if in response to their yearnings, Sabbatai, a pretender rising in the Middle East, offered to release them of everything that rabbinical Judaism had confined or suppressed. He spoke for the tempting doctrine that faith is sufficient for salvation; for the wish to evade the limits of mundane life by forcing a religious transcendence; for the union of erotic with mystical appetites; for the lure of a demonism which the very hopelessness of the Jewish situation rendered plausible. In 1665–66 Sabbatianism came to orgiastic climax, whole communities, out of a conviction that the Messiah was in sight, discarding the moral inhibitions of exile. Their hopes were soon brutally disappointed when Sabbatai, persecuted by the Turkish Sultan, converted to Mohammedanism. His followers were thrown into confusion and despair, and a resurgent rabbinism again took control over Jewish life. Nevertheless, Sabbatianism continued to lead an underground existence among the East European Jews—even, I have been told by *shtetl* survivors, in the late nineteenth and early twentieth century. It became a secret heretical cult celebrating Sabbatai as the apostate savior who had been required to descend to the depths of the world in order to achieve the heights of salvation.

To this buried strand of Jewish experience Singer has been drawn in fascination and repulsion, portraying its manifestations with great vividness and its consequences with stern judgment. It is a kind of experience that rarely figures in traditional Yiddish writing, yet is a significant aspect of the Jewish past. Bringing this material to contemporary readers, Singer writes *in* Yiddish but often quite apart from the Yiddish tradition; indeed, he is one of the few Yiddish writers whose relation to the Jewish past is not determined or screened by that body of values we call Yiddishism.

Singer is a writer of both the pre-Enlightenment and the post-Enlightenment: he would be equally at home with a congregation of medieval Jews and a gathering of twentieth-century intellectuals, perhaps more so than at a meeting of the Yiddish P.E.N. club. He has a strong sense of the mystical and antique, but also a cool awareness of psychoanalytic disenchantment. He has evaded both the religious pieties and the humane rationalism of nineteenth-century East European Judaism. He has skipped over the ideas of the historical epoch which gave rise to Yiddishism, for the truth is, I suppose, that Yiddish literature, in both its writers of acceptance and writers of skepticism, is thoroughly caught up with the Enlightenment. Singer is not. He shares very little in the collective sensibility or the *folkstimlichkeit* of the Yiddish masters; he does not unambiguously celebrate *dos kleine menshele* (the common man) as a paragon of goodness; he is impatient with the sensual deprivations implicit in the values of *edelkeit* (refinement, nobility); and above all he moves away from a central assumption of both Yiddish literature in particular and the nineteenth century in general, the assumption of an immanent fate or end in human existence (what in Yiddish is called *tachlis*).

But again qualifications are needed. It is one thing to decide to break from a tradition in which one has been raised, quite another to make the break completely. For Singer has his ties—slender, subterranean but strong—with the very Yiddish writers from whom he has turned away.

At the center of Yiddish fiction stands the archetypal figure of *dos kleine menshele*. It is he, long-suffering, persistent, lovingly ironic, whom the Yiddish writers celebrate. This poor but proud householder trying to maintain his status in the *shtetl* world even as he keeps sinking deeper and deeper into poverty, appeals to the Yiddish imagination far more than mighty figures like Aeneas or Ahab. And from this representative man of the *shtetl* there emerge a number of significant variations. One extreme variation is the ecstatic wanderer, hopeless in this world because profoundly committed to the other. An equally extreme variation is the wise or sainted fool who has given up the struggle for status and thereby acquired the wry perspective of an outsider. Standing somewhere between *dos kleine menshele* and these offshoots is Peretz's Bontsha Schweig, whose intolerable humbleness makes even the angels in heaven feel guilty and embarrassed. Singer's Gimpel is a literary grandson (perhaps only on one side) of Peretz's Bontsha; and as Gimpel, with the piling up of his foolishness, acquires a halo of comic sadness and comes to seem an epitome of pure spirit, one must keep balancing in one's mind the ways in which he is akin to, yet different from, Bontsha.

The Yiddish critic Shlomo Bickel has perceptively remarked that Singer's dominating principle is an "anti-Prometheanism," a disbelief in the efficacy of striving, defiance, and pride, a doubt as to the sufficiency of knowledge or even wisdom. This seems true, but only if one remembers that in a good many of Singer's fictions the central action does constitute a kind of Promethean ordeal or striving. Singer makes it abundantly clear that his characters have no choice: they must live out their desires, their orgiastic yearnings, their apocalyptic expectations. "Anti-Prometheanism" thus comes to rest upon a belief in the unavoidable recurrence of the Promethean urge.

What finally concerns Singer most is the possibilities for life that remain after the exhaustion of human effort, after failure and despair have come and gone. Singer watches his stricken figures from a certain distance, with enigmatic intent and no great outpouring of sympathy, almost as if to say that before such collapse neither judgment nor sympathy matters very much. Yet in all of his fictions the Promethean effort recurs, obsessional, churning with new energy and delusion. In the knowledge that it will, that it must recur, there may also lie hidden a kind of pity, for that too we would expect, and learn to find, in the writer who created Gimpel.

Part II

Anarchy and Authority
in American Literature

In the beginning was the wilderness. The earth, "almost path-
less," writes Faulkner, was marked only "by the tracks of unalien
shapes—bear and deer and panthers and bison and wolves and
alligators and the myriad smaller beasts. And unalien men to
name them too." America was paradise, the last paradise.

For Faulkner, as for many other American writers, there is a
radical disjunction between social man and the natural world.
The wilderness is primal, source and scene of mobility, freedom,
innocence. Once society appears, it starts to hollow out these
values. And not one or the other form of society, not a better
or worse society, but the very idea of society itself comes to be
regarded with skepticism and distaste.

This myth is lent credence by the hold of the frontier on our
national life. A myth of space, it records the secret voice of a
society regretting its existence, and recalls a time when men
could measure their independence by their physical distance
from one another, for "personal liberty and freedom were almost physical conditions like fire and flood."

Inescapably the settling of the wilderness was a violation. For
a short time afterward, it was still possible to establish a precarious balance between the natural and the social—a balance
which might have preserved a margin of paradise. But the
forest line recedes. In "The Bear," set in the late nineteenth
century, there can still be a return to the wilderness, and within

its narrowed precincts something of our original freedom is recalled. By "Delta Autumn," one must "drive for hours to reach
the woods. . . ." The wilderness is gone. Paradise has been lost,
again.

The Founding Fathers of the United States were hardheaded
and realistic men. They were sincere patriots, almost all of them,
and thoughtful students of government, some of them. They had
a lively sense of their own interests, and meant to create bulwarks for their property; but they also wished to avoid tyranny,
whether aristocratic or popular. As they set about the task of
state-making, they grasped the need to reconcile all of those
conflicting interests and obligations in a society which, precisely
because it *was* a society, could yield only limited satisfactions.

At least some of the men who framed the Constitution believed with John Calvin that evil and damnation are inherent
in the human condition. From Thomas Hobbes they took over
the view that men are contentious; that social struggle is endemic; that interest comes before principle; and that the task of
government is to control the beast in mankind. Yet even as they
absorbed these elements of English political thought, they also
inherited something of seventeenth-century English republican-
ism, as well as the prescriptions of Locke for a limited constitu-
tional government. The Founding Fathers were strongly attached
to the idea of the United States as they were then creating it;
but they were naïvely romantic neither about the New World—
for clearly they found their principles of religion and state-
making in the old—nor about the people—for clearly they believed that popular sovereignty should be limited in behalf of
liberty and property and in accordance with the restraints of
traditional wisdom. They worked into the Constitution a series
of balances which inhibit both the direct expression of the
popular will and tendencies toward autocratic usurpation. It is
a system which rests on the premise that the best way to ensure
stable social conditions and provide adequate protection of
human rights is through a politics of countervailing coalition.
The philosophic premise behind this system was stated with
classical precision by James Madison in *The Federalist Papers*:

Ambition must be made to counteract ambition. . . . It may be a
reflection on human nature that such devices should be necessary to

control the abuses of government. But what is government itself but the greatest of all reflections on human nature? If men were angels, no government would be necessary. . . . In framing a government which is to be administered by men over men, the great difficulty lies in this: you must first enable the government to control the governed; and in the next place oblige it to control itself.

With time there occurred a gradual democratization of American society, in part because Americans displayed in the nineteenth century what Louis Hartz has called "a genius for political participation"; in part because the structure created from Madison's model of limited government could be used advantageously by the agrarian interests for whom Thomas Jefferson spoke, and by the farmers and urban middle class who rallied behind Andrew Jackson; and in part because there continued to course through American life a profound feeling for a radical utopianism.

Now the question we must encounter is this: Could the principles upon which the American government was founded and the expectations that had arisen with the beginning of American settlement be at all reconciled? Can one bring together the worldly realism of *The Federalist Papers* with the Edenic nostalgia coursing through American literature? That the conflict was a real one, and so regarded by the principal actors, may be seen in a caustic passage Alexander Hamilton wrote for *The Federalist Papers*:

Reflections of this kind [in behalf of a balance of power] may have trifling weight with men who hope to see realized in America the halcyon scenes of the poetic or fabulous age; but to those who believe we are likely to experience a common portion of vicissitudes and calamities which have fallen to the lot of other nations . . . etc., etc.*

Yet during the 1820's and 1830's, when the grip of Federalism had been loosened and the powers of capitalism not yet exerted, many Americans must have felt that a harmonious relation between social institutions and moral desires was indeed possible.

---

* See, however, the brilliant essay by Cecelia M. Kenyon, "Alexander Hamilton: Rousseau of the Right" (*Political Science Quarterly*, June 1958), which argues that Hamilton was himself very much an ideologue. Perhaps the point to be stressed is that in the urgent practical task of state-making the Founding Fathers had no choice but to put somewhat to the side their ideological or visionary preoccupations.

Soon, everything changed. The issue of slavery provoked a crisis beyond compromise; the gradual development of commercial capitalism enforced a centralization of power greater than Hamilton could have imagined; and the Populistic hopes which would come to a climax in the late nineteenth and early twentieth centuries were largely fated to disappointment. With time, it became clear that America was trapped in a conflict between its guiding institutions (better though these might seem than any other within sight or memory) and its guiding myth (poignant as this would seem in its absolute unrealizability). And from this conflict there have followed enormous consequences.

In the United States, a country with a passion for political spectacle, the *idea* of politics—to say nothing of the figure of the politician—has been held in ridicule and frequent disrepute. Along the margins of the society there have arisen movements declaring themselves to be political but actually dominated by Edenic and apocalyptic moods that make them profoundly apolitical and even antipolitical. Americans have often been tempted by the possibility of realizing through communities of salvation those ends which other societies assign to politics— and conversely have often been tempted by the idea of assigning to the arena of politics those ends which other societies regard as proper to religion, philosophy, and morality. Yet the very conflicts which make for social impasse and human frustration have served as the themes of our greatest and most poignant literary works. The troubles of life are the convenience of literature.

Classical European literature often displays an extratemporal dimension—its urge to transcendence breaks past the crowded spaces of an old world, to create itself anew in the guise of an ideal future, a heavenly prospect sanctioned by Christianity and removed from the paltriness of time. But at least until the idea of America takes hold of the European imagination there is, for Europeans, no place else to go. Locked into space, they can only transfer their hopes to a time beyond time. Their escape is vertical.

In American literature the urge to break past the limits of the human condition manifests itself through images of space. Our characteristic fictions chart journeys not so much in order to get their heroes out of America as to transport the idea of America into an undefiled space. The urge to transcendence appears as stories of men who move away, past frontiers and borders, into the "territory" or out to sea, in order to preserve their images of possibility. For the enticements of space offer the hope —perhaps only the delusion—of a new beginning: so that, for a time, an individual hero can be seen as re-enacting, within or beyond the society, the myth upon which it rests but which it has not been able to fulfill. In America this new start is seen not so much in terms of an improvement or reordering of the social structure, but as a leap beyond society—a wistful ballet of transcendence.

Now, many critics have noticed these elements in our literature and have discussed them in terms of an Adamic myth, a wish to return to innocence, a nostalgia for a purity we never had. Or they have seen in our writing a wish to escape the guilt brought on by the defilement of the countryside; to put down the burdens of success, family, and women; and to be done with the whole idea of society and sink back into a state of primal fraternity: blood brothers on the raft, the hunting ground, the lonely river, all in common friendliness, black, red, and white.

Let us see what happens, however, if we somewhat shift the terms of this approach to nineteenth-century American literature. Let us see what happens if we acknowledge that many of our major poems and fictions release a hunger for a state of nature not yet soiled by history and commerce; if we further agree that troubled responses to sexuality and perhaps a wish to discard mature sexual life in behalf of a fellowship of innocents are tacitly expressed in these poems and fictions; and if we then look at them in political terms.

It is a special kind of politics that is here at stake: not the usual struggles for power among contending classes within a fixed society; nor the mechanics of power as employed by a stable ruling class; nor even the dynamics of party maneuvering; but rather a politics concerned with the *idea* of society itself, a politics that dares consider—wonderful question—whether society is good and—still more wonderful—whether society is necessary. The paradox of it all is that a literature which on any manifest level is not really political at all should nevertheless be precisely the literature to raise the most fundamental problem in political theory: what is the rationale for society, the justification for the state?

And if we agree for a moment so to regard nineteenth-century American literature, we discover running through it a strong if subterranean current of anarchism. Not anarchism as the political movement known to nineteenth-century Europe, a movement with an established ideology and a spectrum of emphases ranging from Populism to terrorism. That has meant very little in the United States. I have in mind something else: anarchism as a social vision arising spontaneously from the conditions of preindustrial American culture, anarchism as a bias of the American imagination releasing its deepest, which is to say its most frustrated, yearnings.

Anarchism here signifies a vision of a human community beyond the calculation of good and evil; beyond the need for the state as an apparatus of law and suppression; beyond the yardsticks of moral measurement; beyond the need, in fact, for the constraints of authority. It envisages a community of autonomous persons, each secure in his own being and aware of his own mind. It signifies a collective desire to refuse the contaminations of history, precisely at the point where the nation's history begins to seem oppressive and irreversible. The anarchist vision coursing through nineteenth-century American literature speaks for a wish to undo restrictions which violate the deepest myth of the very society that has suffered the necessity of establishing these restrictions. What is novel here is the assumption that because of our blessed locale, we could find space—a little beyond the border, farther past the shore—in which to return, backward and free, to a stateless fraternity, so that the very culture created on the premise of mankind's second chance would, in failing that chance, yet allow its people a series of miniature recurrences. The stuff of tragedy is thereby transformed into an idyll of purity.

The oppressive system of laws, which Herman Melville would later call the "forms" in *Billy Budd*, gives way to the self-ordering discipline of persons in a fraternal relationship. While this relationship is enabled by, and perhaps only possible within, the arena of an unsullied nature, it is not so much the thought of pastoral which excites our major nineteenth-century writers as it is a vision of human comradeship being fulfilled within the setting of pastoral. And thereby the problem of authority, perhaps the most difficult that can be faced in political thought, is—at least on the imaginative plane—simply dissolved: a solution as inadequate as it is entrancing.

In my capsule description of this anarchist vision, the key word is *fraternal*—the notion of a society in which the sense of brotherhood replaces the rule of law, even the best law, since law by its very nature must be unjust insofar as it raises abstract standards above personal relations. The anarchist belief in the fraternal is a belief in the power of love as a mode of discipline, indeed, in an equable relationship which may even replace both love and discipline by something still more lovely: the composure of affection.

Both the theme of a relaxed anarchic community free from the constraints of law and the theme of a return to an unspoiled pastoral America call upon the same imaginative impulse. If the vision of a life without the regulations of the state seems impossible as a basis for a modern politics, it is no more impossible than the pastoral vision of a pansexual, unaggressive, and asocial fraternity in personal relations. To stress the political aspect, however, is a way of sharpening the pathos and underscoring the dilemmas faced by the major nineteenth-century American writers.

The paradisal dream is lodged deeply in their imaginations, as in those of almost all sensitive Americans of the time. Yet they are living in a society Madison helped to form, Jackson to reform, and the expansion of American business to transform. The conviction that injustice and vulgarity grew stronger during the nineteenth century is shared by many of our writers—a conviction, finally, that an America is being created which frustrates both the dream of a new Eden and the idea of a democracy resting upon sturdy, independent citizens. Neither in practice nor thought can our writers find a way of dealing with this sense of disenchantment, if only because the country with which they become disenchanted has itself been the object of enormous expectations. In their bitterness with the social reality and their tacit recognition that they cannot really affect its course, American writers seek to get around or to "transcend" the intractability of what they encounter. Whatever they cannot change head-on, they will now turn away from, clinging meanwhile to that anarchic vision which seems all the more poignant as it recedes into the distance of lost possibilities. And thereby they create an ideal place of the imagination—precarious, transient, unstained—which speaks far more eloquently to the inner desires of our collective life than it can represent, or cope with, its coarse actualities.

Have I not just worked out a paradigm of *Huckleberry Finn*, as Mark Twain turned from the torments of slavery to the idyll of Nigger Jim and Huck on the raft? If American literature in the nineteenth century seldom succeeds in depicting with any complexity or directness the rough textures of our social life, it nevertheless has an enormous relevance to our moral life: it speaks from the heart of a culture.

The idea of a utopian enclave is recurrent among nineteenth-century American intellectuals. What is Thoreau's Walden but a utopia for curmudgeons? Thoreau, who wrote that he would "rather keep a bachelor's hall in hell than go to board in heaven," was not exactly strong in sentiments of fraternity. The proper conclusion to Jefferson's motto, "that government is best which governs least," becomes for Thoreau, "that government is best which governs not at all." His conclusion is not logically binding, but it does indicate his commitment to an absolute selfhood which reflects hostility not only to the idea of government but also to the necessary consequences, the necessary inconveniences, of a democratic society. "Any man more right than his neighbors constitutes a majority of one already," said Thoreau, without troubling to say how that rightness is to be established. Thoreau drives to an extreme those implications of anarchic individualism which in the end must undercut both the fraternal vision and the democratic polity. It is as if Thoreau, temperamentally unable to share in the idea of fraternity which moved Melville and Twain so deeply, were tacitly accepting the skeptical theories of Madison and Hamilton concerning the limitations of man as a social animal and then settling for his own version of anarchy: an anarchy of one.

Lacking that sense of outgoing spaciousness—to say nothing of human trustingness—one finds in Melville and Twain, the New England writers tuck their utopian enclaves into the interstices of their tight little region. In Hawthorne's *The Blithedale Romance* the utopian community is mourned with his characteristic irony and encircling skepticism—though still mourned. Of all our major nineteenth-century writers Hawthorne was least susceptible to visions of paradise, yet as a nineteenth-century American he could not entirely free himself from the sentiments that filled the air; and it is he, after all, not Emerson, who joined Brook Farm. The criticisms he made of this utopian community, a small-scale effort to realize Eden through thrifty New England shareholding, are remarkably cogent. Hawthorne saw that, motives apart, the formation of an isolated utopian community (whether in social actuality or imaginative projection) is seldom a threat to established power; he understood that no matter how unstained its inner morality, the utopian community could not avoid becoming part of the materialistic world it detested—a lesson, by the way, that even Huck and Nigger Jim must learn about their life on the raft as it is related to everything beyond the raft.

I very soon became sensible [writes the central character of *The Blithedale Romance*] that, as regarded society at large, we stood in a position of new hostility, rather than new brotherhood. . . . Constituting so pitiful a minority as now, we were inevitably estranged from the rest of mankind in pretty fair proportion with the strictness of our mutual bond among ourselves.

What Hawthorne is saying here is that, insofar as it is subject to the pressures of the market, the utopian community becomes a competitive unit in a competitive society and will therefore be infected with its corruptions. The utopian who would cut himself off from the ugly world must, to preserve his utopia, become a "practical agriculturist"—which means to model his utopia on the society he rejects. This criticism, striking so hard a blow at the political fancies of many nineteenth-century American intellectuals, is advanced by Hawthorne with a joyless and almost cruel insistence; but that does not make it any the less true.

If Hawthorne criticizes the utopian impulse on the ground that it does not really succeed in avoiding the evil of the great world, he also implies that another trouble is that it does not bring its followers into a sufficiently close relation with the evil of the great world. For the utopian venture at Blithedale, with its transformation of political idealism into pastoral retreat, bears a thoroughly innocent air. It is an innocence peculiar to many nineteenth-century American intellectuals, who believed that politics, when not simply a vulgarity to be avoided, could be undertaken through proclaiming a series of moral ultimates. This innocence was mainly a revulsion from the hopelessly crude and corrupt nature of our ordinary politics, and it showed itself in no more endearing form than the assumption that ordinary politics could be gotten away from or supplanted by the politics of pastoral retreat. America itself having gone astray, utopianism would remake it in the small.

But I have anticipated myself, for I should have begun by examining the anarchist vision in the work of our major writers.

It is in James Fenimore Cooper's fiction that this vision first appears with imaginative strength. Like Hawthorne, Cooper was deeply conservative in his thought; but together with this conscious bias there flows through Cooper's fiction a yearning for a state of social comeliness that he saw embodied in the life of the Indians and, more persuasively, in the habits of his culture-hero, Natty Bumppo.

Cooper's anarchist vision appears as a substratum of feeling, a cluster of wistful images, picturesque set pieces and mythic figures. It is a vision that breaks past his pompous style, as if meant to shatter his conservative opinions. About this ambivalence in Cooper's work no one has written better than Richard Chase:

The forest sequences of *Satanstoe* imply that the ideal young man of the New World, though his values will be formed by a traditional society, will also be at home on the margins of society *where all social values disappear* and are replaced by a strict code of the woods, which entails skill in the lore of the hunt, honor in personal conduct, piety toward nature, stoic forbearance, a sort of programmatic masculinity, and celibacy. This is the habitat and code of Cooper's most vivid hero, Natty Bumppo. . . . Cooper thus has two very different heroes in Corney Littlepage [the central character of *Satanstoe*] and Natty Bumppo. True, there are formal similarities between the aristocratic morals of the one and the stoic code of the other—both involve religion, both insist on hierarchic values. But one of Cooper's heroes is the product of society and the other, though he seems to imply a life not apart from society but on its margins, seems *ultimately to deny the whole idea of society.*

In short, Cooper found it necessary in America to be both a conservative and an anarchist. The vitality of his romances, the very form in which he sees things, the actions that he is able to make vivid—these stem from the political contradictions at the center of his thought. If some of his most moving passages are elegiac, it is because the very terms in which he conceived the quality of life were becoming, even as he wrote, historically outmoded. [Emphases added]

Cooper's best fiction is set either at sea or in the forest, both areas which for him, as for other nineteenth-century American writers, suggest psychic space, moral elbow room. I shall here look only at Cooper in the forest. He is not, of course, a realistic portraitist of the Indians; some of them, in his treatment, seem more sages than savages. But if we think of Cooper's treatment of the Indians as a way of projecting an image of an ideal America, then the material becomes remarkably interesting. In Cooper's fiction the Indian tribes are never burdened with government. Within the tribe, the essential unit of social life is the family, and in many respects a more powerful unit than the tribe itself. Military service is voluntary: when the braves go on the warpath they act out of their own free will. Disputes within the tribe always occur among individuals, so that factions are not formed—Madison's forebodings seem not to be borne out by Cooper's Indians. Indian life is casual in structure, with brief, personal, and temporary relationships the rule. As Cooper portrays it—and historical accuracy need not concern us for a moment—the life of the Indians can be severely bound by tradition, rites, concepts of honor, and limitations of mind, but it is not subject to the institutional authority and the social regulation we associate with the state. Perhaps the most revealing expression of all this comes in a speech made by one of Cooper's Indian chiefs, Susquesus, in *The Redskins*, when he bids farewell to his tribe:

My children, the redman is his own master. He goes and comes as he pleases. If the young men strike the warpath, he can strike it too. He can go on the warpath, or the hunt, or he can stay in the wigwam. All he has to do is to keep his promise, not steal, and not go into another redman's wigwam unasked. . . . How is it with the pale-faces?

They say they are free when the sun rises; they say they are free when the sun goes down behind the hills. They never stop talking of being their own masters. . . . They talk of liberty, and call to one another to put on calico bags, that fifty men may tar and feather one.

The voice is that of a chief, but the words are those of Cooper releasing half-sanctioned fantasies through figures for whom he need take no explicit responsibility. With Natty Bumppo, deer-slayer and pathfinder, Cooper identifies more openly, for in Natty his conservative and anarchist impulses achieve a true union. Natty brings together a version of civilized decorum and the purity of natural man—precisely the unlikelihood of this mixture makes him so poignant a figure. His ideal status depends pretty much on his social ineffectuality. Propertyless as a matter of principle and self-governing through ascetic training, Natty is a monk of the woods living in fraternal closeness with Ching-achgook, his Indian companion. At ease with the natural world and apart from social crowding and hypocrisy, they neither tamper with their feelings nor reduce them to ideas. Natty is the American at once free from historical sophistication and prim-itivist degradation. In Natty self and society are at peace; or better yet, society becomes absorbed into self, in a truce of composure. Natty lives out the anarchist idyll of a life so beauti-fully attuned to its own inner needs and thereby so lucidly harmonious with the external world, there is need for neither rules nor restraints. In the experience of Natty and Chingach-gook we have one of the few instances—imaginary, alas—where the Marxist prescription for the "withering away of the state" has been realized. With this ominous proviso: that you have to keep moving steadily westward as the state keeps reaching farther and farther into the forest.

The serene power of Natty as mythic hero is heightened still further by a contrast Cooper provides in *The Prairie*. There, as Natty slides into advanced age, he meets Ishmael Bush, a vividly drawn squatter, who is also uneasy with civilized society but in whom are embodied the ugly potentialities of a crude individual-ism and a brutal clannishness. As his name suggests, Ishmael is a distorting double of Natty, evidence of Cooper's shrewd in-sight that even the most profound of American visions may have its underside of ugliness. At the end of *The Prairie* Natty ascends to heaven in a virtual apotheosis, yet a shadow has already been cast by the figure of Ishmael, thrust to the forefront of the novel in order to call into question everything Natty stands for.

When Huck Finn and Nigger Jim are alone on that indispensable raft (itself so wonderful a symbol of the isolation, purity, and helplessness upon which the anarchist vision rests), they set up a communal order transcending in value the charms of their personal friendliness. They create a community of equals, because it is a community going beyond the mere *idea* of equality. The idea of equality must be enforced by a state and requires that fixed norms and regulations be imposed on persons of varying needs and powers. The community of equals is established by persons and involves a delicate adjustment, moment by moment, to the desires each perceives in the other.

The community of the raft is a community of friends, quietly competent at the tasks of self-preservation and self-ordering. The impulse embodied in the escape of Huck and Nigger Jim is toward a freedom that can neither be confined to nor adequately described in social terms. It comes into spontaneous existence, not as a matter of status, obligation, or right, but as a shared capacity for sympathetic identification with the natural world, seen as inherently neither good nor bad but a resource which those with the proper sense of reverence can tap. Or it can be a sympathetic identification with other men, which is something to be learned, so that the learning becomes a way of moving past mere learning and received morality. Huck's education is an education of the emotions. And on the raft his emotions are freed because he knows that they—the people of the town, the figures of judgment, the men of authority, the agents of the state—are away. Huck Finn never reaches a conceptual grasp of the problem of slavery: what, as everyone quickly sees, would be so remarkable in his decision to help Nigger Jim gain freedom if he, Huck, concluded that it was the right thing to do? As a decent American boy, he would then have no choice but to offer his help. But made in violation of norms he accepts, Huck's decision becomes a triumph of nature over culture, anarchic fraternity over registered authority. It is, for Huck, a matter of *friendliness*. And in a state of friendliness, men—at least in nineteenth-century American fiction—do not need society. Yet precisely because he does not understand practically the problem he has "surmounted" spiritually, Huck is also helpless before it: he may not want society but society wants him.

As long as Huck and Nigger Jim can float upon the raft there is no need for fixed measurements of right and wrong, good and evil. When Huck and Nigger Jim achieve their moments of fraternal union, we are transported to a kind of ecstasy, a muted rapture enabling them to rise beyond the fixed points of morality. One is reminded of the Hasidic legend which has it that if step by step you move upward on the ladder of morality you will in the end break loose and float away into a buoying space.

Yet Twain was too shrewd and troubled a writer to compose a mere idyll. The precarious community of friends established on the raft is threatened at almost every moment. It is invaded by alien figures, the King and the Duke, who are presented in comic terms but whose significance is steadily felt to be ominous. To the extent that Huck and Nigger Jim overcome them, and fend off assaults from enemies both on the river and on the shore, it is partly as a triumph of innocence, the innocence of friends, and partly as a triumph of shrewdness, Huck's shrewd-ness of social personality which upon need he quickly re-establishes.

Huck is a figure at once fixed and amorphous, recognizable and anonymous. On the raft he sheds his mask—perhaps one might even say his skin—of personality: everything a human being absorbs from his society. The more comfortable he feels, the less individual he seems; for he blends into a state of passive receptivity, he is no longer a demarcated character but a current of experience. The self grows harmonious with its surroundings; it exists as awareness and caress rather than wariness and will. Between Huck and Jim there develops an I-Thou relationship, a sentience so keen that for a few moments the whole American self-violation seems blotted out and we live in the America that might have been, our lost paradise of anarchy. On the river Huck's personality is always in process of dissolution, for there he can leave behind anxiety and shrewdness and ease himself into repose and contemplation. On the land Huck chooses the masquerades of personality, or more accurately, he knows he must choose them. He adopts a variety of names, sometimes passing himself off as Tom Sawyer, the commonplace American boy, and sometimes as the less-than-beatific riverside Huck Finn.

Even on land he is very fine, an admirable moral figure. But on the raft he has no need for disguise, no burden of personality, no strategy of shrewdness. In the community of friends, lawless and stateless, there is storytelling, amiable philosophizing about Sollermun the King, eating, sleeping, and keeping loose.

It cannot last. For all the while Twain is making certain that we remember paradise consists of a few rickety boards nailed together as a raft; that the raft contains a runaway slave worth a sizable number of dollars; that violence threatens at every bend of the shore, and that the paradisal journey is a drift southward, deeper and deeper to slavery. The anarchic enclave must disintegrate under the pressures of the world and perhaps, in the end, contribute to a conservative resignation. Before the world itself, Huck and Nigger Jim are helpless. At one and the same time they represent the power of transcendence, of rising above the crippling grasp of society, and the pitiable vulnerability of a boy and a slave who try to evade the authority of that society. Between these two extremes is there not perhaps a causal relationship, one in which our most splendid yearnings derive from our utter impotence?

From *Huckleberry Finn* to Faulkner's "The Bear" there is a clear line of descent. In "The Bear" the enclave of utopia is seen far more modestly, since Faulkner is aware that it is merely an enclave, "a diminished thing." By now it has been reduced from a drift along the river to an arranged vacation in the woods. The trip to the woods is not a challenge to society, let alone a way of transcending it, but a mixture of refreshment and retreat. In both fictions there is a severe formal problem of finding a resolution for a historically conditioned narrative devoted to celebrating a timeless idyll; but the problem is easier for Faulkner than for Twain. Faulkner never allows the vision of paradise to get out of hand; he never allows it to be seen as anything more than an interval in the course of our usual occupations; and therefore he does not have to face the difficulties Twain encountered once he had yielded himself to the raft. For Twain allowed his vision to become too captivating, too beautiful, *too possible*—all in the face of the evidence he had accumulated to show it as anything but possible. Once you have been on a raft, no other place can matter. Huck will light out for "the territory," and no doubt become a responsible citizen; but he will now have to live, like the rest of us, within the clamps of social limitation.

The early writings of Herman Melville, up to and including *Moby Dick*, are suffused with visions of anarchic bliss. How deeply the paradisal dream remained lodged, or buried, in Melville's imagination we can see from a little-known poem, "To Ned," which he published in 1888, three years before his death. Written in the troubling but impressive style of most of his verse—at once gnarled and strong—"To Ned" addresses itself to Richard Tobias Greene, Melville's companion in the South Pacific adventures related in his first book, *Typee*. Its tone is nostalgic: "Where is the world we roved, Ned Bunn?" Melville sets up a contrast between "Authentic Edens in a Pagan sea" and their invasion by "Paul Pry . . . with Pelf and Trade." In the Marquesas Melville and Ned knew, they "breathed primeval balm/From Eden's eye yet overrun," but now, ends Melville rather sadly, he must marvel whether mortals can twice "Here and hereafter, touch a Paradise." One can only envy a man who supposed he had touched it once.

The picture of Taipa as a tempting if threatening Arcadia; the blood-brotherhood of Ishmael and Queequeg before they submit to Ahab's compulsive authoritarianism, one of the most beautiful enactments of plebeian fraternity in our literature—all these are profoundly radical in stress, far more so than any mere expression of opinion.

They release Melville's distaste for those "forms," those arthritic regulations which in *Billy Budd* finally achieve their dubious victory. The young Melville is full of plebeian hope, utterly American in his democratic impatience with democratic constraints, pledged to a union of men that can surmount the cautions induced by Madison. Even in *Billy Budd* there is far more social irony—a protest muted, despairing, wary—than most critics acknowledge or readers notice. Billy himself is an archetype of innocence, as everyone remarks; but he is imaginable only as a creature of a utopian yearning so intense, so moving, and yet so untenable in the life we must lead that Melville's mature imagination has no choice but fondly to destroy him. And what is Captain Vere, that eminently sane and decent man, but an embodiment of the cruel justice which comprises the state? Captain Vere is a man who does his duty before and above all; and in our time we have learned what such men can be and do. Melville's great perception here is that the personal qualities of Vere, notable as these are, do not finally matter: so long as he acts out the impersonal violence of the state, his virtues as a man come to rather little and he has no choice but to be a judicial killer. Equally haunting is Melville's recognition that Billy in his innocence forgives Captain Vere, while the plebs who are his crew mates, men ground down in the harsh discipline of a state fearful of revolutionary upsurge, neither forgive nor know how to rebel against that which they cannot forgive.

Billy Budd is a work written from Melville's weary disenchantment with the radical utopianism, the gay anarchism of his youthful years, and thereby a work in which the vision of youth is embodied in a figure at once pure and helpless, angelic and speechless, loved and doomed. The power of the story rests in the fact that Melville does what Twain failed to do: he finds a literary resolution for a moral and social problem which, in its own terms, seems insoluble. Melville does not yield himself quite so easily as had Twain to the vision of anarchic bliss, which is perhaps why Billy is not so unforgettable a figure as Huck. But Melville takes the subject from a greater distance than Twain, which is why he presents it in its irreducible pain and complete outrage—as we see in the concluding three chapters, where Billy is dead but neither historical reports nor legends of the sea do his ordeal any justice whatever. By the time Melville came to write *Billy Budd* he could do no more than be the Abraham to his imaginary Isaac, sending to the sacrificial altar the boy who in gesture if not speech summoned the dreams of his youth, perhaps of his nation.

The clash between anarchic yearning and fixed authority leads both to the marvelously open and spacious quality of nineteenth-century American writing and to the choked misanthropy that so often follows. For writers caught up in the utopian vision it is peculiarly hard, as they grow older, to find the modulated resolutions available to the classical European writers. Our literature is schizoid, flaring to ecstasy and falling to misanthropy, but rarely pausing at the middle level of realism and social engage-

ment. The American myth, of which the anarchic vision is one
instance, exerts too great a hold upon our nineteenth-century
masters; and then, as it shatters itself upon the shores of history,
there follows a disenchantment beyond bearing. Where the
traditional treatment of society in the English novel occurs
through class adjustments, contained conflicts, even revolutions,
all within the shared assumption of the inescapability of social
authority and visible power, the American imagination, at its
deepest level, keeps calling into question the idea of society itself. And as the nation moves into the modern world, what can
that come to but absolute despair?

There is no other Western culture of the past two centuries
in which, to my knowledge, so many demands have been expressed for the "creation of values." When one comes to think
of it, that is really an extraordinary fact. The literatures of
Europe either sustain traditional values or enlarge upon revolutionary values; but both are seen as inseparable from the social
order in which the writer writes and the reader reads. In our
culture we have made the unprecedented demand upon writers
that they "create values" quite apart from either tradition or
insurgency. What we have often meant by this is that they
establish a realm of values at a distance from the setting of
actual life, thereby becoming priests of the possible in a world
of shrinking possibilities. We ask them to discover, out of their
desperate clarity, a vision we can cherish, and cherish perhaps
in direct proportion to our knowledge that we will not—or cannot—live by it. The result, I have come to think, is that every
now and again we strike off a fiction of such transcendent
powers it sends the world into enchantment, but also that we
deny ourselves the possibilties of a hard realism in both our
literature and our politics by means of which to transform or
ease our condition. We are tempted to follow the path of Thoreau
in a world utterly unlike that in which Thoreau lived, and we
thereby succeed neither in honoring Thoreau (who already has
too much honor) nor in affecting our circumstances.

Yet, within our literature, the anarchic impulse—together with
the accompanying moral ultimatism and apolitical politics—remains enormously powerful and even those who grow skeptical
as to its social value must grant that it still has a notable

imaginative thrust. If one looks, for example, at the writings of Norman Mailer, it becomes clear that behind all of them lies a fear of stasis, a dread of a future ruled by functional rationality. All of his recent writings seems to ask: Is it possible that "the smooth strifeless world" in which most cultivated Americans live will prove to be a model of tomorrow, a glass enclosure in which there will be a minimum of courage or failure, test or transcendence? For those of us marked, or marred, by the ethic of striving and dissatisfaction, this question seems endlessly haunting.

That Mailer's quest for a new energizing principle leads to gestures of desperation and then a self-mimicry of his own gestures, I need not demonstrate here. Yet despair, if it can remain genuine despair, is not the worst of emotions; it testifies, at least, to the earlier presence of desire. And in our world, the vision of a society of true friends living in composed fraternity is one that can only bring the writer to a ferocious impasse.

An endless dialectic in our life and our literature, this clash between anarchy and authority. Here a poet, Paul Goodman, cries out that he is

> still seeking
> on faces alive in this world
> ideal shapes of heaven,
> vengefully to wrest
> a stolen inheritance back. . . .

and another poet, Robert Frost, writes in a poem significantly entitled "An Answer":

> But Islands of the Blessèd, bless you, son,
> I never came upon a blessèd one.

Henry James
and the
American Scene

In the summer of 1904 Henry James, by then past his sixtieth year and a writer of imposing reputation, made a pilgrimage back to his native land. He had spent much of his adult life in Europe and had become fixed in the style, though as a rule not the snobbism, of the expatriate. He had but recently completed the three great novels of his "late" period—*The Ambassadors, Wings of the Dove,* and *The Golden Bowl*—and had placed these works, all of them wrought to a high sophistication, in a European setting. Yet, as he kept insisting, he remained utterly and forever an American, a writer whose sensibility had been formed in the light of Emerson and the shadow of Lincoln.

James returned to America with an enormous and, as it seemed to his brother William, excessive degree of expectation. He was determined to "take it all in." He was determined to open himself to the realities of his native country quite as, through all his years as a novelist, he had opened himself to the figures and landscapes of his imagination. And he was determined not merely to linger over the places he had loved in his youth but also to confront whatever might now seem brutal and ugly.

To his amusement and mild pleasure, he came as a celebrity of sorts: interviewed by reporters, welcomed to lecture platforms, received by President Theodore Roosevelt. As he traveled through New England, then down the eastern seaboard to Florida, and finally cross-country to Chicago and California, what most stirred and troubled James was the evidence of how deeply the country had changed. He had grown up in an America in which the claims for regional distinctiveness, small-town aloofness and pastoral space could still count for something; he came back to an America well into the age of industrial capitalism. With that taut passivity which always marked the early stages of his creative work, James allowed himself to be overwhelmed by his impressions; and then, once he had had enough of American hotels and American architecture, he decided to "return to England . . . as a saturated sponge and wring myself out there." What then came pouring out of that "sponge" was a remarkable book, *The American Scene*, at once a sparkling account of his travels and a series of speculations about American character and destiny.

Simply as a travel record *The American Scene* is packed with marvelous bits and pieces: pictorial renderings in high gloss, lovely turns of affection, notations of social manners that capture in a sentence insights that duller hands would later thin out into volumes. If *The American Scene* is a brilliant rendering of the surfaces of American civilization at the turn of the century, it is also, regrettably, an incomplete one: James never put down his impressions of the Mid and Far West, which might have enabled him to conclude and not merely stop his book. But in any final reckoning the book is much more than a travel account. It is one of those recurrent attempts to get at "the essence" of the American experience, as if ultimately this country were the working-out of a Platonic idea. It is testimony to our need as a people for the vanity of self-definition or the ordeal of self-interrogation, whichever you wish. Crevecoeur and Cooper, Tocqueville and Bryce had written in this spirit earlier, and many others would try after James. In the past such inquiries had been composed partly by Americans speaking outward and partly by Europeans looking inward; but James could write from both perspectives at once, since he had brought together in his work the purity of nineteenth-century American idealism and the sophistication of traditional European culture, transforming this somewhat eccentric mixture into the materials for his vision of a complex and humane civilization. James was not, of course, the kind of writer who could engage in the sustained sociological speculations of a Tocqueville; only in a passage here and there does he provide explicit statement. His ideas weave through the book rather shyly, and often they do not show themselves in the visible dress of ideas at all. To gain a full sense of what America meant to him one has to read *The American Scene* together with his late novels, all of them together as the fulfillment of his genius.

This may be asking for an ideal reader, but then: why not— *for Henry James, why not?* And if the ideal reader of *The American Scene* does not exist, let us proceed immediately to invent him. He would be a man very much of the contemporary moment, yet willing to spend some months in savoring the pages of this book, two or three an evening, a half-hour at a time, without impatience, haste or anxiety. There is no story to worry about, no uncertainty as to how "it will all come out." There is no message of instant redemption which if only we heed it will transform us, for a day or two, tomorrow morning. For all its brave recognitions of change, *The American Scene* is a conservative book. In motivation, if not always perspective, it is often elegiac, a journey of the imagination backward in time, where all is fixed and irrevocable, beyond the blur of fashion. Toward the present James marches boldly; he grasps it, embraces it, repulses it; but always he is most deeply engaged by the memory of an earlier America.

Even the elaborateness of James's prose, which has been known to disable inexperienced readers, is a strategy meant to encourage reflection and slow reading. All those pyramiding clauses which demand a strict articulation, in the way a good speaker provides his listeners with the invisible chalk marks of his syntax—those clauses move toward rumination, breaks of continuity and returns to fulfillment, starts of surprise that ripen into amusement, and even gaps of comprehension one accepts as evidence that more remains to be absorbed. For the reader of the second half of the twentieth century, the prose of this book may come first as a shock and then as a challenge; at the very least it may restore to us the habit of attentive reading which the most recently certified authorities have announced as obsolete.

Only at a few points does James attempt a prose transparent, simple, and plain, what might be called the style of reportage. Most of the time, everything is filtered through his rich and brooding awareness, and the tacit claim behind this sort of writing is that what the writer sees, remembers, and responds to is intrinsically commanding: impressions that constitute cultural facts of high significance. About all this James is very sly, very amusing. The "restless analyst," as he calls himself, knows he is making heavy demands on his readers; knows he is demanding that we struggle up those plateaus of perception to which years of writing have brought him. He writes openly and with pride as a literary master, perhaps the only American who has ever succeeded in persuading us of his right to assume a role we associate with an older, a European tradition. James composes out of the security of his place and his achievement, and still more, his own measured sense of place and achievement. I am inclined to add: he composes out of the assurance of his eccentricities—that winding, circling, elaborate style which, if only we can *hear* it, comes to seem the essence of lucidity and high civilization.

Let us not pretend that this late style of James's comes easily to us or that a certain kind of training is not necessary before we can feel at ease with it. For all its baroque complications, it must be taken as a spoken style and, in a special way, a style of oratory. Not the oratory of the public speaker, which is utterly alien to James; but the oratory of a formidable and acknowledged literary man addressing a group of friends in a drawing room, speaking with rounded intricacy so as to give pleasure—for his are the kinds of friends that can take pleasure—in syntax as performance. He stands there, this bulky and magisterial man of letters, articulating his web of clauses through stress, through pitch, through tone, and through the rests, those tensed breaks of silence, which help one parse his sentences in the mind's eye. He stands there and he casts a spell.

The center of American society—its economic arrangements and structure, its offices and factories—James never tried to penetrate. Years earlier, in remarking to himself why he would have to forgo an ambition to be the American Balzac, he had acknowledged his ignorance of business life, an ignorance precluding any serious effort to encompass in a sequence of fiction the whole of American society. Now, touring the country, he saw everywhere the consequences of business domination—America as a

"huge Rappacini-garden, rank with each variety of the poison-
plant of the money passion"; the anxiety and rush of a people
caught up in a "foredoomed *grope* of wealth"—yet he did not try
to examine the sources of these apparitions and compulsions.
Only later, in *The Ivory Tower*, that vivid fragment of a novel
left by James at the time of his death, did he attack with equal
directness the American cult of money. "Money is their life," says
the dying millionaire, Mr. Betterman, about the members of his
class. Most of the time, however, James was still too much an
"older American," a somewhat fastidious patrician, to thrust himself imaginatively, as Dreiser would thrust himself, into the arena
of manufacture and money. James was an impressionist painter
of secondary social effects, and in that role, unsurpassed.

He kept shrewdly noting the absence of the privacy in behalf
of which money had presumably been accumulated. He returned again and again to the "so complete abolition of *forms*,"
those enabling devices of social intercourse by which, he felt,
values were articulated. He observed the way Americans mostly
resisted "any exception to the common," perhaps out of a feeling
that sameness of appearance was proof of democratic conviction.
He grew amusingly caustic about the "hotel spirit," wondering
whether it "may not just *be* the American spirit most seeking and
most finding itself." He speculated on "the effects of . . . the
manifestations of wealth in New York . . . nowhere else does
pecuniary power so beat its wings in the void, and so look
around it for the charity of some hint as to the possible awk-
wardness or possible grace of its motion. . . ." And many pages
later, returning to this insight in a subtler way, James moved
into one of his great cryptic passages:

It has a genius, the native spirit, for desiring things of the existence,
even the possibility of which it is actually unaware, and it views the
totality of nature and the general life of man, I think, as more than
anything else commissioned and privileged to wait on these awaken-
ings. Thus new values arise as expansion proceeds; the marked character of which, for comparative sociology, is that they are not at all
as other values. What they "count" for is the particular required
American certainty . . .

No matter how critical James might be of the society he found
at home, he never lapsed into that tiresome baiting of fellow
countrymen which marks a good many literary explorations of

America. If he drew back from the vulgarity, he approved the vigor of the new nation. If he felt distaste for the new rich, he had the good sense to appreciate the comfort in which ordinary people often lived. The two pages in which he described how "two industries, at the most, seemed to rule the American scene. The dentist and the shoe-dealer divided it between them"—these pages are as good a piece of impromptu sociology as we have ever had. He saw that the "far-shining dental gold" expressed more than clumsiness or ostentation, and what he wrote about the American appetite for candy was not merely a piquant touch but led to an important observation:

The whole phenomenon of this omnipresent and essentially "popular" appeal of the confectioner and pastry-cook . . . is more significant of the economic, and even of the social situation of the masses than many a circumstance honored with more attention.

James wrote about New York and New England—these are surely the best parts of the book—with a commanding thrust, a sly humor, a self-assured *brio*. He visibly enjoys the display of his rhetorical powers, as images, conceits and metaphors leap out of the pages like brilliant fish from the sea. He remarks playfully on "the law of the increasing invisibility of [New York] churches." He pictures the "great, gay" Saco river "singing . . . like some reckless adventurer, good-humoured for the hour and with his hands in his pockets. . . ." He sees how the New England "village street and the lonely farm and the hillside cabin . . . twitched with a grim effect the thinness of their mantle, shook out of its folds such crudity and levity as they might, and borrowed, for dignity, a shade of the darkness of Cenci-drama, of monstrous legend, of old Greek tragedy." And he applies, this "restless analyst," a needle sharp and exact: "The condition attested [of the defeated South] is the condition—or, as may be, one of the later, fainter, weaker stages—of having worshipped false gods."

At the forefront of *The American Scene* there is of course James's encounter with the hordes of city strangers, those immigrants of a hundred grating tongues and assertive manner, all of whom—just because he was so distant, so very much an "early American"—he tried to meet with a minimum of preconception. (Only in regard to the Negro, but a few decades freed and in

effect again enslaved, did James's imagination quite fail him.)
The contrast between what he remembered and what he saw
emerges most keenly if one keeps in mind that he knew, in the
literal sense of *knowing*, almost nothing about the immigrants
who flooded the streets of New York. In one respect they were
the strange and the threatening, all that meant an end to the
homeland as he had known it; yet they were also a supreme
testimony to the strength and value of the homeland, and like
many another principled, if slightly bewildered, native American, James felt it a matter of chivalry to turn his eyes toward
these people. His attitude toward them is, finally, complex beyond description, a shifting mixture of curiosity, admiration,
disdain, withdrawal, respect, animus. But above all else, he was
a *writer*, which is to say, a man whose primary obligation
is to encounter the actual regardless of what he might like
it to be. The pages on Ellis Island—"Before this door, which
opens to them there only with a hundred forms and ceremonies,
grindings and grumblings of the key . . ."—have never been sur-
passed in American literature or journalism. Thinking about the
immigrants, James confesses himself dispossessed: "That loud
primary stage of alienism which New York most offers to sight—
operates, for the native, as their note of settled possession . . .
so that *un*settled possession is what we, on our side, seem reduced to . . ." He confesses himself stunned by the sheer rush
of experience the Lower East Side presents. But his eye remains
alert: he notices, as a telling detail, the "complexity of fire-
escapes with which each house-front bristles." And his heart,
if occasionally sinking, remains open:

Truly the Yiddish world was a vast world, with its own deeps and
complexities, and what struck one above all was that it sat there . . .
with a sublimity of good conscience that took away the breath, a
protrusion of elbow never aggressive, but absolutely proof against
jostling.

Yet as one lingers over these splendid pages, one finds them
not quite enough, either in range or penetration, perhaps because James's brilliance is so sustained that it rouses us to un-
reasonable expectations. Finally he cannot move beyond the
humaneness of uncertainty, the ambivalence of cultivation; there
is not in these pages, and there cannot be, the wholeness of feeling James commands when he returns to the places of his youth,

each of them now etched in memory as a landmark. The Hudson seems to

stretch back, with fumbling friendly hand, to the earliest outlook of my consciousness. Many matters had come and gone, innumerable impressions had supervened; yet here, in the stir of the senses, a whole range of small forgotten things revived, things intensely Hudsonian, more than Hudsonian; small echoes and tones and sleeping lights, small sights and sounds and smells that made one, for an hour, *as* small—carried one up the rest of the river, the very river of life, indeed, as a thrilled, roundabout pilgrim, by primitive steamboat, to a mellow, mediaeval Albany.

The same note of piety, though struck more impersonally, can be heard when James ruminates at Concord on the place where Emerson must have walked and thought:

. . . If one had reached a "time of life" one had thereby at least heard him lecture; and not a russet leaf fell for me, while I was there, but fell with an Emersonian drop.

About a writer as richly various as Henry James no single idea can begin to exhaust the interest of his work. It has nevertheless been clear to all his critics, whatever their disagreements about his significance and value, that certain strong preoccupations move steadily through his books, as signatures of concern or tokens of vision. It has seemed to me, for example, that throughout the massing of his fiction James keeps alternating—and I suspect, with experimental deliberateness—between opposite ways of looking upon human affairs, and that these contraries of perspectives were not merely chosen for their "dramatic value" but also were deeply tied in with his own experience.

There is a strand of his fiction in which James submits himself to the imagination of innocence, an imagination firmly and at times, even, sternly moral. At the climax of his career, it becomes an angelic imagination, trying to body forth a goodness almost beyond flesh. These are the novels in which James hovers protectively and lovingly over his heroes and, still more, his heroines, exposing them, as he must, to the treacheries of experience yet remaining eager to share in their ordeals and to be implicated in their fate. I think of novels like *Washington Square*, *Portrait of a Lady*, *What Maisie Knew*, and *Wings of the Dove*, all of which yield, sometimes with irony but sometimes as pure rhapsody, celebrations of the presence and even power of goodness. These are the novels written by James in his "American" self, by which I do not mean that they are necessarily set in America or that James was so naïve as simply to equate this country with goodness, but rather that he found it a useful device, even a usable myth, to connect his moral positives with a lyrical evocation of the homeland.

There is another line of James's fiction at least as distinguished and perhaps more brilliant: *The Europeans, The Bostonians, The Awkward Age,* and *The Ambassadors.* Here James writes as a "European," a man very much at home with the world as it is, in all its hardness, polish, and cultivation. This Henry James is notably relaxed as a moralist. Not that he is indifferent to issues of morality: how could any serious novelist ever be? But he acknowledges the power of the given, the durability of institutions, the attractiveness of forms, and the reality of appetites which cannot readily be silenced by moral injunctions. He sees the social world not as a theater of evil to be destroyed or transcended, but as the arena—the only one we have—in which men act out their lives.

Finally, in his last great novel, James brings together with an almost blinding complexity these opposing strands of his work; and that is one reason *The Golden Bowl* is so remarkable a book. For here the portraitist of European sophistication and the elegist of American innocence, the novelist of the social world and the romancer of unstained morality, enter into a collaboration. Together, the two Jameses create in Maggie Verver, the heroine of *The Golden Bowl,* an overwhelmed young woman who, in behalf of goodness and self-preservation, becomes a figure of overwhelming moral complication. Through "European" tactics, she achieves an "American" transcendence.

Now, what James achieved dramatically in *The Golden Bowl* he touched upon and shyly, deeply buried away in *The American Scene.* Again and again, though with but the slightest stress, he keeps returning in *The American Scene* to the idea of a humane civilization, and for the attentive reader it becomes clear, I think, that this vision signifies nothing less than a union of the American virtues—moral purity, innocence of spirit, freshness of feeling—with the European attractions—nuances of conversation, eloquence of manners, absorbed traditions, and the visible substance of art. The question hovering about *The American Scene* is whether it will be possible, under the pressures of social change, national expansion, and economic power, for this country to become a true civilization, one that might preserve the spirit of Emersonian America while shaking off its provincialism and becoming a worthy heir of Europe.

So flatly stated, this notion cannot be found in *The American Scene*, but endlessly refined and played with, it is, I think, everywhere between the lines. James leaves it, as he must, in the shape of a question, yet a question which lends the book its underlying unity and distinction. That James could not suppose himself able to answer this question, that he may even have wondered whether to ask it betrays a naïve wish for the best of all possible worlds, need not surprise us. But what does seem clear in his book is a recognition that if we Americans do not make the best, we shall certainly end with the worst of all possible worlds.

⋘

Edith Wharton:
Convention and the
Demons of Modernism

"Justice to Edith Wharton"—this was the title, and the motivating plea, of an essay Edmund Wilson wrote soon after Mrs. Wharton's death in 1937. Years have passed; a modest quantity of critical writing about her work has appeared; she still commands the respect of a certain number of readers. But if one judges by the treatment she receives in our standard literary histories, the attention given her in the universities, the influence she exerts upon present-day writers, the feelings serious literary people are likely to have about their faded memories of her novels—then justice has not yet come to Edith Wharton. And this seems particularly true if one believes her to be a writer of wit, force, and maturity—not the peer of Hawthorne, Melville, and James, but several strides ahead of many twentieth-century novelists who have received far more praise than she has.

It is difficult to imagine a study of Mrs. Wharton's apprentice fiction in which sooner or later the word "clever" failed to appear. I quote a few characteristic sentences from her early stories:

The most fascinating female is apt to be encumbered with luggage and scruples.

Her body had been privileged to outstrip her mind, and the two . . . were destined to travel through an eternity of girlishness.

His marriage had been a failure, but he had preserved toward his wife the exact fidelity of act that is sometimes supposed to excuse any divagation of feeling; so that, for years, the tie between them had consisted mainly in his abstaining from making love to other women.

Such writing yields pleasure of a kind, but in context it often seems willful and strained. One senses too quickly the effort behind the cleverness, the claw inside the glove. Dealing with personal relationships among the leisured classes, these stories are usually brittle and contrived, reflections of the conflict in Mrs. Wharton between a worldliness that had not yet been raised to a style and a moralism that had not yet broken past the rationalistic and conventional.

The early stories hardly prepare one for the work to come. For with *The House of Mirth* (1905), a full-scale portrait of a lovely young woman trapped between crass ambitions and disabling refinements of sensibility, Mrs. Wharton composed one of the few American novels that approaches the finality of the tragic. The book is close in philosophic temper to European naturalism, though constructed with an eye toward "well-made" effects that are quite distant from the passion for accumulating evidence that we associate with the naturalistic novel. At its best Mrs. Wharton's style is terse, caustic, and epigrammatic—a prose of aggressive commentary and severe control. At points of emotional stress, however, she succumbs to a fault that is to mar all her novels except *The Age of Innocence*: she employs an overcharged rhetoric to impose upon her story complexities of meaning it cannot support and intensities of feeling it does not need. If not her most finished work, *The House of Mirth* is Mrs. Wharton's most powerful one, the novel in which she dramatizes her sense of the pervasiveness of waste in human affairs and the tyranny that circumstance can exert over human desire.

Technically, Mrs. Wharton was not an audacious writer. She felt little sympathy with the experiments that were being undertaken during her lifetime by the great European and American novelists. In reading her books one is always aware that for Mrs. Wharton the novel is essentially a fixed form, a closely designed if somewhat heavy container of narrative, the presence of which we are never invited to forget. Unlike such impressionist writers as Conrad and Faulkner, she does not seek for that illusion of transparency which might tempt a reader to suppose he is "in" the world of the novel. She wishes her audience always to be aware of her firm guiding hand, to regard it as a force of assurance and control. In the several senses of the term, she is a *formal* writer.

Mrs. Wharton composed the kind of novel in which the plot stands out in its own right, like a clear and visible line of intention; in which the characters are taken to be rationally apprehensible, coherent figures to be portrayed through their actions rather than dissolved into a stream of psychology; and in which the narrative point of view is quickly established and limited, even if most of the time it comes through the austere tones of Mrs. Wharton's own voice. Her locale and subject matter are usually American, but her view of the possibilities and limitations of the novel as a form makes her seem closer to such Europeans as Flaubert than to Americans like Melville and Twain.

She is a writer of limited scope. The historic span of her novels is narrow, usually confined to those late nineteenth-century realignments of power and status that comprise a high moment in the biography of the American *bourgeoisie*. The social range is also narrow, dealing with clashes among segments of the rich or with personal relationships as these have been defined, or distorted, by the conventions of a fixed society. Mrs. Wharton had no gift for the large and "open" narrative forms, those sprawling prose epics which in modern fiction have been employed to depict large areas of national experience. Nor, despite an intense awareness of the pressure of impulse in human life, does she care to encounter the murk and puzzle of the unconscious. She respects it, she fears it, she would as soon keep it at a distance. The arena of her imagination is the forefront of social life, where manners reveal moral stress, and accepted forms of conduct may break under the weight of personal desire. "Civilization and its discontents"—the phrase from Freud could stand as an epigraph for her books. She writes as a convinced rationalist, but in her best work as one who knows how desperately besieged and vulnerable human reason is.

Within these traditional limits, and despite her coolness to modernist innovations, Mrs. Wharton was a restless writer, forever seeking new variations of tone and theme, and in her several important novels after *The House of Mirth* rarely troubling to repeat a success. In *The Reef* (1912) she composed a subtle though tenuous drama of personal relations, Jamesian in manner and diction, which deals largely with the price and advantage of moral scruple. In *The Custom of the Country* (1913) she turned to—I think it fair to say, she was largely the innovator of— a tough-spirited, fierce, and abrasive satire of the barbaric phil- istinism she felt to be settling upon American society and the source of which she was inclined to locate, not with complete accuracy, in the new raw towns of the Midwest. Endless num- bers of American novels would later be written on this theme, and Sinclair Lewis would commonly be mentioned as a writer particularly indebted to *The Custom of the Country;* but the truth is that no American novelist of our time—with the exception of Nathanael West—has been so ruthless, so bitingly cold as Mrs. Wharton in assaulting the vulgarities and failures of our society. Her considerable gifts for caricature reached their fruition in *The Custom of the Country,* a novel that is hard to endure be- cause it provides no consoling reconciliations and has, therefore, never been properly valued or even widely read. And, finally, in the list of her superior novels there is *The Age of Innocence* (1920), a suavely ironic evocation of New York in the 1870's, blending Mrs. Wharton's nostalgia for the world from which she came with her criticism of its genteel timidities and evasions.

On occasion Mrs. Wharton was also a master of the shorter forms of prose fiction. A fine selection could be made from her short stories, and there are three short novels or novelettes— *Ethan Frome* (1911), *Summer* (·1917), and *The Bunner Sisters* (1916)—which are of permanent interest. *Ethan Frome,* a severe depiction of gratuitous human suffering in a New England vil- lage, is a work meant to shock and depress; it has often been criticized, wrongly, for being so successfully the *tour de force* Mrs. Wharton meant it to be—that is, for leaving us with a sense of admiration for the visible rigor of its mechanics and a sense of pain because of its total assault upon our emotions. *Summer,* a more complex and thoughtful piece of writing, is also set in rural New England, displaying a close knowledge of locale and character which would surprise those who suppose Mrs. Whar- ton merely to be the chronicler of the New York rich. *The Bunner Sisters,* an account of the sufferings of two poor women in New York, is not only a masterpiece of compressed realism but a notable example of Mrs. Wharton's ability to release through her fiction a disciplined compassion that is far more impressive than the rhetoric of protest cultivated by many liberal and radical writers. One or two other novelettes by Mrs. Wharton, such as the melodramatic *The Old Maid*, also have a certain interest, for the short novel was a form in which her fondness for economy of effects—a sweeping narrative line, a brisk prose, a rapid disposition of theme and figures—served her well.

The remaining novels? A few are dull and earnest failures, like *The Fruit of the Tree*, and too many others, like *The Glimpses of the Moon*, are barely superior to ladies' magazine fiction. In the novels written during the last fifteen years of her life, Mrs. Wharton's intellectual conservatism hardened into an embittered and querulous disdain for modern life: she no longer really knew what was happening in America; and she lost what had once been her main gift—the accurate location of the target she wished to destroy.

One reason justice has not yet come to Edith Wharton is the widespread assumption that she is primarily a disciple of Henry James—a gifted disciple, to be sure, but not nearly so gifted as the master. Now it is true that if you come to Mrs. Wharton's work with the expectation of finding replicas of the Jamesian novel, you will probably be disappointed; but then the expectation is itself a mistake. The claim that Henry James exerted a major influence upon Mrs. Wharton's fiction, repeated with maddening regularity by literary historians, reveals the reluctance of scholars to suppose that anything can spring directly from the art of a writer without also having some clearly specifiable source in an earlier writer.

I would contend that Mrs. Wharton is not primarily the disciple of James; that James's influence upon her work has either been overstated or misunderstood; and that, within certain obvious limits, she is an original writer.

In one large and pleasant way Mrs. Wharton did regard herself as permanently indebted to Henry James. For her, as for so many later writers, he loomed as a model of artistic conscience; his example made their calling seem a sacred one, his devotion to craft made everything else seem trivial. James persuaded her that the composition of a novel should be not a mere outpouring but a craft to be studied and mastered; he was, as she said, "about the only novelist who had formulated his ideas

about his art." In this respect, then, James was her "inspiration"—
which is something rather different from an influence.

There is *some* evidence of a direct literary influence. A number
of James's early novels left their mark upon that side of Mrs.
Wharton's work which is concerned with the comedy of social
manners. To say this, however, is to indicate a serious qualification: for if James began as a novelist of manners he soon became
something else as well, and although Mrs. Wharton was skillful
at observing manners and in most of her books more dependent
than James upon the use of such observation, it is finally for the
strength of her personal vision and the incisiveness of her mind
that we should value her work. One could say that it was the
lesser James who influenced the lesser Mrs. Wharton.

The point seems to be enforced by E. K. Brown, when he
writes, "The picture of the Faubourg Saint Germain in 'Madame
de Treymes' [a story by Mrs. Wharton] owes as much to
[James's] *The American* and 'Madame de Mauves' as it does to
direct observation." This is largely correct, but it affects only
some minor instances of Mrs. Wharton's work and is not sufficient ground for the usual claim of a pervasive Jamesian influence. Brown is also correct in noting that "from the beginning
to the end *The Reef* is Jamesian." Yet here, too, qualifications
are needed: the refined agonies of conscience which Anna Leath
experiences in this novel are of a kind that depend on Mrs.
Wharton's "feminine" side and thereby are mostly beyond the
reach of James, while the ending of the novel, so painfully
tendentious and damaging to all that has preceded it, is also
dependent on Mrs. Wharton's "feminine" side, as this time it
takes upon itself the privilege of moral retaliation. Still, the
presence of differences between two writers does not remove
the possibility of influence, and in regard to *The Reef* that influence seems clear.

Can we go any farther? In a valuable essay, Q. D. Leavis cites
Mrs. Wharton's remark that James "belonged irrevocably to the
old America out of which I also came," and that he was "essentially a novelist of manners, and the manners he was qualified
by nature and situation to observe were those of the little
vanishing group of people among whom he had grown up."
Such statements form part of Mrs. Leavis's ground for calling
Edith Wharton "the heiress of Henry James," but in taking those

statements at face value she is, I think, being led somewhat
astray.

Mrs. Wharton's description of James's novels is clearly inadequate, for it transforms him into a writer excessively like herself. His dependence on the manners of "the little vanishing
group of people among whom he had grown up" was never very
great and, as his art matured, was left almost entirely behind.
And though a figure of "the old America," James came from a
milieu quite different from the one in which Mrs. Wharton was
raised and upon which she drew so heavily in her fiction. Though
a New Yorker by birth and occasional residence, James had his
closest ties of intellect and temperament with the New England
of philosophical idealism, both as it came down to him in its
own right and as it was recast in the speculations of his father
Henry James, Sr. Now it is precisely this element of American
thought to which the mind of Mrs. Wharton was closed: both to
her literary profit, since she escaped its vapidity, and her literary
loss, since a major lack in her writing is any trace of that urge
to transcendence, that glow of the vision of the possible, which
lights up even the darkest of James's novels. The intellectual
backgrounds of the two writers are quite different, and that is
one reason Mrs. Wharton could not respond favorably to James's
later novels. The whole Emersonian tradition, so important a
formative element in James's sensibility and so pervasive in his
later books, was alien to her.

The truth is that in Mrs. Wharton's most important novels it
is hard to detect any *specific* Jamesian influence. Perhaps it can
be found in her conception of the novel as a form, her wish to
write with plan and economy; perhaps in the style of *The Custom of the Country*, which may owe something to the cold brilliance of James's prose in *The Bostonians*. But Mrs. Wharton's
novelettes are in setting, theme, and characterization quite alien
to James, while each of her three best novels—*The House of
Mirth, The Custom of the Country*, and *The Age of Innocence*—
is a work notably different from either the early or late James.
The somewhat naturalistic method of *The House of Mirth* and
Mrs. Wharton's preoccupation with Lily Bart as victim of her
social milieu, the caustic satire of *The Custom of the Country*
and Mrs. Wharton's impatience with its feeble hero as an agent
of traditional values, the modulated style of *The Age of Inno-*

cence and Mrs. Wharton's involvement with the world of her birth—all this seems her own. Her characteristic style is sharper, clearer, more aggressive, and less metaphorical than James's in all but a few of his novels. Her narrative line is usually more direct than his. And her sense of life is more despondent, less open to the idea or even the possibility of redemption.

Mrs. Wharton's best novels portray the life of New York during the latter third of the nineteenth century. Economically and socially, this world was dominated by an established wealthy class consisting of the sons and grandsons of energetic provincial merchants. In the 1870's and 1880's this class did not yet feel seriously threatened by the competition and clamor of the *nouveaux riches;* it had gained enough wealth to care about leisure, and enough leisure to think of setting itself up as a modest aristocracy. The phrase *modest aristocracy* may seem a contradiction in terms, but it should serve to suggest the difficulty of building an enclave of social precedence in the fluid bourgeois society America was then becoming.

Quite free from any disturbing intensities of belief or aspirations toward grandeur of style, this class was strict in its decorum and narrow in its conventions. With tepid steadfastness it devoted itself to good manners, good English, good form. And it cared about culture, too—culture as a static and finished quantity, something one had to possess but did not have to live by. Its one great passion was to be left alone, untroubled by the motions of history; and this of course was the one privilege history could not bestow. The nation was becoming industrialized; waves of immigrants were descending upon New York; financial empires were being established in the alien cities of the Midwest as well as in Wall Street itself. Such developments made it inevitable that the provincial ruling class of "old New York" should suffer both assault and assimilation by newer, more vigorous, and less cultivated segments of the American *bourgeoisie.*

In "old New York" no one soared and no one was supposed, visibly, to sink. Leisure ruled. Husbands rarely went to their offices "downtown," and there were long midday lunches and solemn entertainments in the evening. Good conversation, though of a not too taxing kind, was felt to be desirable. Taste and form were the reigning gods, not the less tyrannical for their apparent mildness of administration. As Mrs. Wharton remarked with gentle sarcasm in *The Age of Innocence,* it was a world composed of people "who dreaded scandal more than disease, who placed decency above courage, and who considered that nothing was more ill-bred than 'scenes,' except the behavior of those who gave rise to them." In the same novel she wrote: "What was or was not 'the thing' played a part as important in Newland Archer's New York as the inscrutable totem terrors that had ruled the destinies of his forefathers thousands of years ago." And above all, "old New York" was a world that had entered its decline. What was happening in the years of Mrs. Wharton's youth, as Louis Auchincloss remarks, was "the assault upon an old and conservative group by the multitudes enriched, and fabulously enriched, by the business expansion of the preceding decades." Mrs. Wharton kept returning to this theme, half in the cool spirit of the anthropologist studying the death of a tribe, half with the nostalgia of a survivor mourning the loss of vanished graces.

Toward the world in which she grew up Mrs. Wharton retained a mixture of feelings that anticipates those of later American writers toward their immigrant childhood and youth in a new New York. It was too fatally *her* world, beyond choice or escape, and it would serve her as lifelong memory, lifelong subject, perhaps lifelong trauma. She loved "old New York" with that mixture of grieving affection and protective impatience Faulkner would later feel toward Mississippi and Saul Bellow toward the Jewish neighborhoods of Chicago. Yet it also left her dissatisfied, on edge, unfulfilled. Her work, as Edmund Wilson has remarked, "was . . . the desperate product of a pressure of [personal] maladjustments. . . . At her strongest and most characteristic, she is a brilliant example of the writer who relieves an emotional strain by denouncing his generation." She yearned for a way of life that might bring greater intellectual risks and yield greater emotional rewards than her family and friends could imagine, and only after a time did she find it in her dedication to writing. Just as Faulkner's attitudes toward his home country have kept shifting from one ambiguity to another, so Mrs. Wharton combined toward her home city feelings both of harsh rejection and haughty defense. There are moments, especially in

The House of Mirth, when she is utterly without mercy toward "old New York": she sees it as a place of betrayal, failure, and impotence. In her old age, when she came to write her autobiography, she was mellower—though perhaps the word should really be harder—in spirit. "It used to seem to me," she wrote, "that the group in which I grew up was like an empty vessel into which no new wine would ever again be poured. Now I see that one of its uses lay in preserving a few drops of an old vintage too rare to be savored by a youthful palate. . . ."

For a novelist to be so profoundly involved with a known and measured society offers major advantages. Mrs. Wharton wrote about her segment of America with an authority few novelists could surpass, for she was one of the two or three among them who knew, fully and from the inside, what the life of the rich in this country was really like. Henry James had used that life as an occasion for fables of freedom and circumstance in his later books; F. Scott Fitzgerald, an interloper in the world of wealth, was to collect brilliant guesses and fragments of envious insight; John O'Hara has felt his way along the provincial outposts of the America that made its money late and fast. But no American writer has known quite so deeply as Mrs. Wharton what it means, both as privilege and burden, to grow up in a family of the established rich: a family where there was enough money and had been money long enough for talk about it to seem vulgar, and where conspicuous effort to make more of it seemed still more vulgar. One reason for continuing to read *The House of Mirth*, *The Custom of the Country*, and *The Age of Innocence* is the shrewdness with which Mrs. Wharton, through an expert scrutiny of manners, is able to discriminate among the gradations of power and status in the world of the rich. To read these books is to discover how the novel of manners can register both the surface of social life and the inner vibrations of spirit that surface reveals, suppresses, and distorts.

There were other advantages in being so close to her materials. As with Faulkner, the subject seems to have chosen the writer, not the writer the subject; everything came to her with the pressure and inexorability of a felt memory; each return to the locale of her youth raised the possibility of a new essay at self-discovery. And in books like *The House of Mirth* and *The Age of Innocence* she could work on the assumption, so valuable to a writer who prizes economy of structure, that moral values can be tested in a novel by dramatizing the relationships between fixed social groups and mobile characters.

As she herself knew quite well, there was little in Mrs. Wharton's world that could provide her with a subject large in social scope and visibly tragic in its implications. Had "old New York" gone down in blind and bitter resistance to the *nouveaux riches*, that might have been a subject appropriate to moral or social tragedy; but since there was far less conflict than fusion between the old money and the new, she had little alternative to the varieties of comedy that dominate her books. Only once in her novels did she achieve a tragic resonance, and that was in *The House of Mirth,* where Lily Bart is shown as the victim of a world that had made possible her loveliness and inevitable her limitations. Even here we must reduce the traditional notion of the tragic to the pathetic on one side and the bleak on the other, if the term is to be used with approximate relevance. In discussing this novel Mrs. Wharton showed a complete awareness of her problem. How, she asked herself, "could a society of irresponsible pleasure-seekers be said to have, on the 'old woes of the world,' any deeper bearing than the people composing such a society could guess?" And she answered: "A frivolous society can acquire dramatic significance only through what its frivolity destroys. Its tragic implication lies in its power of debasing people and ideas."

Toward the end of her career Mrs. Wharton found it more and more difficult to employ her material with the success that marks her work between 1905 and 1920. Her later novels are shoddy and sometimes mean-spirited in the hauteur with which she dismisses younger generations beyond the reach of her understanding or sympathy. These novels bristle with her impatience before the mysteries of a world she could not enter, the world of twentieth-century America, and are notable for a truculence of temper, a hardening of the moral arteries. I would offer the speculation that Mrs. Wharton, whose intelligence should never be underestimated, was aware that the ground on which she took her moral stand was dissolving beneath her. At best the world of her youth had been an aristocracy of surface ("In that simple society," she recalled, "there was an almost pagan worship of physical beauty"), but she had always wanted it to be something better, something beautiful and truly distinguished. She had wanted to look upon it as potentially an aristocracy of value, and throughout most of her life she struggled with this desire and her recognition that it was an impossible, even unreasonable desire. But even when she recognized this, she still wondered to what extent the style and decorum of "old New York" had at least made possible some of the aspirations she had cherished since childhood. Having a thoroughly earthbound mind, she sought for tangible embodiments, in social groups or communities, of the values to which she clung—for she could not be content with the fabulous imaginings Henry James spun in his later novels. She turned, at times with open savagery and at other times with a feeling as close to wistfulness as she could tolerate, to the world of her birth, hoping to find there some token of security by which to satisfy the needs of her imagination. In the inevitable disappointment that followed, Mrs. Wharton, though extremely conservative in her opinions, proved to be the American novelist least merciful in her treatment of the rich. She kept harassing them, nagging at them in a language they could not, with the best will in the world, understand; and then she became glacial in her contempt, almost too willing to slash away at their mediocrity because she did not know anyone else to turn toward or against.

At the end she was alone. If the incongruity between desire and realization is a recurrent motif in her writing about personal relationships, it is an incongruity she also observed in her dealings with the public world. There were always available to her, once she settled in France, a number of personal friends, men and women of high if somewhat forbidding culture. But what emerges from a scrutiny of her work as a whole is that Mrs. Wharton, like so many of those younger deracinated novelists who both interested and disturbed her, was a solitary, clinging to values for which she could find no place, and holding fast, with tight-lipped stoicism, to the nerve of her pride. She was a writer haunted by what she disliked, haunted by the demons of modernism as they encircled her both in life and literature. She would have nothing to do with them, yet in her most important books they kept reappearing, both as agents of moral dissolution and as possibilities of fresh life that needed to be kept sternly in check.

◆§

The texture of Mrs. Wharton's novels is dark. Like so many writers whose education occurred during the latter decades of the nineteenth century, she felt that the universe—which for her is virtually to say, organized society—was profoundly inhospitable to human need and desire. The malaise which troubled so many intelligent people during her lifetime—the feeling that they were living in an age when energies had run down, meanings collapsed, and the flow of organic life been replaced by the sterile and mechanical—is quite as acute in her novels as in those of Thomas Hardy and George Gissing. Like them, she felt that somehow the world had turned cold, and she could find no vantage point at which to establish a protective distance from it. This condition is somewhat different from the strain of melancholy that runs through American literature, surely different from the metaphysical desperation that overcame Melville in his later years or the misanthropy that beset Twain. What Mrs. Wharton felt was more distinctly "European" in quality, more related to that rationalist conservatism which is a perennial motif in French intellectual life and manifests itself as a confirmed skepticism about the possibilities of human relationships.

In Mrs. Wharton's vision of things—and we can only speculate on the extent to which her personal unhappiness contributed to it—human beings seem always to prove inadequate, always to fail each other, always to be the victims of an innate disharmony between love and response, need and capacity. Men especially have a hard time of it in Mrs. Wharton's novels. In their notorious vanity and faithlessness, they seldom "come through"; they fail Mrs. Wharton's heroines less from bad faith than from weak imagination, a laziness of spirit that keeps them from a true grasp of suffering; and in a number of her novels one finds a suppressed feminine bitterness, a profound impatience with the claims of the ruling sex. This feminist resentment seems, in turn, only an instance of what Mrs. Wharton felt to be a more radical and galling inequity at the heart of the human scheme. The inability of human beings to achieve self-sufficiency drives them to seek relationships with other people, and these relationships necessarily compromise their freedom by subjecting them to the pain of a desire either too great or too small. Things, in Mrs. Wharton's world, do not work out. In one of her books she speaks of "the sense of mortality," and of "its loneliness, the way it must be borne without help." I am convinced she meant by this more than the prospect of death. What "must be borne without help" is the inexorable disarrangement of everything we seek through intelligence and will to arrange.

Mrs. Wharton's general hostility toward "modern" ideas must have predisposed her against Freudian psychology, yet one is repeatedly struck by the fact that, at least in regard to the *possibilities* of the human enterprise, there is an underlying closeness of skepticism between her assumptions and Freud's theories. Mrs. Wharton had a highly developed, perhaps over-developed, sense of the power of everything in organized social existence which checks our desires. Like Freud, she believed that we must endure an irremediable conflict between nature and culture, and while she had at least as healthy a respect as he did for the uses of sublimation, she also knew that the human capacity for putting up with substitute gratifications is limited. From this impasse she could seldom find a way out.

A good many of Mrs. Wharton's critics have assumed that she was simply a defender of harsh social conventions against all those who, from romantic energy or mere hunger for meaning in life, rebel against the fixed patterns of their world. But this is not quite true for many of her books, and in regard to some of them not true at all. What is true is that most of her plots focus upon a clash between a stable society and a sensitive person who half belongs to and half rebels against it. At the end he must surrender to the social taboos he had momentarily challenged or wished to challenge, for either he has not been able to summon the resources of courage through which to act out his rebellion, or he has discovered that the punitive power of society is greater than he had supposed, or he has learned that the conventions he had assumed to be lifeless still retain a certain wisdom. Yet much of Mrs. Wharton's work contains a somewhat chill and detached sympathy for those very rebels in whose crushing she seems to connive. Her sense of the world is hardly such as to persuade her of its goodness; it is merely such as to persuade her of its force.

Mrs. Wharton understands how large is the price, how endless the nagging pain, that must be paid for a personal assertion against the familiar ways of the world, and she believes, simply, that most of us lack the strength to pay. Yet she has no respect for blind acceptance, and time after time expresses her distaste for "sterile pain" and "the vanity of self-sacrifice." It is hard to imagine another American writer for whom society, despite its attractions of surface and order, figures so thoroughly as a prison of the human soul. And there, she seems to say, there it is: the doors locked, the bars firm. "Life," she wrote in *The Fruit of the Tree*, "is not a matter of abstract principles, but a succession of pitiful compromises with fate, of concessions to old traditions, old beliefs, old tragedies, old failures." This sense of fatality has, in her best work, a certain minor magnificence, what might be called the magnificence of the bleak.

In a final reckoning, of course, Mrs. Wharton's vision of life has its severe limitations. She knew only too well how experience can grind men into hopelessness, how it can leave them persuaded that the need for choice contains within itself the seeds of tragedy and the impossibility of choice the sources of pain. Everything that reveals the power of the conditioned, everything that shreds our aspirations, she brought to full novelistic life. Where she failed was in giving imaginative embodiment to the human will seeking to resist defeat or move beyond it. She lacked James's ultimate serenity. She lacked his gift for summoning through images of conduct the purity of children and the selflessness of girls. She lacked the vocabulary of happiness.

But whatever Mrs. Wharton could see, she looked at with absolute courage. She believed that what the heart desires brings with it a price, often an exorbitant price. Americans are not trained to accept this view of the human situation, and there is nothing to recommend it except the fact that it contains at least a fraction of the truth. How well, with what sardonic pleasure, Mrs. Wharton would have responded to the lines of W. H. Auden:

> Every farthing of the cost
> All the bitter stars foretell
> Shall be paid.

◈₃

Dreiser:
The Springs
of Desire

Do I exaggerate in saying that Theodore Dreiser has dropped
out of the awareness of cultivated Americans? If so, it is but a
slight exaggeration. Few young writers now model themselves
on his career, and not many readers think of him as one of those
literary figures whose word can transform the quality of their
experience. Dreiser has suffered the fate that often besets writers
caught up in cultural dispute: their work comes to seem inseparable from what has been said about it, their passion gets
frozen into history.

Mention Dreiser to a bright student of literature, mention him
to a literate older person, and only seldom will the response be
a swift turning of memory to novels that have brought pleasure
and illumination. Far more likely is a series of fixed associations:
to a cragged, brooding, bearlike figure who dragged himself out
of nineteenth-century poverty and provincialism, and in *Sister
Carrie* composed a pioneering novel of sexual candor; or to a
vague notion that the author of *The Financier* and *The Titan*
turned out quantities of ill-tuned and turgid social documenta-
tion; or to a prepared judgment against a writer taken to be
sluggish in thought and language, sluggishly accumulating data
of destruction and failure, but deaf to the refinements of consciousness, dull to the play of sensibility, and drab, utterly and
hopelessly drab in the quality of his mind.

The decline of Dreiser's reputation has not been an isolated

event. It has occurred in the context, and surely as a consequence, of the counterrevolution in American culture during the
forties and fifties. For readers educated in these years, Dreiser
became a symbol of everything a superior intelligence was
supposed to avoid. For the New Critics, to whom the very possibility of a social novel seemed disagreeable; for literary students trained in the fine but narrow school of the Jamesian sensibility; for liberals easing into a modest gentility and inclined
to replace a belief in social commitment with a search for personal distinction; for intellectuals delighted with the values of
ambiguity, irony, complexity and impatient with the pieties of
radicalism—for all such persons Dreiser became an object of
disdain. He stood for an earlier age of scientism, materialism,
agnosticism: all of which were now seen as hostile to the claims
of moral freedom and responsibility. He represented the boorish-
ness of the Populist mentality, as it declined into anti-Semitism
or veered toward a peculiarly thoughtless brand of Communism.
He could not think: he could only fumble with the names of
ideas. He could not write: he could only pile words on top of
each other. He cared not for art as such, but only for the novel
as a vehicle of social and "philosophical" ideas. He was unedu-
cated, insensitive—the novelist as mastodon.

So the indictment went, frequently right in its details, and
when coming from so temperate a critic as Lionel Trilling often
persuasive in result. If a few literary men, like the novelist James
T. Farrell and the critic Alfred Kazin, continued to praise
Dreiser as a writer of massive and poignant effects, if they insisted that attention be paid to the novels he wrote rather than
to his foolish public declamations, they were not much heeded.

But now, when Dreiser's prejudices have begun to be forgotten and all that remains—all that need remain—are his three
or four major novels, it is time for reconsideration. The early
praise these books received may have been undiscriminating: we
are not obliged to repeat it. Dreiser's role in assaulting the taboos
of gentility can no longer excite us as once it did his admirers.
And as for his faults, no great critical insight is required to
identify them, since they glare out of every chapter, especially
his solemnities as a cosmic voice and his habit of crushing the
English language beneath a leaden embrace. Yet these faults are
interwoven with large creative powers, and it can be argued that

for the powers to be released there had first to be the triggering presence of the faults. Let me cite an example.

As a philosopher Dreiser can often be tiresome; yet his very lust for metaphysics, his stubborn insistence upon learning "what it's all about," helped to deepen the emotional resources from which he drew as a novelist. For he came to feel that our existence demands from us an endless contemplativeness, even if—perhaps because—we cannot think through our problems or solve our mysteries. In the frustrations he encountered when trying to extract some conceptual order from the confusion and trouble of existence, he grew more closely involved, more *at one*, with the characters he created, also confused and troubled. Somewhat like Hardy, he learned to stand back a little from the human spectacle and watch the endlessly repeated sequence of desire, effort, and disintegration; and from this distance—perhaps the sole reward of his philosophical gropings—he gained a sense of the shared helplessness of men, he learned how brutal and irrelevant the impulse to moral judgment can become, and he arrived at his profoundly inclusive compassion for the whole of human life.

In the first task of the novelist, which is to create an imaginary social landscape both credible and significant, Dreiser ranks among the American giants, the very few American giants we have had. Reading *An American Tragedy* once again, after a lapse of more than twenty years, I have found myself greatly moved and shaken by its repeated onslaughts of narrative, its profound immersion in human suffering, its dredging up of those shapeless desires which lie, as if in fever, just below the plane of consciousness. How much more vibrant and tender this book is than the usual accounts of it in recent criticism might lead one to suppose! It is a masterpiece, nothing less.

Dreiser published *An American Tragedy* in 1925. By then he was fifty-four years old, an established writer with his own fixed and hard-won ways, who had written three first-rate novels: *Sister Carrie, Jennie Gerhardt* and *The Financier*. These books are crowded with exact observation—observation worked closely into the grain of narrative—about the customs and class structure of American society in the phase of early finance capitalism. No other novelist has absorbed into his work as much knowledge as

Dreiser had about American institutions: the mechanisms of business, the stifling rhythms of the factory, the inner hierarchy of a large hotel, the chicaneries of city politics, the status arrangements of rulers and ruled. For the most part, Dreiser's characters are defined through their relationships to these institutions. They writhe and suffer to win a foothold in the slippery social world or to break out of the limits of established social norms. They exhaust themselves to gain success, they destroy themselves in acts of impulsive deviance. But whatever their individual lot, they all act out the drama of determinism—which, in Dreiser's handling, is not at all the sort of listless fatality that hostile critics would make it seem, but is rather a struggle by human beings to discover the harsh limits of what is possible to them and thereby perhaps to enlarge those limits by an inch or two. That mostly they fail is the tribute Dreiser pays to reality.

This controlling pattern in Dreiser's novels has been well described by Bernard Rosenberg, a sociologist with a literary eye:

> Emile Durkheim had suggested in Dreiser's day that when men speak of a force external to themselves which they are powerless to control, their subject is not God but social organization. This is also Dreiser's theme, and to it he brings a sense of religious awe and wonder. "So well defined," he writes, "is the sphere of social activity, that he who departs from it is doomed." . . . Durkheim identified social facts, i.e., the existence of norms, precisely as Dreiser did: by asking what would happen if they were violated. . . . Norms develop outside the individual consciousness and exist prior to it; we internalize them and are fully aware of their grip only when our behavior is deviant. Durkheim illustrated this proposition in a dozen different ways, and so did Dreiser.

In Dreiser's early novels most of the central characters are harried by a desire for personal affirmation, a desire they can neither articulate nor suppress. They suffer from a need that their lives assume the dignity of dramatic form, and they suffer terribly, not so much because they cannot satisfy this need, but because they do not really understand it. Money, worldly success, sensual gratification, are the only ends they know or can name, but none of these slakes their restlessness. They grapple desperately for money, they lacerate themselves climbing to success, yet they remain sullen and bewildered, always hopeful for some unexpected sign by which to release their bitter craving for a state of grace or, at least, illumination. Dreiser's characters are romantics who behave as if the Absolute can be found, immaculately preserved, at the very summit of material power. Great energies can flow from this ingrained American delusion, both for the discharge of ambition and the aggressiveness of ego. And Dreiser too, because he had in his own experience shared these values and struggled, with varying effectiveness, to burn them out of his system—Dreiser too lived out, with an intense dramatic complicity, the longings and turmoil of his characters.

Yet there is usually present in his early novels a governing intelligence more copious and flexible than that of the characters. This governing intelligence is seldom revealed through direct statement, either by characters or author. So thoroughly does Dreiser recognize the bond of vulnerability between a Carrie and himself, he never moralizes. So patiently does he join a Cowperwood and a Jennie through the course of their experience, he never condescends. Taking upon himself the perils and sharing in the miseries of his characters, he leaves the privilege of admonition to others. Yet there is never really a question as to what his novels "mean," nor any serious possibility that the characters will usurp control. Through the logic of the narrative, the working-out of its implications, we are enabled to grasp with an almost visceral intensity how shallow are the standards by which the characters live.

In these early novels society figures largely as a jungle; and with good reason—the capitalism of the early twentieth century closely resembled a jungle. The characters may begin with a hard struggle for survival, but far more quickly than most of Dreiser's critics allow, they leave it behind them. Having emerged from the blunt innocence of their beginnings, they are now cursed with a fractional awareness. They can find neither peace nor fulfillment. In their half-articulate way, Dreiser's characters are beset by the same yearnings that trouble the characters of Fitzgerald and many other American novelists: a need for some principle of value by which to overcome the meanness, the littleness of their lives. To know, however, that the goals to which one has pledged one's years are trivial, yet not to know in what their triviality consists—this is a form of suffering which overcomes Dreiser's characters again and again. In all its dumb misery, it is the price, or reward, of their slow crawl to awareness. One sometimes feels that in the novels of Dreiser there is being re-enacted the whole progression of the race toward the idea of the human.

The prose in these early novels is often as wretched as unsympathetic critics have said. Dreiser had little feeling for the sentence as a rhythmic unit (though he had a strong intuitive grasp of the underlying rhythm of narrative as a system of controlled variation and incremental development). He had a poor ear for the inflections of common speech, or even for the colloquial play of language. And worst of all, he had a weakness, all too common among semieducated writers, for "elegant" diction and antique rhetoric. Yet, despite the many patches of gray and the occasional patches of purple prose,* Dreiser manages to accumulate large masses of narrative tension; he pulls one, muttering and bruised, into the arena of his imagination; and finally one has no recourse but surrender to its plenitude, its coarse and encompassing reality.

Not even Dreiser's philosophical excursions—bringing together nativist American prejudice with the very latest ideas of 1900—can break the thrust of these narratives. Dreiser's thought has by now been analyzed, mauled, and ridiculed: his distortion of social life through metaphors of brute nature, his reduction of human motive to the malignant pressure of "chemisms," his toying with notions about "the superman" in the Cowperwood novels. But it hardly matters. One brushes all this aside, resigned to the malice of a fate that could yoke together such intellectual debris with so much creative power. One brushes aside, and reads on.

Though surely Dreiser's major achievement, *An American Tragedy* is not the work of a master who, at the approach of old age, decides upon a revolutionary break from the premises and

---

* "The function of language is much more largely referential in the novel than in other literary forms . . . the genre itself works by exhaustive presentation rather than by elegant concentration. This fact would no doubt explain . . . why the novel is the most translatable of genres; why many undoubtedly great novelists, from Richardson and Balzac to Hardy and Dostoevsky, often write gracelessly, and sometimes with downright vulgarity. . . ." —Ian Watt, *The Rise of the Novel* (Berkeley and Los Angeles: University of California Press, 1959).

patterns of his earlier writing. For that order of boldness Dreiser lacked a sufficient self-awareness and sophistication as an artist; he was cut off from too much of the tradition of Western, even of American, culture to do anything but continue with his version of naturalism. He was the kind of writer who must keep circling about the point of his beginnings, forever stirred by memories of his early struggles and preoccupations. All such a writer can hope for—a very great deal—is to mine his talent to its very depth; and that Dreiser did in *An American Tragedy*. Still, there are some changes from the earlier novels, and most of them to the good.

The prose, while quite as clotted and ungainly as in the past, is now more consistent in tone and less adorned with "literary" paste gems. Solecisms, pretentiousness, and gaucherie remain, but the prose has at least the negative virtue of calling less attention to itself than in some of the earlier books. And there are long sections packed with the kind of specification that in Dreiser makes for a happy self-forgetfulness, thereby justifying Philip Rahv's remark that one finds here "a prosiness so primary in texture that if taken in bulk it affects us as a kind of poetry of the commonplace and ill-favored."

For the first and last time Dreiser is wholly in the grip of his vision of things, so that he feels little need for the buttress of comment or the decoration of philosophizing. Dreiser is hardly the writer whose name would immediately occur to one in connection with T. S. Eliot's famous epigram that Henry James had a mind so fine it could not be violated by ideas; yet if there is one Dreiser novel about which a version of Eliot's remark might apply, it is *An American Tragedy*. What Eliot said has sometimes been taken, quite absurdly, as if it were a recommendation for writers to keep themselves innocent of ideas; actually he was trying to suggest the way a novelist can be affected by ideas yet must not allow his work to become a mere illustration for them. And of all Dreiser's novels *An American Tragedy* is the one that seems least cluttered with unassimilated formulas and preconceptions.

Where the earlier novels dealt with somewhat limited aspects of American life, *An American Tragedy*, enormous in scope and ambition, requires to be judged not merely as an extended study of the American lower middle class during the first years of the twentieth century but also as a kind of parable of our national experience. Strip the story to its bare outline, and see how much of American desire it involves: an obscure youth, amiable but weak, is lifted by chance from poverty to the possibility of winning pleasure and wealth. To gain these ends he must abandon the pieties of his fundamentalist upbringing and sacrifice the tender young woman who has given him a taste of pure affection. All of society conspires to persuade him that his goals are admirable, perhaps even sacred; he notices that others, no better endowed than himself, enjoy the privileges of money as if it were in the very nature of things that they should; but the entanglements of his past now form a barrier to realizing his desires, and to break through this barrier he must resort to criminal means. As it happens, he does not commit the murder he had planned, but he might as well have, for he is trapped in the machinery of social punishment and destroyed. "So well defined is the sphere of social activity that he who departs from it is doomed."

Now this story depends upon one of the most deeply grounded fables in our culture. Clyde Griffiths, the figure in Dreiser's novel who acts it out, is not in any traditional sense either heroic or tragic. He has almost no assertive will, he lacks any large compelling idea, he reveals no special gift for the endurance of pain. His puny self is little more than a clouded reflection of the puny world about him. His significance lies in the fact that he represents not our potential greatness but our collective smallness, the common denominator of our foolish tastes and tawdry ambitions. He is that part of ourselves in which we take no pride, but know to be a settled resident. And we cannot dismiss him as a special case or an extreme instance, for his weakness is the essential shoddiness of mortality. By a twist of circumstance he could be a junior executive, a country-club favorite; he almost does manage to remake himself to the cut of his fantasy; and he finds in his rich and arrogant cousin Gilbert an exasperating double, the young man he too might be. Clyde embodies the nothingness at the heart of our scheme of things, the nothingness of our social aspirations. If Flaubert could say, *Emma Bovary, c'est moi*, Dreiser could echo, Clyde Griffiths, he is us.

We have, then, in Clyde a powerful representation of our unacknowledged values, powerful especially since Dreiser keeps a majestic balance between sympathy and criticism. He sees Clyde as a characteristic reflex of "the vast skepticism and apathy of life," as a characteristic instance of the futility of misplaced desire in a society that offers little ennobling sense of human potentiality. Yet he manages to make the consequences of Clyde's mediocrity, if not the mediocrity itself, seem tragic. For in this youth there is concentrated the tragedy of human waste: energies, talents, affections all unused—and at least in our time the idea of human waste comprises an essential meaning of tragedy. It is an idea to which Dreiser kept returning both in his fiction and his essays:

When one was dead one was dead for all time. Hence the reason for the heartbreak over failure here and now; the awful tragedy of a love lost, a youth never properly enjoyed. Think of living and yet not living in so thrashing a world as this, the best of one's hours passing unused or not properly used. Think of seeing this tinkling phantasmagoria of pain and pleasure, beauty and all its sweets, go by, and yet being compelled to be a bystander, a mere onlooker, enhungered and never satisfied.

The first half of *An American Tragedy* is given to the difficult yet, for Dreiser's purpose, essential task of persuading us that Clyde Griffiths, through his very lack of distinction, represents a major possibility in American experience. Toward this end Dreiser must accumulate a large sum of substantiating detail. He must show Clyde growing up in a family both materially and spiritually impoverished. He must show Clyde reaching out for the small pleasures, the trifles of desire, and learning from his environment how splendid are these induced wants. He must show Clyde, step by step, making his initiation into the world of sanctioned America, first through shabby and then luxury hotels, where he picks up the signals of status and sin. He must show Clyde as the very image and prisoner of our culture, hungering with its hungers, empty with its emptiness.

Yet all the while Dreiser is also preparing to lift Clyde's story from this mere typicality, for he wishes to go beyond the mania for the average which is a bane of naturalism. Everything in this story is ordinary, not least of all the hope of prosperity through marriage—everything but the fact that Clyde begins to act out, or is treated as if he had acted out, the commonplace fantasy of violently disposing of a used-up lover. This is the sole important departure from ordinary verisimilitude in the entire novel, and Dreiser must surely have known that it was. In the particular case upon which he drew for *An American Tragedy*, the young man did kill his pregnant girl; but Dreiser must nevertheless have realized that in the vast majority of such crises the young man dreams of killing and ends by marrying. Dreiser understood, however, that in fiction the effort to represent common experience requires, at one or two crucial points, an effect of heightening, an intense exaggeration. Clyde's situation may be representative, but his conduct must be extreme. And is that not one way of establishing the dramatic: to drive a representative situation to its limits of possibility?

In *An American Tragedy* Dreiser solved a problem which vexes all naturalistic novelists: how to relate harmoniously a large panorama of realism with a sharply contoured form. Dreiser is endlessly faithful to common experience. No one, not even the critics who have most harshly attacked the novel, would care to deny the credibility of Clyde and Roberta Alden, the girl he betrays; most of the attacks on Dreiser contain a mute testimony to his achievement, for in order to complain about his view of life they begin by taking for granted the "reality" of his imagined world. Yet for all its packed detail, the novel is economically structured—though one must understand that the criterion of economy for this kind of novel is radically different from that for a James or Conrad novel. In saying all this, I do not mean anything so improbable as the claim that whatever is in the book belongs because it is there; certain sections, especially those which prepare for Clyde's trial, could be cut to advantage; but the overall architecture has a rough and impressive craftsmanship.

The action of the novel moves like a series of waves, each surging forward to a peak of tension and then receding into quietness, and each, after the first one, re-enacting in a more complex and perilous fashion the material of its predecessor. Clyde in Kansas City, Clyde in Chicago, Clyde alone with Roberta in Lycurgus, Clyde on the edge of the wealthy set in Lycurgus—these divisions form the novel until the point where Roberta is drowned, and each of them acts as a reflector on the others, so that there is a mounting series of anticipations and variations upon the central theme. Clyde's early flirtation with a Kansas City shopgirl anticipates, in its chill manipulativeness, the later and more important relationship with Sondra Finchley, the rich girl who seems to him the very emblem of his fantasy. Clyde's childhood of city poverty is paralleled by the fine section presenting the poverty of Roberta's farm family. The seduction and desertion of Clyde's unmarried sister anticipates Clyde's seduction and desertion of Roberta. Clyde receives his preliminary education in the hotels where he works as bellboy, and each of these serves as a microcosm of the social world he will later break into. Clyde's first tenderness with Roberta occurs as they float in a rowboat; the near-murder, equally passive, also in a rowboat. The grasping Clyde is reflected through a series of minor hotel figures and then through the antithetic but complementary figures of his cousin Gilbert and Sondra; while the part of him that retains some spontaneous feeling is doubled by Roberta, thereby strengthening one's impression that Clyde and Roberta are halves of an uncompleted self, briefly coming together in a poignant unity but lacking the emotional cultivation that would enable them to keep the happinesss they have touched. There are more such balancings and modulations, which in their sum endow the novel with a rhythm of necessity.

Reinforcing this narrative rhythm is Dreiser's frequent shifting of his distance from the characters. At some points he establishes an almost intolerable closeness to Clyde, so that we feel locked into the circle of his moods, while at other points he pulls back to convey the sense that Clyde is but another helpless creature among thousands of helpless creatures struggling to get through their time. In the chapters dealing with Clyde upon his arrival at Lycurgus, Dreiser virtually *becomes* his character, narrowing to a hairline the distance between Clyde and himself, in order to make utterly vivid Clyde's pleasure at finding a girl as yielding as Roberta. By contrast, there are sections in which Dreiser looks upon his story from a great height, especially in the chapters after Roberta's death, where his intent is to suggest how impersonal is the working of legal doom and how insignificant Clyde's fate in the larger motions of society. Through these shifts in perspective Dreiser can show Clyde in his double aspect, both as solitary figure and symbolic agent, confused sufferer and victim of fate.

In the first half of the novel Dreiser prepares us to believe that Clyde *could* commit the crime: which is to say, he prepares us to believe that a part of ourselves could commit the crime. At each point in the boy's development there occurs a meeting between his ill-formed self and the surrounding society. The impoverishment of his family life and the instinctual deprivation of his youth leave him a prey to the values of the streets and the hotels; yet it is a fine stroke on Dreiser's part that only through these tawdry values does Clyde nevertheless become aware of his impoverishment and deprivation. Yearning gives way to cheap desire and false gratification, and these in turn create new and still more incoherent yearnings. It is a vicious circle and the result is not, in any precise sense, a self at all, but rather the beginning of that poisonous fabrication which in America we call a "personality." The hotels are his college, and there he learns to be "insanely eager for all the pleasures which he saw swirling around him." The sterile moralism of his parents cannot provide him with the strength to resist his environment or a principle by which to overcome it. The first tips he receives at the Green-Davidson hotel seem to him "fantastic, Aladdinish really." When he tries to be romantic with his first girl, the images that spring to his mind are of the ornate furnishings in the hotel. Later, as he contemplates killing Roberta, the very idea for the central act in his life comes from casual reading of a newspaper. It would be hard to find in American literature another instance where the passivity, rootlessness, and self-alienation of urban man is so authoritatively presented. For in one sense Clyde does not exist, but is merely a creature of his milieu. And just as in Dreiser's work the problem of human freedom becomes critically acute through a representation of its decline, so the problem of awareness is brought to the forefront through a portrait of its negation.

Even sexuality, which often moves through Dreiser's world like a thick fog, is here diminished and suppressed through the power of social will. Clyde discovers sex as a drugstore clerk, "never weary of observing the beauty, the daring, the self-sufficiency and the sweetness" of the girls who come to his counter. "The wonder of them!" All of these fantasies he then focuses on the commonplace figure of Sondra Finchley: Héloïse as a spoiled American girl. Apart from an interval with Roberta, in which he yields to her maternal solicitude, Clyde's sexuality never breaks out as an irresistible force; it is always at the service of his fears, his petty snobbism, his calculations.

Now all of this is strongly imagined, yet what seems still more notable is Dreiser's related intuition that even in a crippled psyche there remain, eager and available, the capacities we associate with a life of awareness. False values stunt and deform these capacities, but in some pitiful way also express and release them. Clyde and Roberta are from the beginning locked in mutual delusion, yet the chapters in which they discover each other are extremely tender as an unfolding of youthful experience. That this can happen at all suggests how indestructible the life force is; that Dreiser can portray it in his novels is the reward of his compassion. He is rarely sentimental, he reckons human waste to the bitter end; but at the same time he hovers over these lost and lonely figures, granting them every ounce of true feeling he possibly can, insisting that they too—clerk and shopgirl, quite like intellectual and princess—can know "a kind of ecstasy all out of proportion to the fragile, gimcrack scene" of the Starlight Amusement Park.

Dreiser surrenders himself to the emotional life of his figures, not by passing over their delusions or failures but by casting all his energy into evoking the fullness of their experience. And how large, finally, is the sense of the human that smolders in this book! How unwavering the feeling for "the sensitive and seeking individual in his pitiful struggle with nature—with his enormous urges and his pathetic equipment!" Dreiser's passion for detail is a passion for his subject; his passion for his subject, a passion for the suffering of men. As we are touched by Clyde's early affection for Roberta, so later we participate vicariously in his desperation to be rid of her. We share this desire with some shame, but unless we count ourselves among the hopelessly pure, we share it.

Other naturalists, when they show a character being destroyed by overwhelming forces, frequently leave us with a sense of littleness and helplessness, as if the world were collapsed. Of Dreiser that is not, in my own experience, true. For he is always on the watch for a glimmer of transcendence, always concerned with the possibility of magnitude. Clyde is pitiable, his life and fate are pitiable; yet at the end we feel a somber exaltation, for we know that *An American Tragedy* does not seek to persuade us that human existence need be without value or beauty.

No, for Dreiser life is something very different. What makes him so absorbing a novelist, despite all of his grave faults, is that he remains endlessly open to experience. This is something one cannot say easily about most modern writers, including those more subtle and gifted than Dreiser. The trend of modern literature has often been toward a recoil from experience, a nausea before its flow, a denial of its worth. Dreiser, to be sure, is unable to make the finer discriminations among varieties of experience; and there is no reason to expect these from him. But he is marvelous in his devotion to whatever portion of life a man can have; marvelous in his conviction that something sacred resides even in the transience of our days; marvelous in his feeling that the grimmest of lives retain the possibility of "a mystic something of beauty that perennially transfigures the world." Transfigures—that is the key word, and not the catch-phrases of mechanistic determinism he furnishes his detractors.

In a lecture on Spinoza, Santayana speaks of "one of the most important and radical of religious perceptions":

It has perceived that though it is living, it is powerless to live; that though it may die, it is powerless to die; and that altogether, at every instant and in every particular, it is in the hands of some alien and inscrutable power.

Of this felt power I profess to know nothing further. To me, as yet, it is merely the counterpart of my impotence. I should not venture, for instance, to call this power almighty, since I have no means of knowing how much it can do: but I should not hesitate, if I may coin a word, to call it *omnificent*: it is to me, by definition, the doer of everything that is done. I am not asserting the physical validity of this sense of agency or cause: I am merely feeling the force, the friendliness, the hostility, the unfathomableness of the world.

The power of which Santayana speaks is the power that flows, in all its feverish vibrations, through *An American Tragedy*.

The Quest
for
Moral Style

"I went to the woods," wrote Henry David Thoreau, "because I wished to live deliberately, to front only the essential facts of life, and see if I could not learn what it had to teach and not, when I came to die, discover that I had not lived." It is no mere fancy to suggest that in this one sentence Thoreau released the dominant concern of nineteenth-century American writing, especially that segment of it composed in New England under the influence of the transcendental philosophers. Not many American writers have cared, literally, to go to the woods: Hawthorne would have preferred a warm study. But in the mid-nineteenth century most of them believed that, by discovering a new freedom in the openness of the natural world, man could reach out toward both God and his inmost self—the two were not always kept distinct in Ralph Waldo Emerson's New England —without having first to be greatly concerned about the intervening barriers of society. The first major outburst of American writing, as it comes to us in the work of Emerson, Hawthorne, Melville, and Whitman, is at once intimate, dealing with problems of personal being, and metaphysical, seeking to establish a fresh sense of man's relation to the universe. But of social forms, conventions, institutions, ambitions, and burdens there is very little.

Only during the last decades of the nineteenth century does the idea of society as an overwhelming and inescapable force appear in American literature. The important writers of this period differ radically in their responses to society: Mark Twain looks upon it as insidiously enclosing and asphyxiating, Henry James regards it as both the solvent of innocence and the necessary theater for high drama, William Dean Howells treats it simply as the neutral and sometimes benign medium of daily existence, and for Frank Norris it becomes a mysterious agency dispensing pleasure and destruction with promiscuous brutishness. But all of these writers, both those who announce their contempt and those who relax in acceptance, confront society with a vigilance that is new to American literature.

In two later novelists, Theodore Dreiser and Edith Wharton, the *idea* of society becomes a central preoccupation. Though utterly different in literary method and social opinion, Dreiser in *Sister Carrie* and Mrs. Wharton in *The House of Mirth* assume that society exists, intractably, and that it can be examined in terms of relationships of power, economic interest and social status. For such novelists society becomes a force, an actor apart from the central characters and not to be reduced to a mere "background." It breaks the will of the characters or bends to their desires; and it takes on a "thickness," a hovering and often menacing presence, that cannot be found in the earlier American novelists.

In their eagerness to observe social detail and their commitment to the view that the power of circumstance is a power over the human soul, Dreiser and Mrs. Wharton are closer to the central tradition of the nineteenth-century novel both in England and in continental Europe than they are to the American writers preceding or following them. Unlike the Melville of *Moby Dick* or the Hemingway of *The Sun Also Rises*, they believe that the web of society is the true locale of man's destiny and that his salvation can be found, if found at all, within society. But Dreiser and Mrs. Wharton are not mere passive recorders, mere photographers of the world as it is. Like every other sensitive writer of the past hundred years, they also need to question—even if, in some of Mrs. Wharton's novels, strongly to reaffirm—traditional views governing our moral existence. They, too, are involved in that peculiarly anxious and persistent search for values which forms so prominent an aspect of the moral history of our time—the search for secure assumptions, unbroken justifications, which can give direction and coherence to human conduct.

That search is by now not only a familiar but an expected component of the serious novel; a tradition has been established in which it figures conspicuously and often omnivorously, so that readers have come, with a certain loss of historical perspective, to regard it as a necessary part of literary experience.

For the generation of American writers, however, that began publishing shortly after World War I, the crisis of traditional values was no longer a problem in quite the way it had been for writers in the late nineteenth century. By now the crisis of values was an accepted fact, and therefore not so much a painful conclusion toward which their novels and poems might reach as a necessary assumption from which their novels and poems had to begin.

This attitude found an important anticipation in the stories of Sherwood Anderson, a writer who began to publish only a few years before Hemingway and Fitzgerald but who was clearly a man of an older generation, his mind and temper having been formed in the rural Midwest. The younger writers would soon be brushing Anderson aside as a sentimentalist, which in part he was; but at his best, in the haunting tales and sketches he wrote about American loneliness, he helped prepare the way for the modernist writing of the twenties.

Anderson did this through the example of his life, particularly that moment of climax, soon to become a legend in our culture, when at the age of thirty-six he abandoned his paint factory, wife, and children to strike out for the bohemia of Chicago, devote himself to the culture of art and thereby, as he might have said, "front only the essential facts of life." His work, too, set a significant example. *Winesburg, Ohio* is a classic American portrait of human bewilderment, conveying a vision of the native landscape cluttered with dead stumps, twisted oddities, grotesque and pitiful remnants of human creatures. Confronted with this world of back-street grotesques, for whom nothing can happen because everything is too late, one hardly feels it enough to speak of a crisis of values. Things have gone beyond that, and what *Winesburg* reveals is the debris of crisis, the cost of collapse. As it abandons the naturalist impulse of a Dreiser to represent society in overwhelming detail and moves toward an expressionist tableau of human deformity, *Winesburg* helps to confirm the younger writers in their sense of American life and their desire to find a way of imaginatively transcending it.

Perhaps the most vivid account of this new generation of writers, a generation that begins to publish after World War 1 and reaches its finest achievement during the mid-twenties, has come from the poet and critic John Peale Bishop. In his essay "The Missing All"—the title is taken from an Emily Dickinson poem that begins "The missing All prevented me from missing minor things"—Bishop described how the young literary men returning from the war felt they had been cheated not merely of health and time but more important, of truth and honor. They formed "really the first literary generation in America. There had been groups before, but they were not united by a communion of youth, a sense of experience shared and enemies encountered. . . ." They felt themselves to be cut off from the world of all who had come immediately before them, all who held power and spoke with authority. They were not in rebellion against the political order of Western capitalism, but in revulsion from its moral disorder. As Bishop wrote:

The most tragic thing about the war was not that it made so many dead men, but that it destroyed the tragedy of death. Not only did the young suffer in the war, but every abstraction that would have sustained and given dignity to their suffering. The war made the traditional morality inacceptable; it did not annihilate it; it revealed its immediate inadequacy. So that at its end the survivors were left to face, as they could, a world without values.

This sense of having been betrayed and left adrift was powerful among young people in all the Western countries, where it formed the psychic foundation for that "communion of youth" Bishop so keenly observed. It is one of the strongest feelings behind the writing of the twenties, and nowhere has it been expressed so poignantly as in the introduction T. E. Lawrence would write for *The Seven Pillars of Wisdom:*

We were wrought up with ideas inexpressible and vaporous, but to be fought for. We lived many lives in those whirling campaigns, never sparing ourselves any good or evil: yet when we achieved and the new world dawned, the old men came out again and took from us our victory and remade it in the likeness of the former world they knew. Youth could win, but had not learned to keep, and was pitiably weak against age. We stammered that we had worked for a new heaven and a new earth, and they thanked us kindly and made their peace.

When Emily Dickinson spoke of "the missing All," she meant the God of her fathers, the God of Christianity; when Bishop borrowed her phrase, he had in mind not merely the image of God but a whole way of life that had been the heritage of classical Christianity, even if hardened and distorted in America by puritanism, and that was now clearly in the process of crumbling. This perception—it is more a perception than a belief or idea—is seldom the dominant subject in the work of Hemingway and his contemporaries, but it is the dominant fact that needs to be known about their work. It is the premise from which they start, a premise that strikes them as so entirely obvious they feel no need to demonstrate or dramatize it. They do not even discuss it—only their critics do. The hopelessness of the familiar social world, the pointlessness of trying to change it, and the necessity for some credo of private disaffiliation (Hemingway's "separate peace") are assumptions in their work quite as the need to grapple with inherited but fading Christian pieties form an assumption in the work of Hawthorne and Melville.

For writers like Hemingway, Fitzgerald, Cummings, and the early Dos Passos there could no longer be any question of clinging to traditional values. But more important, there could not even be a question of trying to find a new set of values; they were beyond such ambitions or delusions, they knew it was their lot to spend their lives in uncertainty, and the problem that troubled them most was how to do this without violating their feelings about courage and dignity. To be sure, the very desire to find an honorable style of survival in a time of moral confusion indicates a certain strength of moral intent; and the hope of preserving courage and dignity while experiencing a crack-up of values implies the continued hold of certain values. Even these, however, become extremely problematic when they are raised to the level of a troubled self-consciousness.

The writers we are here discussing went through just this kind of crisis. Almost by instinct they backed away from large-scale beliefs or ideals: they had had enough of rhetoric, enough of "idealism," and lived in a magnified fear of platitudes. They had given up, if they had ever had it, the hope of achieving a coherent and ordered moral perspective; they were concerned with something more desperate, more fragmentary, more immediate. They were struggling to survive, as men of sensibility who had lost their way and knew it. They saw their task as a defensive one: the preservation of residual decencies even when they could not quite provide sufficient reasons for wishing to preserve them. And if that seemed too ambitious, they were ready to settle for a severe insistence upon keeping honest among, and with, themselves. Though often bohemian and sometimes dissolute, these writers nourished a sense of their calling as austere and, finally, as monastic as Flaubert's. It was as if they had taken upon themselves the obligation to keep alive an undefiled word, not because they grasped its full meaning but because they felt that to keep it alive would allow others, later on, to grasp it.

The best of these writers were in search of what I propose to call a *moral style*. I mean by this improvised phrase a series of tentative embodiments in conduct of a moral outlook they could not bring to full statement; or a series of gestures and rituals made to serve as a substitute for a moral outlook that could no longer be summoned; or a fragmentary code of behavior by which to survive decently, as if there were—the drama consisting in the fact that there is not—a secure morality behind it. The search for a moral style, which I take to be fundamental to the best American writing between World War I and the Depression years, is a search undertaken by men who have learned that a life constricted to the standard of *faute de mieux* can still be a rigorous, even an exalting obligation. Or, to put it in more homely terms, the idea of moral style is a twentieth-century equivalent—only far more urgent and desperate—of the New England notion of "making do." How one "makes do," whether with grace or falsity, courage or evasion, is the great problem.

The great problem, above all, in the work of the most influential American novelist of our time, Ernest Hemingway. Of all the writers who began to publish after the war, Hemingway seems best to have captured the tone of human malaise in an era of war and revolution; yet it is noteworthy that, while doing so, he rarely attempted a frontal or sustained representation of life in the United States, for he seems always to have understood that common experience was not within his reach. By evoking the "essence" of the modern experience through fables of violence that had their settings in Africa and Europe, Hemingway touched the imagination of American readers whose lives, for all their apparent ordinariness, were also marked by the desperation which would become his literary signature and which is, indeed, central to all "modernist" writing. These readers, in turn, often tried to endow their lives with meaning and value by copying the gestures of defiance, the devotion to clenched styles of survival, which they found in Hemingway's work. Because he had penetrated so deeply to the true dilemmas of the age, Hemingway soon began to influence its experience—not for the first time life came to imitate art.

Who, by now, is not familiar with the shape and colors of Hemingway's world? His recurrent figures are literary expatriates in the wastes of *nada*, bullfighters who have lost their nerve and skill, rich young men without purpose, wounded soldiers who would sign "a separate peace" in order to withdraw from the world's battles, distraught young women grasping at physical sensations as if they were a mode of salvation, tired gangsters, homeless café-sitters, stricken Spaniards: men and women always on the margin, barely able to get by from day to day. There emerges from this gallery the characteristic hero of the Hemingway world: the hero who is wounded but bears his wound in silence, who is sensitive but scorns to devalue his feelings into words, who is defeated but finds a remnant of dignity in an honest confrontation of defeat. In almost all of Hemingway's books there is a tacit assumption that the deracination of our life is so extreme, everyone must find a psychic shelter of his own, a place in which to make a last stand.

But note: to make a last stand; for if defeat is accepted in Hemingway's world, humiliation and rout are not. His fictions present moments of violence, crisis, and death, yet these become occasions for a stubborn, quixotic resistance through which the human capacity for satisfying its self-defined obligations is both asserted and tested. "Grace under pressure": this becomes the ideal stance, the hoped-for moral style, of Hemingway's characters. Or, as he puts it in describing Romero's bullfighting in *The Sun Also Rises*: "the holding of his purity of line through the maximum of exposure." All of Hemingway's novels and stories can be read as variants upon this theme, efforts to find improvised gestures and surrogate codes for the good, the true, even the heroic.

The Hemingway hero is a man who has surrendered the world in order to remake a tiny part of it, the part in which he can share honor and manner with a few chosen comrades. Jake Barnes, Frederick Henry, most of Hemingway's heroes, are men who have seen too much, who want no more of this world and now seek to act out the choreography of heroism as a kind of private charade. The bull ring becomes, for some of them, a substitute for the social world; the combat with the bull, a version of the manly testing which this world does not allow; the circle of *aficionados*, a monastic order of crippled heroes.

It may be true, as Edmund Wilson claims, that Hemingway shows a taste for scenes of killing, but at his best he wishes to squeeze from them some precarious assertion—or perhaps more accurately, some credible facsimile—of value. The Hemingway hero turns to his code, a mixture of stylized repression and inarticulate decencies, so that manners become the outer sign of an inexpressible heroism and gestures the substance of a surviving impulse to moral good. And what is this code? The determination to be faithful to one's own experience, not to fake emotions or pretend to sentiments that are not there; the belief that loyalty to one's few friends matters more than the claims and dogmas of the world; the insistence upon avoiding self-pity and public displays; the assumption that the most precious feelings cannot be articulated and that if the attempt is made they turn "rotten"; the desire to salvage from the collapse of social life a version of stoicism that can make suffering bearable; the hope that in direct physical sensation, the cold water of the creek in which one fishes or the purity of the wine made by Spanish peasants, there will be found an experience that can resist corruption (which is one reason Hemingway approaches these sensations with a kind of propitiatory awe, seldom venturing epithets more precise than "fine" and "nice," as if he feared to risk a death through naming). Life now consists in keeping an equilibrium with one's nerves, and that requires a tight control over one's desires, so that finally one learns what one cannot have and then even not to want it, and above all, not to make a fuss while learning. As Jake Barnes says in *The Sun Also Rises*, "I did not care what it was all about. All I wanted was how to live in it."

Hemingway was always a young writer, and always a writer for the young. He published his best novel, *The Sun Also Rises*, in his mid-twenties and completed most of his great stories by the age of forty. He started a campaign of terror against the fixed vocabulary of literature, a purge of style and pomp, and in the name of naturalness he modeled a new artifice for tension. He struck past the barriers of culture and seemed to disregard the reticence of civilized relationships. He wrote for the nerves.

In his very first stories Hemingway struck to the heart of our nihilism, writing with that marvelous courage he then had, which allowed him to brush past received ideas and show Nick Adams alone, bewildered, afraid, and bored; Nick Adams finding his bit of peace through fishing with an exact salvaging ritual in the big two-hearted river. Hemingway struck to the heart of our nihilism through stories about people who have come to the end of the line, who no longer know what to do or where to turn: nihilism not as an idea or a sentiment, but as an encompassing condition of moral disarray in which one has lost those tacit impulsions which permit life to continue. There is a truth which makes our faith in human existence seem absurd, and no one need contemplate it for very long: Hemingway, in his early writing, did. Nick Adams, Jake Barnes, Lady Brett, Frederick Henry, and then the prizefighters, matadors, rich Americans, and failed writers: all are at the edge, almost ready to surrender and be done with it, yet holding on to whatever fragment of morale, whatever scrap of honor, they can.

Hemingway was not so foolish as to suppose that fear can finally be overcome: all his best stories, from "Fifty Grand" to "The Short Happy Life of Francis Macomber" are concerned to improvise a momentary truce in the hopeless encounter with

fear. But Hemingway touched upon something deeper, something that broke forth in his fiction as the most personal lonely
kind of experience but was formed by the pressures of twentieth-
century history. His great subject was panic, the panic that follows upon the dissolution of nihilism into the blood stream of
consciousness, the panic that finds unbearable the thought of
the next minute and its succession by the minute after that. We
all know this experience, even if, unlike Jake Barnes, we can
sleep at night: we know it because it is part of modern life, perhaps of any life, but also because Hemingway drove it into our
awareness.

Hemingway's early fiction made his readers turn in upon
themselves with the pain of measurement and consider the question of their sufficiency as men. He touched the quick of our
anxieties, and for the moment of his excellence he stood ready
to face whatever he saw. The compulsive stylization of his prose
was a way of letting the language tense and retense, group and
regroup, while beneath it the panic that had taken hold of the
characters and then of the reader kept spreading inexorably. The
prose served as barrier to that shapelessness which is panic by
definition, and through its very tautness allowed the reader
finally to establish some distance and then perhaps compassion.

The poet John Berryman once said that we live in a culture
where a man can go through his entire life without having once
to discover whether he is a coward. Hemingway forced his readers to consider such possibilities, and through the clenched shape
of his stories he kept insisting that no one can escape, moments
of truth come to all of us. Fatalistic as they often seem, immersed
in images of violence and death, his stories are actually incite-
ments to personal resistance and renewal.

A code pressing so painfully on the nervous system and so constricted to symbolic gratifications is almost certain to break
down—indeed, in his best work Hemingway often shows that
it does. After a time, however, his devotion to this code yields
him fewer and fewer psychic returns, since it is in the nature of
the quest for a moral style that the very act of approaching or
even finding it sets off a series of discoveries as to its radical
limitations. As a result the later Hemingway, in his apparent
satisfaction with the moral style he has improvised, begins to

imitate and caricature himself: the manner becomes that of the tight-lipped tough guy, and the once taut and frugal prose turns corpulent.

At first glance F. Scott Fitzgerald's novels seem closer to the social portraiture of Edith Wharton than to the moral fables of Hemingway. Few American writers have commanded so fine a sense of social gradation, not merely in terms of class relationships but even more in the subtle nuances of status which in our country often replace or disguise class relationships. Fitzgerald is a writer very much of the historical moment, the laureate of the twenties, the *wunderkind* of the jazz age, and his talent, profligacy, and tragic personal fate seem symbolic tokens of that historical moment. But in addition to the Fitzgerald who made of his "extreme environmental sense" a foundation of his gift for rendering social manners, there was the Fitzgerald who had been seized and driven by a vision of earthly beatitude which, all through his life, allowed him neither rest nor fulfillment.

Fitzgerald was an eternal adolescent infatuated with the surfaces of material existence. He worshiped money, he worshiped glamour, he worshiped youth, but above all, he worshiped the three together in a totality of false values. Like Keats before the candy shop, he stared with a deep yearning at the blessings of the rich, the ease and security with which they moved through the years, apparently free from the tyranny of work and the burden of circumstance, and thereby enabled to cultivate their own sense of what life might be. He thought that in the American dream of money there lay imbedded a possibility of human realization, because money means power and when you have power you can do anything—you can even, as Jay Gatsby supposes, obliterate the past. He felt that youth was the greatest of human possessions, indeed a kind of *accomplishment* for which the young should be praised. His work was a glittering celebration of immaturity, the American fear of aloneness and limitation.

The preceding paragraph condenses the kind of critical attacks to which Fitzgerald was subject during his career: it is true, all of it true, but not the whole truth about his writing.

For the man who composed *The Great Gatsby* and *The Last*

Tycoon was a writer who had gone to war against the unexamined convictions of his youth, and at a terrible price in suffering and blood, had triumphed. This was the writer who noted that "all the stories that came into my head had a touch of disaster in them—the lovely young creatures in my novels went to ruin, the diamond mountains of my short stories blew up, my millionaires were as beautiful and damned as Thomas Hardy's peasants." Fitzgerald knew—it was to anchor this knowledge that he put Nick Carraway into *The Great Gatsby* as narrator—that the vitality and ambition of Jay Gatsby were lavished on a "vast, vulgar and meretricious beauty." He knew—it was to release this knowledge that he created the looming figure of Monroe Stahr in *The Last Tycoon*—that "life is essentially a cheat and its conditions are those of defeat, and that the redeeming things are not 'happiness and pleasure' but the deeper satisfactions that come out of struggle." As one of Fitzgerald's critics, Andrews Wanning, has remarked: "His style keeps reminding you . . . of his sense of the enormous beauty of which life, suitably ornamented, is capable; and at the same time of his judgment as to the worthlessness of the ornament and the corruptibility of the beauty."

The preceding paragraph condenses the kind of critical praise with which Fitzgerald was honored in the years after his death; it is true, all of it true, but only if one also remembers how accurate were the attacks against him.

Yet there is more to Fitzgerald than his counterposition of early illusion and later self-discovery. In his best writing—which consists not merely of one or two novels and several stories but also of a succession of extraordinary passages appearing almost anywhere in his books, like sudden flares of beauty and wisdom —Fitzgerald confronted both early illusion and later self-discovery from a certain ironic distance. ("The test of a first-rate intelligence," he once wrote, "is the ability to hold two opposed ideas in his mind at the same time, and still retain the ability to function.") Supremely American that he was, Fitzgerald tried to preserve something of the sense of human potentiality which had first led him to be enticed by the vulgarity of money and the shallowness of youth. He knew how impotent, and finally irrelevant, was that depreciation of material values in the name of some moralistic ideal which had become a set attitude in American thought and writing. He sensed that, endlessly rehearsed, this depreciation had actually come to reinforce the power of material values, partly because it could not come to grips with the society that drove men to concern themselves with money and partly because any claim of indifference to such a concern was in America likely to be a mere Sunday pose. As Fitzgerald had worshiped wealth, youth and glamour, they were surely false; as he later turned upon them, his turning was true; but even in his turning he kept some essential part of his earlier worship, and—one is inclined to say—he was right to do so.

Where Hemingway had tried to salvage a code for men at the margin of society, Fitzgerald tried to construct a vision of human possibility at its center. He enjoyed neither doctrinal support in religion nor a buoying social goal nor even a firm awareness of traditional culture that might have helped him sustain and enlarge this vision. Necessarily, it was sporadic, marred, and precarious, more a series of flickering intuitions than assured values. Fitzgerald was struggling to achieve something of vast importance for our society, even though he could hardly have named it and we, in turn, can seldom enlarge upon it. He tried to create a moral style out of the urgencies of desire and talent, and finally it came to a search, at the very least, for a mode of gracefulness in outer life and, at the very best, for some token of grace in a world where grace could no longer be provided by anyone but man himself.

William Faulkner, last of the three major American novelists to begin writing in the decade after World War I, enjoyed a more secure sense of social place and moral tradition than either Hemingway or Fitzgerald. The impact of the fundamentalist Protestantism of the South was still fresh to his imagination, even if more as a discipline than a dogma; the power of a commanding historical myth, the myth of heroic Southern resistance and defeat in the Civil War, was everywhere to be felt in the world of his youth; and the idea of kinship, a deep tacit awareness of the bonds of family and clan, was still a reality in his early experience, as it would later be in the series of novels set in Yoknapatawpha County.

In one major respect, however, Faulkner began as a thoroughly "modern" writer, caught up with the same emotion of uprootedness and uncertainties of value that afflicted Hemingway: his early novels *Soldier's Pay* and *Sartoris* reflect, though not nearly so well as those of Hemingway, the belief of a generation that it is adrift, "lost" in the aftermath of a terrible war. Provincial though the early Faulkner was, he had nevertheless been bruised by the troubles of the outer world, and for all his attachment to the Southern homeland he always retained a lively conviction as to the pervasiveness of malaise in modern life. But he had available, both as man and writer, resources which Hemingway and Fitzgerald lacked. Where Hemingway turned in his novels and stories to a marginal world he had partly observed and partly imagined, and Fitzgerald tried to impose his vision of human possibility upon such recalcitrant material as the lives of the very rich and very young, Faulkner could still turn back to a living segment of American society—back to the familiar places of the South, the homeland he knew with an intimacy beyond love or hate.

Each of Faulkner's novels written during his great creative outburst—from *The Sound and the Fury* in 1929 to *Go Down, Moses* in 1942—represents an increasingly severe and fundamental criticism of the homeland. Not merely of the South alone, to be sure; for when Faulkner composed his despairing estimate of social loss in *The Sound and the Fury* he was also portraying some of the central disabilities of modern civilization. But the foreground subject in the Yoknapatawpha novels is the immediate present and recent past of the South: the way in which its claims to grandeur prove to be aspects of delusion; its pretensions to gentility, elements of corruption; and its compulsive racialism, a poison coursing through its whole moral life. In the novels written during this period Faulkner ranged through almost every area of Southern life, beginning with a wish for nostalgia and ending with the bleakness of accepted truth.

At every point in these novels Faulkner had available—or wrote as if there were still available—persons, places, and principles to which he could look for moral support and standards. He *turned back*, as neither Hemingway nor Fitzgerald could, to the hillsmen, the poor farmers, the Negroes, and the children, all of whom seemed to him apart and pure, surviving in the interstices of a decadent society, unable significantly to change its course, yet vital enough to serve as figures of moral and dramatic contrast. The MacCallums, Dilsey, Cash Bundren, Lena Grove, Ike McCaslin, Lucas Beauchamp, Miss Habersham, Ratliff—these are some of the characters in Faulkner's world who embody in their conduct some portion of goodness and charity. Defeated as they may often be, they are nevertheless *there*, and because they are there Faulkner did not yet need to invent a moral style in the sense Hemingway and Fitzgerald did.

Now, in what is obviously a simplification, one can regard the whole development of Faulkner's Yoknapatawpha saga as a gradual discovery that these figures, for all their attractions and virtues, prove less and less competent as moral guides for the contemporary world. That Faulkner clearly sees as much is suggested by the history of Ratliff, the choric figure in the Snopes trilogy who is so marvelously self-assured in *The Hamlet* but so fumbling in *The Mansion* when he must approach the modern South. Slowly, Faulkner has been exhausting the psychic and moral resources he had supposed to be present for him in the world of Yoknapatawpha; slowly, he has been emerging to the same needs and bewilderments that other writers now feel. The idea of a return to primitive simplicity retains its strength in Faulkner's books insofar as it is kept by him at a certain distance from the present, or can be recognized as metaphor rather than prescription. In his later books Faulkner still turns for moral contrast and support to the kinds of characters he had admired in the earlier ones—the back-country saints, the earthy madonnas, the Negroes, the children, the good simple men. But now it is with very little of the old conviction: you need only contrast his use of Nancy in *Requiem for a Nun* with Dilsey in *The Sound and the Fury*. He turns to such figures because he has nowhere else to go, and he turns to them not with any firm conviction as to their moral power but simply in the hope of imposing on and through them his own hopes and standards. With the figures who had once been for him the bulwarks of life he must now try to "make do," late in his career; and not very skillfully, learn to improvise a moral style.

The search for moral style is recurrent in modern writing. It places a tremendous burden upon literature, almost the burden of demanding that literature provide us with norms of value we find impossible to locate in experience. It tends to demand from literature a kind of prophetic gratification which would have seemed decidedly strange to earlier generations of readers. Yet precisely this aspect of the work of such modern figures as Hemingway, Fitzgerald, and Faulkner makes them seem close to us, writers whom we continue to regard as the spokesmen for our needs and our desires.

Black Boys
and
Native Sons

James Baldwin first came to the notice of the American literary
public not through his own fiction but as author of an impas-
sioned criticism of the conventional Negro novel. In 1949 he
published in *Partisan Review* an essay called "Everybody's Protest Novel," attacking the kind of fiction, from *Uncle Tom's
Cabin* to *Native Son*, that had been written about the ordeal of
the American Negroes; and two years later he printed in the
same magazine "Many Thousands Gone," a tougher and more
explicit polemic against Richard Wright and the school of naturalistic "protest" fiction that Wright represented. The protest
novel, wrote Baldwin, is undertaken out of sympathy for the
Negro, but through its need to present him merely as a social
victim or a mythic agent of sexual prowess, it hastens to confine
the Negro to the very tones of violence he has known all his life.
Compulsively re-enacting and magnifying his trauma, the protest
novel proves unable to transcend it. So choked with rage has this
kind of writing become, it cannot show the Negro as a unique
person or locate him as a member of a community with its own
traditions and values, its own "unspoken recognition of shared
experience which creates a way of life." The failure of the protest novel "lies in its insistence that it is [man's] categorization
alone which is real and which cannot be transcended."

Like all attacks launched by young writers against their famous elders, Baldwin's essays were also a kind of announcement

167

of his own intentions. He wrote admiringly about Wright's courage ("his work was an immense liberation and revelation for me"), but now, precisely because Wright had prepared the way for the Negro writers to come, he, Baldwin, would go further, transcending the sterile categories of "Negro-ness," whether those enforced by the white world or those defensively erected by the Negroes themselves. No longer mere victim or rebel, the Negro would stand free in a self-achieved humanity. As Baldwin put it some years later, he hoped "to prevent myself from becoming *merely* a Negro; or even, merely a Negro writer." The world "tends to trap and immobilize you in the role you play," and for the Negro writer, if he is to be a writer at all, it hardly matters whether the trap is sprung from motives of hatred or condescension.

Baldwin's rebellion against the older Negro novelist who had served him as a model and had helped launch his career, was not, of course, an unprecedented event. The history of literature is full of such painful ruptures, and the issue Baldwin raised is one that keeps recurring, usually as an aftermath to a period of "socially engaged" writing. The novel is an inherently ambiguous genre: it strains toward formal autonomy and can seldom avoid being a public gesture. If it is true, as Baldwin said in "Everybody's Protest Novel," that "literature and sociology are not one and the same," it is equally true that such statements hardly begin to cope with the problem of how a writer's own experience affects his desire to represent human affairs in a work of fiction. Baldwin's formula evades, through rhetorical sweep, the genuinely difficult issue of the relationship between social experience and literature.

Yet in *Notes of a Native Son*, the book in which his remark appears, Baldwin could also say: "One writes out of one thing only—one's own experience." What, then, was the experience of a man with a black skin, what *could* it be in this country? How could a Negro put pen to paper, how could he so much as think or breathe, without some impulsion to protest, be it harsh or mild, political or private, released or buried? The "sociology" of his existence formed a constant pressure on his literary work, and not merely in the way this might be true for any writer, but with a pain and ferocity that nothing could remove.

James Baldwin's early essays are superbly eloquent, displaying virtually in full the gifts that would enable him to become one of the great American rhetoricians. But these essays, like some of the later ones, are marred by rifts in logic, so little noticed when one gets swept away by the brilliance of the language that it takes a special effort to attend their argument.

Later Baldwin would see the problems of the Negro writer with a greater charity and more mature doubt. Reviewing in 1959 a book of poems by Langston Hughes, he wrote: "Hughes is an American Negro poet and has no choice but to be acutely aware of it. He is not the first American Negro to find the war between his social and artistic responsibilities all but irreconcilable." All but irreconcilable: the phrase strikes a note sharply different from Baldwin's attack upon Wright in the early fifties. And it is not hard to surmise the reason for this change. In the intervening years Baldwin had been living through some of the experiences that had goaded Richard Wright into rage and driven him into exile; he, too, like Wright, had been to hell and back, many times over.

"Gawd, Ah wish all them white folks was dead."

The day *Native Son* appeared, American culture was changed forever. No matter how much qualifying the book might later need, it made impossible a repetition of the old lies. In all its crudeness, melodrama, and claustrophobia of vision, Richard Wright's novel brought out into the open, as no one ever had before, the hatred, fear, and violence that have crippled and may yet destroy our culture.

A blow at the white man, the novel forced him to recognize himself as an oppressor. A blow at the black man, the novel forced him to recognize the cost of his submission. *Native Son* assaulted the most cherished of American vanities: the hope that the accumulated injustice of the past would bring with it no lasting penalties, the fantasy that in his humiliation the Negro somehow retained a sexual potency—or was it a childlike good nature?—that made it necessary to envy and still more to suppress him. Speaking from the black wrath of retribution, Wright insisted that history can be a punishment. He told us the one thing even the most liberal whites preferred not to hear: that Negroes were far from patient or forgiving, that they were scarred by fear, that they hated every moment of their suppression even when seeming most acquiescent, and that often enough they hated *us*, the decent and cultivated white men who from complicity or neglect shared in the responsibility for their plight. If such younger novelists as Baldwin and Ralph Ellison were to move beyond Wright's harsh naturalism and toward more supple modes of fiction, that was possible only because Wright had been there first, courageous enough to release the full weight of his anger.

In *Black Boy*, the autobiographical narrative he published several years later, Wright would tell of an experience he had while working as a bellboy in the South. Many times he had come into a hotel room carrying luggage or food and seen naked white whores lounging about, unmoved by shame at his presence, for "blacks were not considered human beings anyway . . . I was a non-man . . . I felt doubly cast out." With the publication of *Native Son*, however, Wright forced his readers to acknowledge his anger, and in that way, if none other, he wrested for himself a sense of dignity as a man. He forced his readers to confront the disease of our culture, and to one of its most terrifying symptoms he gave the name of Bigger Thomas.

Brutal and brutalized, lost forever to his unexpended hatred and his fear of the world, a numbed and illiterate black boy stumbling into a murder and never, not even at the edge of the electric chair, breaking through to an understanding of either his plight or himself, Bigger Thomas was a part of Richard Wright, a part even of the James Baldwin who stared with horror at Wright's Bigger, unable either to absorb him into his consciousness or eject him from it. Enormous courage, a discipline of self-conquest, was required to conceive Bigger Thomas, for this was no eloquent Negro spokesman, no admirable intellectual or formidable proletarian. Bigger was drawn—one would surmise, deliberately—from white fantasy and white contempt. Bigger was the worst of Negro life accepted, then rendered a trifle conscious and thrown back at those who had made him what he was. "No American Negro exists," Baldwin would later write, "who does not have his private Bigger Thomas living in the skull."

Wright drove his narrative to the very core of American phobia: sexual fright, sexual violation. He understood that the fantasy of rape is a consequence of guilt, what the whites suppose themselves to deserve. He understood that the white man's notion of uncontaminated Negro vitality, little as it had to do with the bitter realities of Negro life, reflected some ill-formed and buried feeling that our culture has run down, lost its blood, become febrile. And he grasped the way in which the sexual issue has been intertwined with social relationships, for even as the white people who hire Bigger as their chauffeur are decent and charitable, even as the girl he accidentally kills is a liberal of sorts, theirs is the power and the privilege. "We black and they white. They got things and we ain't. They do things and we can't."

The novel barely stops to provision a recognizable social world, often contenting itself with cartoon simplicities and yielding almost entirely to the nightmare incomprehension of Bigger Thomas. The mood is apocalyptic, the tone superbly aggressive. Wright was an existentialist long before he heard the name, for he was committed to the literature of extreme situations both through the pressures of his rage and the gasping hope of an ultimate catharsis.

Wright confronts both the violence and the crippling limitations of Bigger Thomas. For Bigger the whites are not people at all, but something more, "a sort of great natural force, like a stormy sky looming overhead." And only through violence does he gather a little meaning in life, pitifully little: "He had murdered and created a new life for himself." Beyond that Bigger cannot go.

At first *Native Son* seems still another naturalistic novel: a novel of exposure and accumulation, charting the waste of the undersides of the American city. Behind the book one senses the molding influences of Theodore Dreiser, especially the Dreiser of *An American Tragedy*, who knows there are situations so oppressive that only violence can provide their victims with the hope of dignity. Like Dreiser, Wright wished to pummel his readers into awareness; like Dreiser, to overpower them with the sense of society as an enclosing force. Yet the comparison is finally of limited value, and for the disconcerting reason that Dreiser had a white skin and Wright a black one.

The usual naturalistic novel is written with detachment, as if by a scientist surveying a field of operations; it is a novel in which the writer withdraws from a detested world and coldly piles up the evidence for detesting it. *Native Son*, though preserving some of the devices of the naturalistic novel, deviates sharply from its characteristic tone: a tone Wright could not possibly have maintained and which, it may be, no Negro novelist can really hold for long. *Native Son* is a work of assault rather than withdrawal; the author yields himself in part to a vision of nightmare. Bigger's cowering perception of the world becomes the most vivid and authentic component of the book. Naturalism pushed to an extreme turns here into something other than itself, a kind of expressionist outburst, no longer a replica of the familiar social world but a self-contained realm of grotesque emblems.

That *Native Son* has grave faults anyone can see. The language is often coarse, flat in rhythm, syntactically overburdened, heavy with journalistic slag. Apart from Bigger, who seems more a brute energy than a particularized figure, the characters have little reality, the Negroes being mere stock accessories and the whites either "agit-prop" villains or heroic Communists whom Wright finds it easier to admire from a distance than establish from the inside. The long speech by Bigger's radical lawyer Max (again a device apparently borrowed from Dreiser) is ill-related to the book itself: Wright had not achieved Dreiser's capacity for absorbing everything, even the most recalcitrant philosophical passages, into a unified vision of things. Between Wright's feelings as a Negro and his beliefs as a Communist there is hardly a genuine fusion, and it is through this gap that a good part of the novel's unreality pours in.

Yet it should be said that the endlessly repeated criticism that Wright caps his melodrama with a party-line oration tends to oversimplify the novel, for Wright is too honest to allow the propagandistic message to constitute the last word. Indeed, the last word is given not to Max but to Bigger. For at the end Bigger remains at the mercy of his hatred and fear, the lawyer retreats helplessly, the projected union between political consciousness and raw revolt has not been achieved—as if Wright were persuaded that, all ideology apart, there is for each Negro an ultimate trial that he can bear only by himself.

Black Boy, which appeared five years after *Native Son*, is a slighter but more skillful piece of writing. Richard Wright came from a broken home, and as he moved from his helpless mother to a grandmother whose religious fanaticism (she was a Seventh-Day Adventist) proved utterly suffocating, he soon picked up a precocious knowledge of vice and a realistic awareness of social power. This autobiographical memoir, a small classic in the literature of self-discovery, is packed with harsh evocations of Negro adolescence in the South. The young Wright learns how wounding it is to wear the mask of a grinning nigger boy in order to keep a job. He examines the life of the Negroes and judges it without charity or idyllic compensation—for he already knows, in his heart and his bones, that to be oppressed means to lose out on human possibilities. By the time he is seventeen, preparing to leave for Chicago, where he will work on a WPA project, become a member of the Communist Party, and publish his first book of stories, *Uncle Tom's Children*, Wright has managed to achieve the beginnings of consciousness, through a slow and painful growth from the very bottom of deprivation to the threshold of artistic achievement and a glimpsed idea of freedom.

Baldwin's attack upon Wright had partly been anticipated by the more sophisticated American critics. Alfred Kazin, for example, had found in Wright a troubling obsession with violence:

If he chose to write the story of Bigger Thomas as a grotesque crime story, it is because his own indignation and the sickness of the age combined to make him dependent on violence and shock, to astonish the reader by torrential scenes of cruelty, hunger, rape, murder and flight, and then enlighten him by crude Stalinist homilies.

The last phrase apart, something quite similar could be said about the author of *Crime and Punishment*; it is disconcerting to reflect upon how few novelists, even the very greatest, could pass this kind of moral inspection. For the novel as a genre seems to have an inherent bias toward extreme effects, such as violence, cruelty, and the like. More important, Kazin's judgment rests on the assumption that a critic can readily distinguish between the genuine need of a writer to cope with ugly realities and the damaging effect these realities may have upon his moral and psychic life. But in regard to contemporary writers one finds it very hard to distinguish between a valid portrayal of violence and an obsessive involvement with it. A certain amount of obsession may be necessary for the valid portrayal—writers devoted to themes of desperation cannot keep themselves morally intact. And when we come to a writer like Richard Wright, who deals with the most degraded and inarticulate sector of the Negro world, the distinction between objective rendering and subjective immersion becomes still more difficult, perhaps even impossible. For a novelist who has lived through the searing experiences that Wright has there cannot be much possibility of approaching his subject with the "mature" poise recommended by high-minded critics. What is more, the very act of writing his novel, the effort to confront what Bigger Thomas means to him, is for such a writer a way of dredging up and then perhaps shedding the violence that society has pounded into him. Is Bigger an authentic projection of a social reality, or is he a symptom of Wright's "dependence on violence and shock"? Obviously both; and it could not be otherwise.

For the reality pressing upon all of Wright's work was a nightmare of remembrance, everything from which he had pulled himself out, with an effort and at a cost that is almost unimaginable. Without the terror of that nightmare it would have been impossible for Wright to summon the truth of the reality—not the only truth about American Negroes, perhaps not even the deepest one, but a primary and inescapable truth. Both truth and terror rested on a gross fact which Wright alone dared to confront: that violence is central in the life of the American Negro, defining and crippling him with a harshness few other Americans need suffer. "No American Negro exists who does not have his private Bigger Thomas living in the skull."

Now I think it would be well not to judge in the abstract, or with much haste, the violence that gathers in the Negro's heart as a response to the violence he encounters in society. It would be well to see this violence as part of a historical experience that is open to moral scrutiny but ought to be shielded from presumptuous moralizing. Bigger Thomas may be enslaved to a hunger for violence, but anyone reading *Native Son* with mere courtesy must observe the way in which Wright, even while yielding emotionally to Bigger's deprivation, also struggles to transcend it. That he did not fully succeed seems obvious; one may doubt that any Negro writer can.

More subtle and humane than either Kazin's or Baldwin's

criticism is a remark made by Isaac Rosenfeld while reviewing *Black Boy*: "As with all Negroes and all men who are born to suffer social injustice, part of [Wright's] humanity found itself only in acquaintance with violence, and in hatred of the oppressor." Surely Rosenfeld was not here inviting an easy acquiescence in violence; he was trying to suggest the historical context, the psychological dynamics, which condition the attitudes all Negro writers take, or must take, toward violence. To say this is not to propose the condescension of exempting Negro writers from moral judgment, but to suggest the terms of understanding, and still more, the terms of hesitation for making a judgment.

There were times when Baldwin grasped this point better than anyone else. If he could speak of the "unrewarding rage" of *Native Son*, he also spoke of the book as "an immense liberation." Is it impudent to suggest that one reason he felt the book to be a liberation was precisely its rage, precisely the relief and pleasure that he, like so many other Negroes, must have felt upon seeing those long-suppressed emotions finally breaking through?

The kind of literary criticism Baldwin wrote was very fashionable in America during the postwar years. Mimicking the Freudian corrosion of motives and bristling with dialectical agility, this criticism approached all ideal claims—especially those made by radical and naturalist writers—with a weary skepticism, and proceeded to transfer the values such writers were attacking to the perspective from which they attacked. If Dreiser wrote about the power hunger and dream of success corrupting American society, that was because he was really infatuated with them. If James Farrell showed the meanness of life in the Chicago slums, that was because he could not really escape it. If Wright portrayed the violence gripping Negro life, that was because he was really obsessed with it. The word "really" or more sophisticated equivalents could do endless service in behalf of a generation of intellectuals soured on the tradition of protest but suspecting they might be pygmies in comparison to the writers who had protested. In reply, there was no way to "prove" that Dreiser, Farrell, and Wright were not contaminated by the false values they attacked; probably, since they were mere mortals, living in the present society, they were contaminated; and so one had to keep insisting that such writers were nevertheless presenting actualities of modern experience, not merely phantoms of their neuroses.

If Bigger Thomas, as Baldwin said, "accepted a theology that denies him life," if in his Negro self-hatred he "*wants* to die because he glories in his hatred," this did not constitute a criticism of Wright unless one were prepared to assume what was simply preposterous: that Wright, for all his emotional involvement with Bigger, could not see beyond the limitations of the character he had created. This was a question Baldwin never seriously confronted in his early essays. He would describe accurately the limitations of Bigger Thomas and then, by one of those rhetorical leaps at which he is so gifted, would assume that these were also the limitations of Wright or his book.

Still another ground for Baldwin's attacks was his reluctance to accept the clenched militancy of Wright's posture as both novelist and man. In a remarkable sentence appearing in "Everybody's Protest Novel," Baldwin wrote, "Our humanity is our burden, our life; we need not battle for it; we need only to do what is infinitely more difficult—that is, accept it." What Baldwin was saying here was part of the outlook so many American intellectuals took over during the years of a postwar liberalism not very different from conservatism. Ralph Ellison expressed this view in terms still more extreme: "Thus to see America with an awareness of its rich diversity and its almost magical fluidity and freedom, I was forced to conceive of a novel unburdened by the narrow naturalism which has led after so many triumphs to the final and unrelieved despair which marks so much of our current fiction." This note of willed affirmation—as if one could *decide* one's deepest and most authentic response to society!—was to be heard in many other works of the early fifties, most notably in Saul Bellow's *Adventures of Augie March*. Today it is likely to strike one as a note whistled in the dark. In response to Baldwin and Ellison, Wright would have said (I virtually quote the words he used in talking to me during the summer of 1958) that only through struggle could men with black skins, and for that matter, all the oppressed of the world, achieve their humanity. It was a lesson, said Wright with a touch of bitterness yet not without kindness, that the younger writers would have to learn in their own way and their own time. All that has happened since, bears him out.

One criticism made by Baldwin in writing about *Native Son,* perhaps because it is the least ideological, remains important. He complained that in Wright's novel "a necessary dimension has been cut away; this dimension being the relationship that Negroes bear to one another, that depth of involvement and unspoken recognition of shared experience which creates a way of life." The climate of the book, "common to most Negro protest novels . . . has led us all to believe that in Negro life there exists no tradition, no field of manners, no possibility of ritual or intercourse, such as may, for example, sustain the Jew even after he has left his father's house." It could be urged, perhaps, that in composing a novel verging on expressionism Wright need not be expected to present the Negro world with fullness, balance, or nuance; but there can be little doubt that in this respect Baldwin did score a major point: the posture of militancy, no matter how great the need for it, exacts a heavy price from the writer, as indeed from everyone else. For "Even the hatred of squalor / Makes the brow grow stern / Even anger against injustice / Makes the voice grow harsh . . ." All one can ask, by way of reply, is whether the refusal to struggle may not exact a still greater price. It is a question that would soon be tormenting James Baldwin, and almost against his will.

In his own novels Baldwin hoped to show the Negro world in its diversity and richness, not as a mere specter of protest; he wished to show it as a living culture of men and women who, even when deprived, share in the emotions and desires of common humanity. And he meant also to evoke something of the distinctiveness of Negro life in America, as evidence of its worth, moral tenacity, and right to self-acceptance. How can one not sympathize with such a program? And how, precisely as one does sympathize, can one avoid the conclusion that in this effort Baldwin has thus far failed to register a major success?

His first novel, *Go Tell It on the Mountain,* is an enticing but minor work: it traces the growing-up of a Negro boy in the atmosphere of a repressive Calvinism, a Christianity stripped of grace and brutal with fantasies of submission and vengeance.

No other work of American fiction reveals so graphically the way in which an oppressed minority aggravates its own oppression through the torments of religious fanaticism. The novel is also striking as a modest *Bildungsroman*, the education of an imaginative Negro boy caught in the heart-struggle between his need to revolt, which would probably lead to his destruction in the jungles of New York, and the miserly consolations of black Calvinism, which would signify that he accepts the denial of his personal needs. But it would be a mistake to claim too much for this first novel, in which a rhetorical flair and a conspicuous sincerity often eat away at the integrity of event and the substance of character. The novel is intense, and the intensity is due to Baldwin's absorption in that religion of denial which leads the boy to become a preacher in his father's church, to scream out God's word from "a merciless resolve to kill my father rather than allow my father to kill me." Religion has, of course, played a central role in Negro life, yet one may doubt that the special kind of religious experience dominating *Go Tell It on the Mountain* is any more representative of that life, any more advantageous a theme for gathering in the qualities of Negro culture, than the violence and outrage of *Native Son*. Like Wright before him, Baldwin wrote from the intolerable pressures of his own experience; there was no alternative; each had to release his own agony before he could regard Negro life with the beginnings of objectivity.

Baldwin's second novel, *Giovanni's Room*, seems to me a flat failure. It abandons Negro life entirely (not in itself a cause for judgment) and focuses upon the distraught personal relations of several young Americans adrift in Paris. The problem of homosexuality, which is to recur in Baldwin's fiction, is confronted with a notable courage, but also with a disconcerting kind of sentimentalism, a quavering and sophisticated submission to the ideology of love. It is one thing to call for the treatment of character as integral and unique; but quite another for a writer with Baldwin's background and passions to succeed in bringing together his sensibility as a Negro and his sense of personal trouble.

Baldwin has not yet succeeded—the irony is a stringent one —in composing the kind of novel he counterpoised to the work of Richard Wright. He has written three essays, ranging in tone from disturbed affection to disturbing malice, in which he tries to break from his rebellious dependency upon Wright, but he remains tied to the memory of the older man. The Negro writer who has come closest to satisfying Baldwin's program is not Baldwin himself but Ralph Ellison, whose novel *Invisible Man* is a brilliant though flawed achievement, standing with *Native Son* as the major fiction thus far composed by American Negroes.

What astonishes one most about *Invisible Man* is the apparent freedom it displays from the ideological and emotional penalties suffered by Negroes in this country. I say "apparent" because the freedom is not quite so complete as the book's admirers like to suppose. Still, for long stretches *Invisible Man* does escape the formulas of protest, local color, genre quaintness, and jazz chatter. No white man could have written it, since no white man could know with such intimacy the life of the Negroes from the inside; yet Ellison writes with an ease and humor which are now and again simply miraculous.

Invisible Man is a record of a Negro's journey through contemporary America, from South to North, province to city, naïve faith to disenchantment and perhaps beyond. There are clear allegorical intentions (Ellison is "literary" to a fault) but with a book so rich in talk and drama it would be a shame to neglect the fascinating surface for the mere depths. The beginning is both nightmare and farce. A timid Negro boy comes to a white smoker in a Southern town: he is to be awarded a scholarship. Together with several other Negro boys he is rushed to the front of the ballroom, where a sumptuous blonde tantalizes and frightens them by dancing in the nude. Blindfolded, the Negro boys stage a "battle royal," a free-for-all in which they pummel each other to the drunken shouts of the whites. Practical jokes, humiliations, terror—and then the boy delivers a prepared speech of gratitude to his white benefactors. At the end of this section, the boy dreams that he has opened the briefcase given him together with his scholarship to a Negro college and that he finds an inscription reading: "To Whom It May Concern: Keep This Nigger-Boy Running."

He keeps running. He goes to his college and is expelled for having innocently taken a white donor through a Negro gin mill that also happens to be a brothel. His whole experience is to follow this pattern. Strip down a pretense, whether by choice or accident, and you will suffer penalties, since the rickety structure of Negro respectability rests upon pretense and those who profit from it cannot bear to have the reality exposed (in this case, that the college is dependent upon the Northern white millionaire). The boy then leaves for New York, where he works in a white paint factory, becomes a soapboxer for the Harlem Communists, the darling of the fellow-traveling bohemia, and a big wheel in the Negro world. At the end, after witnessing a frenzied race riot in Harlem, he "finds himself" in some not entirely specified way, and his odyssey from submission to autonomy is complete.

Ellison has an abundance of that primary talent without which neither craft nor intelligence can save a novelist: he is richly, wildly inventive; his scenes rise and dip with tension, his people bleed, his language sings. No other writer has captured so much of the hidden gloom and surface gaiety of Negro life.

There is an abundance of superbly rendered speech: a West Indian woman inciting her men to resist an eviction, a Southern sharecropper calmly describing how he seduced his daughter, a Harlem street vender spinning jive. The rhythm of Ellison's prose is harsh and nervous, like a beat of harried alertness. The observation is expert: he knows exactly how zoot-suiters walk, making stylization their principle of life, and exactly how the antagonism between American and West Indian Negroes works itself out in speech and humor. He can accept his people as they are, in their blindness and hope: here, finally, the Negro world does exist, seemingly apart from plight or protest. And in the final scene Ellison has created an unforgettable image: "Ras the Destroyer," a Negro nationalist, appears on a horse dressed in the costume of an Abyssinian chieftain, carrying spear and shield, and charging wildly into the police—a black Quixote, mad, absurd, unbearably pathetic.

But even Ellison cannot help being caught up with *the idea* of the Negro. To write simply about "Negro experience" with the esthetic distance urged by the critics of the fifties, is a moral and psychological impossibility, for plight and protest are inseparable from that experience, and even if less political than Wright and less prophetic than Baldwin, Ellison knows this quite as well as they do.

If *Native Son* is marred by the ideological delusions of the thirties, *Invisible Man* is marred, less grossly, by those of the fifties. The middle section of Ellison's novel, dealing with the Harlem Communists, does not ring quite true, in the way a good portion of the writings on this theme during the postwar years does not ring quite true. Ellison makes his Stalinist figures so vicious and stupid that one cannot understand how they could ever have attracted him or any other Negro. That the party leadership manipulated members with deliberate cynicism is beyond doubt, but this cynicism was surely more complex and guarded than Ellison shows it to be. No party leader would ever tell a prominent Negro Communist, as one of them does in *Invisible Man*: "You were not hired [as a functionary] to think" —even if that were what he felt. Such passages are almost as damaging as the propagandist outbursts in *Native Son*.

Still more troublesome, both as it breaks the coherence of the novel and reveals Ellison's dependence on the postwar *Zeitgeist*, is the sudden, unprepared, and implausible assertion of unconditioned freedom with which the novel ends. As the hero abandons the Communist Party he wonders, "Could politics ever be an expression of love?" This question, more portentous than profound, cannot easily be reconciled to a character who has been presented mainly as a passive victim of his experience. Nor is one easily persuaded by the hero's discovery that "my world has become one of infinite possibilities," his refusal to be the "invisible man" whose body is manipulated by various social groups. Though the unqualified assertion of self-liberation was a favorite strategy among American literary people in the fifties, it is also vapid and insubstantial. It violates the reality of social life, the interplay between external conditions and personal will, quite as much as the determinism of the thirties. The unfortunate fact remains that to define one's individuality is to stumble upon social barriers which stand in the way, all too much in the way, of "infinite possibilities." Freedom can be fought for, but it cannot always be willed or asserted into existence. And it seems hardly an accident that even as Ellison's hero asserts the "infinite possibilities" he makes no attempt to specify them.

Throughout the fifties Richard Wright was struggling to find his place in a world he knew to be changing but could not grasp

with the assurance he had felt in his earlier years. He had resigned with some bitterness from the Communist Party, though
he tried to preserve an independent radical outlook, tinged occasionally with black nationalism. He became absorbed in the
politics and literature of the rising African nations, but when
visiting them he felt hurt at how great was the distance between
an American Negro and an African. He found life in America
intolerable, and he spent his last fourteen years in Paris, somewhat friendly with the intellectual group around Jean-Paul
Sartre but finally a loner, a man who stood by the pride of his
rootlessness. And he kept writing, steadily experimenting, partly,
it may be, in response to the younger men who had taken his
place in the limelight and partly because he was truly a dedi-
cated writer.

These last years were difficult for Wright, since he neither
made a true home in Paris nor kept in imaginative touch with
the changing life of the United States. In the early fifties he
published a very poor novel, *The Outsider,* full of existentialist
jargon applied to, but not really absorbed in, the Negro theme.
He was a writer in limbo, and his better fiction, such as the
novelette "The Man Who Lived Underground," is a projection
of that state.

In the late fifties Wright published another novel, *The Long
Dream,* which is set in Mississippi and displays a considerable
recovery of his powers. This book has been criticized for presenting Negro life in the South through "old-fashioned" images
of violence, but one ought to hesitate before denying the relevance of such images or joining in the criticism of their use.
For Wright was perhaps justified in not paying attention to the
changes that have occurred in the South these past few decades.
When Negro liberals write that despite the prevalence of bias
there has been an improvement in the life of their people, such
statements are reasonable and necessary. But what have these
to do with the way Negroes feel, with the power of the memories
they must surely retain? About this we know very little and
would be well advised not to nourish preconceptions, for their
feelings may be much closer to Wright's rasping outbursts than
to the more modulated tones of some younger Negro novelists.
Wright remembered, and what he remembered other Negroes

must also have remembered. And in that way he kept faith with the experience of the boy who had fought his way out of the depths, to speak for those who remained there.

His most interesting fiction after *Native Son* is to be found in a posthumous collection of stories, *Eight Men,* written during the last twenty-five years of his life. Though they fail to yield any clear line of chronological development, these stories give evidence of Wright's literary restlessness, his often clumsy efforts to break out of the naturalism which was his first and, I think, necessary mode of expression. The unevenness of his writing is highly disturbing: one finds it hard to understand how the same man, from paragraph to paragraph, can be so brilliant and inept. Time after time the narrative texture is broken by a passage of sociological or psychological jargon; perhaps the later Wright tried too hard, read too much, failed to remain sufficiently loyal to the limits of his talent.

Some of the stories, such as "Big Black Good Man," are enlivened by Wright's sardonic humor, the humor of a man who has known and released the full measure of his despair but finds that neither knowledge nor release matters in a world of despair. In "The Man Who Lived Underground" Wright shows a sense of narrative rhythm, which is superior to anything in his full-length novels and evidence of the seriousness with which he kept working.

The main literary problem that troubled Wright in recent years was that of rendering his naturalism a more terse and supple instrument. I think he went astray whenever he abandoned naturalism entirely: there are a few embarrassingly bad experiments with stories employing self-consciously Freudian symbolism. Wright needed the accumulated material of circumstance which naturalistic detail provided his fiction; it was as essential to his ultimate effect of shock and bruise as dialogue to Hemingway's ultimate effect of irony and loss. But Wright was correct in thinking that the problem of detail is the most vexing technical problem the naturalist writer must face, since the accumulation that makes for depth and solidity can also create a pall of tedium. In "The Man Who Lived Underground" Wright came close to solving this problem, for here the naturalistic detail is put at the service of a radical projective image

—a Negro trapped in a sewer—and despite some flaws, the story is satisfying both for its tense surface and elasticity of suggestion.

Richard Wright died at fifty-two, full of hopes and projects. Like many of us, he had somewhat lost his intellectual way, but he kept struggling toward the perfection of his craft and toward a comprehension of the strange world that in his last years was coming into birth. In the most fundamental sense, however, he had done his work: he had told his contemporaries a truth so bitter they paid him the tribute of trying to forget it.

Looking back to the early essays and fiction of James Baldwin, one wishes to see a little farther than they at first invite: to see past their brilliance of gesture, by which older writers could be dismissed, and past their aura of gravity, by which a generation of intellectuals could be enticed. What strikes one most of all is the sheer pathos of these early writings, the way they reveal the desire of a greatly talented young man to escape the scars—and why should he not have wished to escape them?—which he had found upon the faces of his elders and knew to be gratuitous and unlovely.

Chekhov once said that what the aristocratic Russian writers assumed as their birthright, the writers who came from the lower orders had to pay for with their youth. James Baldwin did not want to pay with his youth, as Richard Wright had paid so dearly. He wanted to move, as Wright had not been able to, beyond the burden or bravado of his stigma; he wanted to enter the world of freedom, grace, and self-creation. One would need a heart of stone, or be a brutal moralist, to feel anything but sympathy for this desire. But we do not make our circumstances; we can, at best, try to remake them. And all the recent writing of Baldwin indicates that the wishes of his youth could not be realized, not in *this* country. The sentiments of humanity which had made him rebel against Richard Wright have now driven him back to a position close to Wright's rebellion.

Baldwin's *Another Country* is a "protest novel" quite as much as *Native Son,* and anyone vindictive enough to make the effort, could score against it the points Baldwin scored against Wright. No longer is Baldwin's prose so elegant or suave as it was once; in this book it is harsh, clumsy, heavy-breathing with the pant of suppressed bitterness. In about half of *Another Country*—the best half, I would judge—the material is handled in a manner somewhat reminiscent of Wright's naturalism: a piling on of the details of victimization, as the jazz musician Rufus Scott, a sophisticated distant cousin of Bigger Thomas, goes steadily down the path of self-destruction, worn out in the effort to survive in the white man's jungle and consumed by a rage too extreme to articulate, yet too amorphous to act upon. The narrative voice is a voice of anger, rasping and thrusting, not at all "literary" in the somewhat lacquered way the earlier Baldwin was able to achieve. And what that voice says, no longer held back by the proprieties of literature, is that the nightmare of the history we have made allows us no immediate escape. Even if all the visible tokens of injustice were erased, the Negroes would retain their hatred and the whites their fear and guilt. Forgiveness cannot be speedily willed, if willed at all, and before it can even be imagined there will have to be a fuller discharge of those violent feelings that have so long been suppressed. It is not a pretty thought, but neither is it a mere "unrewarding rage"; and it has the sad advantage of being true, first as Baldwin embodies it in the disintegration of Rufus, which he portrays with a ferocity quite new in his fiction, and then as he embodies it in the hard-driving ambition of Rufus's sister Ida, who means to climb up to success even if she has to bloody a good many people, whites preferably, in order to do it.

Another Country has within it another novel: a nagging portrayal of that entanglement of personal relationships—sterile, involuted, grindingly rehearsed, pursued with quasi-religious fervor, and cut off from any dense context of social life—which has come to be a standard element in contemporary fiction. The author of *this* novel is caught up with the problem of communication, the emptiness that seeps through the lives of many cultivated persons and in response to which he can only reiterate the saving value of true and lonely love. These portions of *Another Country* tend to be abstract, without the veined milieu, the filled-out world, a novel needs: as if Baldwin, once he moves away from the Negro theme, finds it quite as hard to lay hold of contemporary experience as do most other novelists. The two pulls upon his attention are difficult to reconcile, and Baldwin's future as a novelist is decidedly uncertain.

During the last few years James Baldwin has emerged as a national figure, the leading intellectual spokesman for the Negroes, whose recent essays, as in *The Fire Next Time,* reach heights of passionate exhortation unmatched in modern American writing. Whatever his ultimate success or failure as a novelist, Baldwin has already secured his place as one of the two or three greatest essayists this country has ever produced. He has brought a new luster to the essay as an art form, a form with possibilities for discursive reflection and concrete drama which make it a serious competitor to the novel, until recently almost unchallenged as the dominant literary genre in our time. Apparently drawing upon Baldwin's youthful experience as the son of a Negro preacher, the style of these essays is a remarkable instance of the way in which a grave and sustained eloquence— the rhythm of oratory, but that rhythm held firm and hard—can be employed in an age deeply suspicious of rhetorical prowess. And in pieces like the reports on Harlem and the account of his first visit south, Baldwin realizes far better than in his novels the goal he had set himself of presenting Negro life through an "unspoken recognition of shared experience." Yet it should also be recognized that these essays gain at least some of their resonance from the tone of unrelenting protest in which they are written, from the very anger, even the violence Baldwin had begun by rejecting.

Like Richard Wright before him, Baldwin has discovered that to assert his humanity he must release his rage. But if rage makes for power it does not always encourage clarity, and the truth is that Baldwin's most recent essays are shot through with intellectual confusions, torn by the conflict between his assumption that the Negro must find an honorable place in the life of American society and his apocalyptic sense, mostly fear but just a little hope, that this society is beyond salvation, doomed with the sickness of the West. And again like Wright, he gives way on occasion to the lure of black nationalism. Its formal creed does not interest him, for he knows it to be shoddy, but he is impressed by its capacity to evoke norms of discipline from followers at a time when the Negro community is threatened by a serious inner demoralization.

In his role as spokesman, Baldwin must pronounce with certainty and struggle with militancy; he has at the moment no other choice; yet whatever may have been the objective inadequacy of his polemic against Wright, there can be no question but that the refusal he then made of the role of protest reflected faithfully some of his deepest needs and desires. But we do not make our circumstances; we can, at best, try to remake them; and the arena of choice and action always proves to be a little narrower than we had supposed. One generation passes its dilemmas to the next, black boys on to native sons.

"It is in revolt that man goes beyond himself to discover other people, and from this point of view, human solidarity is a philosophical certainty." The words come from Camus: they might easily have been echoed by Richard Wright: and today one can imagine them being repeated, with a kind of rueful passion, by James Baldwin. No more important words could be spoken in our century, but it would be foolish, and impudent, not to recognize that for the men who must live by them the cost is heavy.

October 1969

Because "Black Boys and Native Sons" has a history of its own and, in some small way, has even entered recent literary history, I have resisted the temptation to modify a phrase here or there and have printed it quite as it first appeared in the Autumn 1963 *Dissent*. Shortly after its publication, Ralph Ellison, the distinguished novelist, wrote a long and sharp attack on this essay, which appeared in *The New Leader*, December 9, 1963. I then replied briefly in the same journal and Ellison rebutted in the February 3, 1964, issue. There the debate rests. It has never been published in its entirety, and perhaps the time has come for the whole discussion, with retrospective comment by the two participants, to be reissued under one cover.

It was Ellison's view that I had locked Negro writers into a narrow and asphyxiating box called "the protest novel" and thereby deprived them of those copious possibilities for creative work that white writers enjoyed. "Unrelieved suffering," charged Ellison, "is the only 'real' Negro experience" I credited. And, he continued, "To deny in the interest of revolutionary posture that such possibilities of human richness exist for others, even in

Mississippi, is not only to deny us our humanity but to betray the critic's commitment to social reality." How accurate or valid Ellison's attack is I leave for others to judge.

What is, however, especially interesting is that in the few years that have passed since we disagreed in print, the cultural atmosphere has changed radically. When our essays first appeared, the literary world was overwhelmingly sympathetic to Ellison: here, it would seem, was a Negro novelist defending creative authority against a radical critic who was said to insist that militancy and protest were the necessary, perhaps desirable, condition of the Negro writer. Every piety of the moment was prepared for enlistment.

By the late 1960's, however, all has changed. White literary intellectuals are often eager to declare an uncritical—which is, I think, a patronizing—acceptance of Black Power ideology. They jostle one another to join the New Left parade, if not as participants then as its Adult Corps; and at least some of them, I imagine, would dismiss both Ellison and me as old-fashioned, irrelevant, and—most shattering of blows!—"mere liberal" advocates of "integration."

Among Negro writers the fashion has also changed. Instead of working, in the style of the early Baldwin, to break away from the naturalistic crudeness and racial anger of a Richard Wright and toward the novel of personal sensibility, most young black writers are now caught up in a separatist and nationalist ideology. They must surely be hostile, if also uneasily respectful, toward Ellison, and impatient, if not contemptuous, toward the distinctions of attitude that Ellison and I, each in his own way, were trying to make. Ellison's claim that he shares quite as much as any white writer in the heritage of Western culture, these black writers would dismiss as a token of inauthenticity, if not worse. My view that the Negro writer, while trapped in a historical situation that makes protest all but unavoidable, nevertheless seeks to find ways of mediating between the gross historical pressures that surround him and his needs and feelings as a unique individual, would strike them as a token of equivocation, if not worse.

So it may be that, with the passage of only five or so years, the dispute between Ellison and me has taken on a new significance. The differences between us remain, and they matter;

but both of us believe in the unity of experience and culture, both of us believe that the works of literature produced by black men should be judged by the same aesthetic criteria as those produced by white men, both of us resist attempts by whoever it may be to reinstitute a new version of social and cultural segregation, and both of us believe in the value of liberal discourse. That, in any case, is the way it now seems to me; how it seems to Ellison I cannot really say, though I should very much like to know.

Mass Society
and
Postmodern Fiction

Raskolnikov is lying on his bed: feverish, hungry, despondent. The servant Nastasya has told him that the landlady plans to have him evicted. He has received a letter from his mother in which she writes that for the sake of money his sister Dounia is to marry an elderly man she does not love. And he has already visited the old pawnbroker and measured the possibility of murdering her.

There seems no way out, no way but the liquidation of the miserly hunchback, whose disappearance from the earth would cause no one any grief. Tempted by the notion that the strong, simply because they are strong, may impose their will upon the weak, Raskolnikov lies there, staring moodily at the ceiling. It must be done: so he tells himself and so he resolves.

Suddenly—but here I diverge a little from the text—the door-bell rings. A letter. Raskolnikov tears it open:

Dear Sir,
It is my pleasure to inform you, on behalf of the Guggenheim Foundation, that you have been awarded a fellowship for the study of color imagery in Pushkin's poetry and its relation to the myths of the ancient Muscovites. If you will be kind enough to visit our offices, at Nevsky Prospect and Q Street, arrangements can be made for commencing your stipend immediately.

(signed) Raevsky

Trembling with joy, Raskolnikov sinks to his knees and bows his head in gratitude. The terrible deed he had contemplated can now be forgotten; he need no longer put his theories to the test; the way ahead, he tells himself, is clear.

But Dostoevsky: is the way now clear for him? May not Raskolnikov's salvation prove to be Dostoevsky's undoing? For Dostoevsky must now ask himself: how, if the old pawnbroker need no longer be destroyed, can Raskolnikov's pride be brought to a visible dramatic climax? The theme remains, for we may imagine that Raskolnikov will still be drawn to notions about the rights of superior individuals; but a new way of realizing this theme will now have to be found.

It is a common assumption of modern criticism that Dostoevsky's ultimate concern was not with presenting a picture of society, nor merely with showing us the difficulties faced by an impoverished young intellectual in czarist Russia. He was concerned with the question of what a human being, acting in the name of his freedom or disenchantment, may take upon himself. Yet we cannot help noticing that the social setting of his novel "happens" to fit quite exactly the requirements of his theme: it is the situation in which Raskolnikov finds himself that embodies the moral and metaphysical problems which, as we like to say, form Dostoevsky's deepest interest.

The sudden removal of Raskolnikov's poverty, as I have imagined it a moment ago, does not necessarily dissolve the temptation to test his will through killing another human being; but it does eliminate the immediate cause for committing the murder. Gliding from fellowship to fellowship, Raskolnikov may now end life as a sober professor of literature. Like the rest of us, he will occasionally notice in himself those dim urges and quavers that speak for hidden powers beyond the assuagement of reason. He may remember that once, unlikely as it has now come to seem, he was even tempted to murder an old woman. But again like the rest of us, he will dismiss these feelings as unworthy of a civilized man.

The case is not hopeless for Dostoevsky: it never is for a writer like him. He can now invent other ways of dramatizing the problem that had concerned him in the novel as it was to be, the novel before Raevsky's letter arrived. But it is questionable whether even he could imagine circumstances—imagine circumstances, as distinct from expressing sentiments—which would lead so persuasively, so inexorably to a revelation of Raskolnikov's moral heresy as do those in what I am tempted to call the unimproved version of *Crime and Punishment.*

From which it will not be concluded, I hope, that a drop in our standard of living is needed in order to provide novelists with extreme or vivid situations. I am merely trying to suggest that in reading contemporary fiction one sometimes feels that the writers find themselves in situations like the one I have here fancied for Dostoevsky.

Let us assume for a moment that we have reached the end of one of those recurrent periods of cultural unrest, innovation, and excitement that we call "modern." Whether we really have no one can say with assurance, and there are strong arguments to be marshaled against such a claim. But if one wishes to reflect upon some—the interesting minority—of the novels written in America during the late forties and the fifties, there is a decided advantage in regarding them as "postmodern," significantly different from the kind of writing we usually call modern. Doing this helps one to notice the distinctive qualities of recent novels: what makes them new. It tunes the ear to their distinctive failures. And it lures one into patience and charity.

That modern novelists—those, say, who began writing after the early work of Henry James—have been committed to a peculiarly anxious and persistent search for values, everyone knows. By now this search for values has become not only a familiar but also an expected element in modern fiction. It has been a major cause for that reaching, sometimes a straining toward, moral surprise, for that inclination to transform the art of narrative into an act of cognitive discovery, which sets modern fiction apart from a large number of eighteenth- and even nineteenth-century novels.

Not so frequently noticed, however, is the fact that long after the modern novelist had come to suspect and even assault traditional values there was still available to him—I would say, until about World War II—a cluster of stable assumptions as to the nature of our society. If the question, "How shall we live?"

agitated novelists without rest, there was a remarkable consensus in their answers to the question, "How do we live?"—a consensus not so much in explicit opinion as in a widely shared feeling about Western society.

Indeed, the turn from the realistic social novel among many of the modern writers would have been most unlikely had there not been available such a similarity of response to the familiar social world. At least some of the novelists who abandoned realism seem to have felt that modern society had been exhaustively, perhaps even excessively portrayed (so D. H. Lawrence suggests in one of his letters) and that the task of the novelist was now to explore a chaotic multiplicity of meanings rather than to continue representing the surfaces of common experience.

No matter what their social bias, and regardless of whether they were aware of having any, the modern novelists tended to assume that the social relations of men in the world of capitalism were established, familiar, knowable. If Joyce could write of Stephen Dedalus that "his destiny was to be elusive of social or religious orders," that was partly because he knew and supposed his readers to know what these orders were. If Lawrence in his later works could write a new kind of novel that paid as little attention to the external phenomena of the social world as to the fixed conventions of novelistic "character," that was partly because he had already registered both of these—the social world and the recognizable solid characters—in *Sons and Lovers*. The observations of class relationships in the earlier novels are not discarded by Lawrence in the later ones; they are tacitly absorbed to become a basis for a new mode of vision.

Values, as everyone now laments, were in flux; but society, it might be remembered, was still there: hard, tangible, ruled by a calculus of gain. One might not know what to make of this world, but at least one knew what was happening in it. Every criticism that novelists might direct against society had behind it enormous pressures of evidence, enormous accumulations of sentiment; and this is the tradition that has been available to and has so enriched modern fiction. A novelist like F. Scott Fitzgerald, whose gifts for conceptual thought were rather meager, could draw to great advantage upon the social criticism that for over a century had preceded him, the whole lengthy and bitter assault upon bourgeois norms that had been launched by the spokesmen for culture. That Fitzgerald may have known little more than the names of these spokesmen, that he drew upon their work with only a minimum of intellectual awareness, serves merely to confirm my point. The rapidity with which such criticism was accumulated during the nineteenth century, whether by Marx or Carlyle, Nietzsche, or Mill, enabled the modern novelists to feel they did not need to repeat the work of Flaubert and Dickens, Balzac, and Zola: they could go beyond them.

Between radical and conservative writers, as between both of these and the bulk of nonpolitical ones, there were many bonds of shared feeling—a kinship they themselves were often unable to notice but which hindsight permits us to see. The sense of the banality of middle-class existence, of its sensuous and spiritual meanness, is quite the same among the conservative as the radical writers, and their ideas about the costs and possibilities of rising in the bourgeois world are not so very different, either.

If one compares two American novelists so different in formal opinion, social background, and literary method as Theodore Dreiser and Edith Wharton, it becomes clear that in such works as *Sister Carrie* and *The House of Mirth* both are relying upon the same crucial assumption: that values, whether traditional or modernist, desirable or false, can be tested in a novel by dramatizing the relationships between mobile characters and fixed social groups. Neither writer felt any need to question, neither would so much as think to question, the presence or impact of these social groups as they formed part of the examined structure of class society. In both novels "the heart of fools is in the house of mirth," the heartbreak house of the modern city; and as Carrie Meeber and Lily Bart make their way up and down the social hierarchy, their stories take on enormous weights of implication because we are ready to assume *some* relationship— surely not the one officially proclaimed by society, nor a mere inversion of it, but still some complex and significant relationship—between the observed scale of social place and the evolving measure of moral value. It is this assumption that has been a major resource of modern novelists; for without some such assumption there could not occur the symbolic compression of incident, the readiness to assume that X stands for Y, which is a prerequisite for the very existence of the novel.

Beset though they might be by moral uncertainties, the modern novelists could yet work through to a relative assurance in their treatment of the social world; and one reason for this assurance was that by the early years of our century the effort to grasp this world conceptually was very far advanced. The novelists may not have been aware of the various theories concerning capitalism, the city, and modern industrial society; it does not matter. These ideas had so thoroughly penetrated the consciousness of thinking men, and even the folklore of the masses, that the novelists could count on them without necessarily being able to specify or elaborate them. In general, when critics "find" ideas in novels, they are transposing to a state of abstraction those assumptions which had become so familiar to novelists that they were able to seize them as sentiments.

Part of what I have been saying runs counter to the influential view that writers of prose fiction in America have written romances and not novels because, in words of Lionel Trilling that echo a more famous complaint of Henry James, there has been in this country "no sufficiency of means for the display of a variety of manners, no opportunity for the novelist to do his job of searching out reality, not enough complication of appearance to make the job interesting." I am not sure that this was ever true of American fiction—the encounter between Ishmael and Queequeg tells us as much about manners (American manners), and through manners about the moral condition of humanity, as we are likely to find in a novel by Jane Austen or Balzac. But even if it is granted that the absence of clear-cut distinctions of class made it impossible in the nineteenth century to write novels about American society and encouraged, instead, a species of philosophical romance, this surely ceased to be true by about 1890. Since then, at least, there has been "enough complication of appearance to make the job interesting."

Nor am I saying—what seems to me much more dubious—that the presumed absence in recent years of a fixed, stratified society or of what one critic, with enviable naïveté, calls "an agreed picture of the universe" makes it impossible to study closely our social life, or to develop (outside of the South) human personalities rooted in a sense of tradition, or to write good novels dealing with social manners and relationships. That all of these things can be done we know, simply because they have been done. I wish merely to suggest that certain assumptions concerning modern society, which have long provided novelists with symbolic economies and dramatic conveniences, are no longer quite so available as they were a few decades ago. To say this is not to assert that we no longer have recognizable social classes in the United States, or that distinctions in manners have ceased to be significant. It is to suggest that the modern theories about society—theories that for novelists have usually been present as tacit assumptions—have partly broken down; and that this presents a great many new difficulties for the younger writers. New difficulties, which is also to say: new possibilities.

In the last two decades there has occurred a series of changes in American life, the extent, durability, and significance of which no one has yet measured. No one can. We speak of the growth of a "mass society," a term I shall try to define in a moment; but at best this is merely a useful hypothesis, not an accredited description. It is a notion that lacks common consent, for it does not yet merit common consent. Still, one can say with some assurance that the more sensitive among the younger writers, those who feel that at whatever peril to their work and careers they must grapple with something new in contemporary experience, even if, like everyone else, they find it extremely hard to say what that "newness" consists of—such writers recognize that the once familiar social categories and place marks have now become as uncertain and elusive as the moral imperatives of the nineteenth century seemed to novelists of fifty years ago. And the something new which they notice or stumble against is, I would suggest, the mass society.

By the mass society we mean a relatively comfortable, half-welfare and half-garrison society in which the population grows passive, indifferent, and atomized; in which traditional loyalties, ties, and associations become lax or dissolve entirely; in which coherent publics based on definite interests and opinions gradually fall apart; and in which man becomes a consumer, himself mass-produced like the products, diversions, and values that he absorbs.

No social scientist has yet come up with a theory of mass society that is entirely satisfying; no novelist has quite captured its still amorphous symptoms—a peculiar blend of frenzy and sluggishness, amiability, and meanness. I would guess that a novelist unaware of the changes in our experience to which the theory of mass society points, is a novelist unable to deal successfully with recent American life; while one who focused only upon those changes would be unable to give his work an adequate sense of historical depth and social detail.

This bare description of the mass society can be extended by noting a few traits or symptoms:

1) Social classes continue to exist, and the society cannot be understood without reference to them; yet the visible tokens of class are less obvious than in earlier decades and the correlations between class status and personal condition, assumed both by the older sociologists and the older novelists, become elusive and problematic—which is not, however, to say that such correlations no longer exist.

2) Traditional centers of authority, like the family, tend to lose some of their binding-power upon human beings; vast numbers of people now float through life with a burden of freedom they can neither sustain nor legitimately abandon to social or religious groups.

3) Traditional ceremonies that have previously marked moments of crisis and transition in human life, thereby helping men to accept such moments, are now either neglected or debased into mere occasions for public display.

4) Passivity becomes a widespread social attitude: the feeling that life is a drift over which one has little control and that even when men do have shared autonomous opinions they cannot act them out in common.

5) As perhaps never before, opinion is manufactured systematically and "scientifically."

6) Opinion tends to flow unilaterally, from the top down, in measured quantities: it becomes a market commodity.

7) Disagreement, controversy, polemic are felt to be in bad taste; issues are "ironed out" or "smoothed away"; reflection upon the nature of society is replaced by observation of its mechanics.

8) Direct and first-hand experience seems to evade human beings, though the quantity of busy-ness keeps increasing and the number of events multiplies with bewildering speed.

9) The pressure of material need visibly decreases, yet there follows

neither a sense of social release nor a feeling of personal joy; instead, people become increasingly aware of their social dependence
and powerlessness.

Now this is a social cartoon and by no means a description of
American society; but it is a cartoon that isolates an aspect of our
experience with a suggestiveness that no other mode of analysis
is likely to match. Nor does it matter that no actual society may
ever reach the extreme condition of a "pure" mass society; the
value of the theory lies in bringing to our attention a major historical drift.

If there is any truth at all in these speculations, they should
help illuminate the problems faced by the novelists whose work
began to appear shortly after World War II. They had to confront not merely the chronic confusion of values which has
gripped our civilization for decades. In a sense they were quite
prepared for that—the whole of modern literature taught them
to expect little else. But they had also to face a problem which,
in actually composing a novel, must have been still more troublesome: our society no longer lent itself to assured definition, one
could no longer assume as quickly as in the recent past that a
spiritual or moral difficulty could find a precise embodiment in
a social conflict. Raskolnikov, fellowship in hand, might still be
troubled by the metaphysical question of what a human being
can allow himself; but Raskolnikov as a graduate student with
an anxious young wife and a two-year-old baby—what was the
novelist to make of him? Something fresh and valuable, no
doubt; but only if he were aware that this new Raskolnikov had
to be seen in ways significantly different from those of the traditional modern novelists.

How to give shape to a world increasingly shapeless and an
experience increasingly fluid; how to reclaim the central assumption of the novel that telling relationships can be discovered between a style of social behavior and a code of moral judgment,
or if that proves impossible, to find ways of imaginatively projecting the code in its own right—these were the difficulties that
faced the young novelists. It was as if the guidelines of both our
social thought and literary conventions were being erased. Or,
as a young German writer has recently remarked:

There's no longer a society to write about. In former years you knew where you stood: the peasants read the Bible; the maniacs read *Mein Kampf*. Now people no longer have any opinions; they have refrigerators. Instead of illusions we have television, instead of tradition, the Volkswagen. The only way to catch the spirit of the times is to write a handbook on home appliances.

Taken literally, this is close to absurd; taken as half-comic hyperbole, it reaches a genuine problem.

The problem, in part, is the relationship between the writer and his materials. Some years ago Van Wyck Brooks had spoken of the conflict between the life of the spirit and the life of commerce, and had called upon American writers to make their choice. Most of them did. Almost every important writer in twentieth-century America, whether or not he read Brooks, implicitly accepted his statement as the truth and chose, with whatever lapses or qualifications, to speak for the life of the spirit.

But was the conflict between spirit and commerce, between culture and society still so acute during the postwar years? Was not a continued belief in this conflict a stale and profitless hangover from the ideologies of the thirties? Might there not be ground for feeling, among the visible signs of our careless postwar prosperity, that a new and more moderate vision of society should inform the work of our novelists? It hardly matters which answers individual writers gave to these questions; the mere fact that they were now being seriously raised had a profound impact upon their work.

Those few who favored a bluntly "positive" approach to American society found it hard to embody their sentiments in vibrant —or even credible—fictional situations. The values of accommodation were there for the asking, but they seemed, perversely, to resist creative use. For almost two decades after the war there was an outpouring of "affirmative" novels about American businessmen—Executive Suites in various shades; but I do not know of a single serious critic who found these books anything but dull and mediocre. At least in our time, the novel seems to lend itself irrevocably to the spirit of criticism; as Camus has remarked, it "is born simultaneously with the spirit of rebellion and expresses, on the aesthetic plane, the same ambition."

But what has been so remarkable and disconcerting is that

those writers who wished to preserve the spirit of rebellion also found it extremely hard to realize their sentiments in novels dealing with contemporary life. Most of them were unable, or perhaps too shrewd, to deal with the postwar experience directly; they preferred tangents of suggestion to frontal representation; they could express their passionate, though often amorphous, criticism of American life not through realistic portraiture but through fable, picaresque, prophecy, and nostalgia.

Morally the young novelists were often more secure than their predecessors. Few of them were as susceptible to money and glitter as Fitzgerald; few had Hemingway's weakness for bravado and swagger; few succumbed to hallucinatory rhetoric in the manner of Faulkner. Yet, as novelists, they were less happily "placed" than the writers who began to publish in the twenties and early thirties. They lacked the pressure of inevitable subjects as these take shape in situations and locales. They lacked equivalents of Fitzgerald's absorption with social distinctions, Hemingway's identification with expatriates, Faulkner's mourning over the old South. Sentiments they had in abundance and often fine ones; but to twist a remark of Gertrude Stein's, literature is not made of sentiments.

Literature is not made of sentiments; yet a good portion of what is most fresh in recent American fiction derives from sentiments. Better than any other group of literate Americans, our novelists resisted the mood of facile self-congratulation which came upon us during the postwar years. To be novelists at all, they had to look upon our life without ideological delusions; and they saw—*often better than they could say*—the hovering sickness of soul, the despairing contentment, the prosperous malaise. They were not, be it said to their credit, taken in. Yet the problem remained: how can one represent malaise, which by its nature is vague and without shape? It can be done, we know. But to do it one needs to be Chekhov; and that is hard.

My point is not that novelists need social theories or philosophical systems. They do, however, need to live in an environment about which they can make economical assumptions that, in some ultimate way, are related to the ideas of speculative thinkers. Let me borrow a useful distinction that C. Wright Mills made between troubles and issues. Troubles signify a strong but unfocused sense of disturbances and pain, while issues refer to troubles that have been articulated as general statements. Novelists, as a rule, concern themselves with troubles, not issues. But to write with assurance and economy about troubles, they need to be working in a milieu where there is at least some awareness of issues. And in the troubled years after World War II, it was precisely this awareness that was often lacking.

A few serious writers did try to fix in their novels the amorphous "troubledness" of postwar American experience. In *The Violated*, an enormous realistic narrative about some ordinary people who reach adulthood during the war, Vance Bourjailly seemed consciously to be dramatizing a view of American society quite similar to the one I have sketched here. He chose to write one of those full-scale narratives composed of parallel strands of plot—a technique which assumes that society is distinctly articulated, that its classes are both sharply visible and intrinsically interesting, and that a novelist can arrange a conflict between members of these classes which will be dramatic in its own right and emblematic of large issues. But for the material Bourjailly chose—the lives of bewildered yet not uncharacteristic drifters during the postwar decades—these assumptions could not operate with sufficient force; and as his characters, in the sameness of their misery, melted into one another, so the strands of his narrative, also having no inevitable reason for separate existence, collapsed into one another.

Norman Mailer, trying in *The Deer Park* to compose a novel about the malaise of our years, avoided the cumbersomeness of the traditional social novel but could find no other structure that would give coherence to his perceptions. Mailer tried to embody his keen if unstable vision in a narrative about people whose extreme dislocation of experience and feeling would, by the very fact of their extreme dislocation, come to seem significant. But in its effort to portray our drifting and boredom fullface, in its fierce loyalty to the terms of its own conception, *The Deer Park* tended to become a claustrophobic work, driving attention inward, toward its own tonal peculiarities, rather than outward, as an extending parable. Throughout the novel Mailer had to fall back upon his protagonist, through whom he tried to say that which he found hard to show.

᪜

A whole group of novelists, among the best of recent years, found itself responding to immediate American experience by choosing subjects and locales apparently far removed from that experience yet, through their inner quality, very close to it. These writers were sensitive to the moods and tones of postwar American life; they knew that something new, different, and extremely hard to describe was happening to us. Yet they did not usually write about postwar experience *per se:* they did not confront it as much as they tried to ambush it. The film critic Stanley Kauffmann has noted a similar phenomenon:

When Vittorio de Sica was asked why so many of his films deal with adultery, he is said to have replied, "But if you take adultery out of the lives of the *bourgeoisie,* what drama is left?" It is perhaps this belief that has impelled Tennessee Williams into the areas that his art inhabits. He has recognized that most of contemporary life offers limited dramatic opportunities . . . so he has left "normal" life to investigate the highly neurotic, the violent and the grimy. It is the continuing problem of the contemporary writer who looks for great emotional issues to move him greatly. The anguish of the advertising executive struggling to keep his job is anguish indeed, but its possibilities in art are not large-scale. The writer who wants to "let go" has figuratively to leave the urban and suburban and either go abroad, go into the past, or go into those few pockets of elemental emotional life left in this country.

Abroad, the past, or the few pockets of elemental emotional life—many of our writers pursued exactly these strategies in order to convey their attitudes toward contemporary experience. In *The Assistant* Bernard Malamud wrote a somber story about a Jewish family during the Depression years, yet it soon becomes clear that one of his impelling motives is a wish to recapture intensities of feeling we have apparently lost but take to be characteristic of an earlier time. Herbert Gold's *The Man Who Was Not With It* is an account of marginal figures in a circus as they teeter on the edge of *lumpen* life; but soon one realizes that he means his story to indicate possibilities for personal survival in a world increasingly compressed. The precocious and bewildered boy in J. D. Salinger's *Catcher in the Rye* expresses something of the moral condition of adolescents during the forties and fifties—or so they tell us; but clearly his troubles are not meant to refer to his generation alone. In *A Walk on the Wild Side* Nelson Algren turns to down-and-outers characteristic of an earlier social moment, but if we look to the psychic pressures breaking through the novel we see that he is really searching for a perspective for estrangement that will continue to be relevant. In *The Field of Vision* Wright Morris moves not backward in time but sideways in space: he contrives to bring a dreary Nebraskan middle-class family to a Mexican bullfight so that the excitement of the blood and ritual will stir it to self-awareness. And while, on the face of it, Saul Bellow's *The Adventures of Augie March* is a picaresque tale about a cocky Jewish boy moving almost magically past the barriers of American society, it is also a kind of paean to the idea of personal freedom in hostile circumstances. Bellow's next novel, *Henderson the Rain King*, seems an even wilder tale about an American millionaire venturing into deepest Africa, in part, the deepest Africa of boys' books; but when he writes that men need a shattering experience to "wake the spirit's sleep" we soon realize that his ultimate reference is to America, where many spirits sleep.

Though vastly different in quality, these novels of the fifties have in common a certain obliqueness of approach. They do not represent directly the postwar American experience, yet refer to it constantly. They tell us rather little about the surface tone, the manners, the social patterns of recent American life, yet are constantly projecting moral criticisms of its essential quality. They approach that experience on the sly, yet are colored and shaped by it throughout. And they gain from it their true subject: the recurrent search—in America, almost a national obsession—for personal identity and freedom. In their distance from fixed social categories and their concern with the metaphysical implications of that distance, these novels constitute what I would call postmodern fiction.

But the theme of personal identity, if it is to take on fictional substance, needs some kind of placement, a setting in the world of practical affairs. And it is here that the postmodern novelists ran into serious troubles: the connection between subject and setting cannot always be made, and the "individual" of their novels, because he lacks social definition and is sometimes a creature of literary or ideological fiat, tends to be not very individualized. Some of the best postwar novels, like *The Invisible Man* and *The Adventures of Augie March*, are deeply concerned with the fate of freedom in a mass society; but the assertiveness of idea and vanity of style which creep into such books are the result, I think, of willing a subject onto a novel rather than allowing it to grow out of a sure sense of a particular moment and place. These novels merit admiration for defending the uniqueness of man's life, but they suffer from having to improvise the terms of this uniqueness. It is a difficulty that seems to have been unavoidable and I have no wish to disparage writers who faced it courageously. Still, it had better be said that the proclamation of personal identity in postwar American fiction tends, if I may use a fashionable phrase, to be more a product of the will than of the imagination.

It may help strengthen my point—critics ought not to strengthen such points too much—if I turn for a moment to the two most discussed literary groups of the postwar years: the "angry young men" in England and the "beat generation" writers of San Francisco.

Partly because they wrote in and about England, Kingsley Amis, John Braine, and John Wain were blessed with something precious to a writer: a subject urgently imposing itself upon their imaginations. They earned the scorn of a good many American critics—notable, of course, for their asceticism—who pointed out that it is not clear whether these writers want a better or just a bigger share of the material and cultural goods in contemporary England. But while you can feel righteous or even hostile toward Amis and Braine, you can hardly deny that in their early novels one finds something of the focused desire, the quick apprehension and notation of contemporary life which, for reasons I have tried to suggest, have become somewhat rare in a serious American fiction. These English writers faced a predicament of the welfare state: it rouses legitimate desires in people of the "lower orders"; it partly satisfies these desires, but it satisfies them only to the point of arousing new demands beyond its power of meeting. For society this may be irksome; for writers it can be exhilarating. Gripes are transformed into causes, ambitions cloaked as ideals. And the angry young men were particularly fortunate in that their complaints led them to deal with some of the traditional materials of the novel: frustrated ambition, frozen snobbery, fake culture, decaying gentility. Through comedy they were able to *structure* their complaints. Their work touched upon sore spots in English life, hurting some people and delighting others. It threatened the Establishment, perhaps its survival, more likely its present leaders. It created tension, opposition, a dialectic of interests. All of which is to say it rested upon a coherent, though very limited, vision of English social relations.

By contrast, the young men in San Francisco seem largely to have been a reflex of the circumstances of mass society. They suffered from psychic and social disturbance: and as far as that goes, they were right—there is much in American life to give one a pain. But they had no clear sense of why or how they were troubled, and some of them seemed opposed in principle to a clear sense of anything. The angry young men in England, even though their protest proved to be entirely opportunistic and momentary, could say what it is that hurts. The San Francisco writers failed to understand, as Paul Goodman has remarked, that

It is necessary to have some contact with institutions and people in order to be frustrated and angry. They [the San Francisco writers] have the theory that to be affectless, not to care, is the ultimate rebellion, but this is a fantasy; for right under the surface is burning shame, hurt feelings, fear of impotence, speechless and powerless tantrum, cowering before papa, being rebuffed by mama; and it is these anxieties that dictate their behavior in every crisis.

These writers illustrate the painful, though not inevitable, predicament of rebellion in a mass society—the ease with which they can turn themselves, all too fashionably, into the other side of the American hollow. In their contempt for mind, they are at one with the middle-class suburbia they think they scorn. In their incoherence of feeling and statement, they mirror the incoherent society that clings to them like a mocking shadow. In their yearning to keep "cool" they sing out an eternal shopkeeper's fantasy. Lonely and estranged, they huddle together in gangs, create a Brook Farm of Know-Nothings, and send back ecstatic reports to the squares: Having a Wonderful Time, Having Wonderful Kicks! But alas, all the while it is clear that they are terribly lost and don't even have the capacity for improvising vivid fantasies. As they raced meaninglessly back and forth across the continent, veritable mimics of the American tourist, they did not have a Wonderful Time. They did not get happily drunk, many of them preferring milk shakes and tea; and their sexual revelations, particularly in Kerouac's *The Subterraneans*, were as sad as they were unintentional. They couldn't, that is, dream themselves out of the shapeless nightmare of California; and for that, perhaps, we should not blame them, since it is not certain that anyone can.

No wonder, then, that in Kerouac's novels one is vaguely aware that somewhere, in the unmapped beyond, a society does exist: a society with forms, requirements, burdens, injustices, duties, and pleasures; but that in the space of the novels themselves we can find only a series of distraught and compulsive motions. The themes of what I have called postmodern fiction are reflected in the San Francisco writers as caricature and symptom; for if you shun consciousness as if it were a plague, then a predicament may ravage you but you cannot cope with it.*

Where, finally, does this leave us? In the midst, I hope, of the promise and confusion of contemporary American writing. No settled ending is possible here, because the tendencies I have been noticing are still in flux, still open to many pressures and possibilities. But it may not be too rash to say that the more serious of the postmodern novelists—those who grapple with problems rather than merely betraying their effects—have begun to envisage that we may be on the threshold of enormous changes in human history. These changes, merely glanced by the idea of the "mass society," fill our novelists with a sense of foreboding; and through the strategy of obliqueness, they bring to bear a barrage of moral criticisms, reminders of human potentiality, and tacit exhortations.

* Both of these literary tendencies—the English "angries" and American "beats"—have all but disintegrated during the sixties. The achievement of the first now seems a very modest one, and that of the second almost invisible. Yet the contrast made above remains, I think, a useful way of indicating how and why the English novelists found it easier to articulate their sense of social complaint than the Americans.

One of the possibilities that appears to them is that we are moving toward a quiet desert of moderation, where men will forget the passion of moral and spiritual restlessness which has characterized Western society. That the human creature, no longer a Quixote or a Faust, will become a docile attendant to an automated civilization. That the "aura of the human" will be replaced by the nihilism of satiety. That the main question will no longer be the conditions of existence but existence itself. That high culture as we understand it will become increasingly problematical and perhaps reach some point of obsolescence.

But before such prospects—they form the bad dreams of thoughtful men, the nightmares our postmodern novelists are trying to exorcise—the mind grows dizzy and recalcitrant. It begins to solace itself with rumblings about eternal truths, and like the exacerbated judge in Faulkner's *The Hamlet*, cries out, "I can't stand no more. . . . This case is adjourned!"

October 1969

Hardly a decade has passed since the kind of fiction discussed in this essay seemed to dominate the imagination of the more serious American writers. When a school or style is in favor, it can seem invulnerable to change, beyond decay. But then, as we always know yet seldom believe, there occurs one of those startling shifts in cultural temper which are both hard to explain and certain to occur. Until seven or eight years ago the kind of writing I've called "postmodern fiction" was the most distinctive and serious in American literature; yet during the last few years it has been replaced by a style radically different, a style discussed in the last third of the following essay. These two kinds of fiction share, I think, some essential elements: both come after the great achievements of literary modernism, both are dependent on what they deviate from, and both can be regarded as signs of the gradual breakdown of the modernist impulse. How it happens that we experience so sharp a turn from the fiction described in this essay to the kind sketched in the concluding portion of the next—that, indeed, is a problem cultural historians might conjure with.

Part III

The
New York
Intellectuals

We do not yet have a full-scale history of intellectuals in the
United States, but when that book comes to be written one of
its central themes will surely be that our intellectuals have done
their work mostly in isolation. Even the groups we locate in the
past—the Transcendentalists encircling Emerson, the writers and
critics following Van Wyck Brooks during the *Seven Arts* period
—are groups mainly by courtesy of retrospect. The figures we
see within them were not nearly so close to one another in experience nor so allied in opinion as our need for historical reconstruction makes them out to have been. The kind of inner
fraternity we associate with literary groups in Paris and London
has rarely been characteristic of American intellectual life. It is
hardly an accident that one of our most poignant cultural legends
concerns the brief friendship between Hawthorne and Melville
and then its long sequel of separation. Ours is a culture in which
people rattle around.

A seeming exception is the group of writers who have come
to be known, these past few decades, as the New York intellectuals. They appear to have a common history, prolonged now for
more than thirty years; a common political outlook, even if
marked by ceaseless internecine quarrels; a common style of
thought and perhaps composition; a common focus of intellectual
interests; and once you get past politeness—which becomes,
these days, easier and easier—a common ethnic origin. They are,

or until recently have been, anti-Communist; they are, or until some time ago were, radicals; they have a fondness for ideological speculation; they write literary criticism with a strong social emphasis; they revel in polemic; they strive self-consciously to be "brilliant"; and by birth or osmosis, they are Jews.

The New York intellectuals are perhaps the only group America has ever had that could be described as an *intelligentsia*. This term comes awkwardly to our lips, and for good reason: it suggests, as Martin Malia, a historian of Russian culture, writes, "more than intellectuals in the ordinary sense. Whether merely 'critical-thinking' or actively oppositional, their name indicates that [in Russia] they thought of themselves as the embodied 'intelligence' . . . or 'consciousness' of the nation. They clearly felt an exceptional sense of apartness from the society in which they lived."

Malia's phrase about "consciousness of the nation" seems special to the problems of the Russian intellectuals under czarism, but the rest of his description fits the New York intellectuals rather well: the stress upon "critical thinking," the stance of active opposition, the sense of apartness. Or, perhaps more accurately, it is a description which fits the past of the New York intellectuals. And just as the Russian "intelligentsia" was marked by a strongly Westernizing outlook, a wish to bring Russian culture out of its provincial limits and into a close relationship with the culture of Western Europe, so the New York intellectuals have played a role in the internationalization of American culture, serving as a liaison between American readers and Russian politics, French ideas, European writing.

A more complicated approach to the problem of the intelligentsia is provided by Renato Poggioli in his book *The Theory of the Avant Garde*. He describes the Russian intelligentsia as "an intellectual order from the lower ranks . . . created by those who were rejected by other classes: an intellectual order whose function was not so much cultural as political. . . ." Poggioli remarks that in Russia the term referred to a "cultural proletariat," but

these intellectuals are not so much proletarian as proletarianizing . . . they may become ideologically and politically bound to the mass of workers and peasants but they are not, at bottom, an order economically bound to the interests of those masses. A member of the intelligentsia is not born but made.

I suspect there may be a contradiction between regarding the intelligentsia as an order "from the lower ranks" and concluding that a member of this order "is not born but made." But Poggioli's description is valuable insofar as it suggests that the intelligentsia is defined primarily by its position in society rather than by its relation to culture. Poggioli wishes sharply to distinguish the intelligentsia from an "intellectual elite," which he regards as a self-mobilized group whose *raison d'être* is a cultural attitude, and in our time, a positive commitment to modernist literature. In respect to late nineteenth- and early twentieth-century Russia, this distinction is useful; when we turn to America, we are obviously dealing with loose analogies, yet useful ones, too, for Poggioli's distinction should help us, a little later, to see the precise nature and limits of the New York intellectuals as a group.

Reflecting upon the experience of these writers, one begins to wonder whether—apart from a few years during the late thirties—they ever did constitute a coherent and self-defined group. The steady exchange of ideas, the reading of manuscripts, the preliminary discussion of work, all these characteristics of European intellectuals were not often evident in New York. On the contrary. In their work habits the New York intellectuals have mostly been loners, and in their relationships with one another, closer to the vision of life we associate with Hobbes than with Kropotkin. Repeatedly I have been struck by the way writers commonly associated with this group will hotly deny that it exists, or will say that if indeed it does exist they—*they!*—would not be so docile as to be part of it. Certain New York intellectuals like Harold Rosenberg and Lionel Abel have never been very strong in sentiments of group fraternity; and Rosenberg, in the course of a polemic against other New York writers, once coined the memorable phrase, "a herd of independent minds." Some, like myself, have seen themselves as only in part and then ambivalently related, since we are also caught up with a separate political milieu.* After a time, in Europe, it became a source of pride for writers to say they had once been associated

---

* Is it "they" or "we"? To speak of the New York intellectuals as "they" might seem coy or disloyal; to speak of "we" self-assertive or cozy. Well, let it be "they," with the proviso that I do not thereby wish, even if I could, to exempt myself from judgment.

with the Bloomsbury group or the *Scrutiny* critics or the socialists led by Gorky before the Revolution; but for whatever reasons, that point has not been reached among the New York writers. I doubt that it ever will be. Contentious and, by virtue of their origins and history, uncertain as to their relationship with American culture, the New York intellectuals wish, so far as I can tell, to form a loose and unacknowledged tribe.

Yet the mere fact that there does exist a commonly shared perception of a New York intellectual group, even if that perception is held mainly by hostile academics and a parasitic mass media, must be taken as decisive. That people "out there" believe in the reality of the New York group, makes it a reality of sorts. And in all candor there is something else: the New York writers dislike being labeled, they can speak bitterly about each other's work and opinions, they may not see one another from year's start to year's end, but they are nervously alert to one another's judgments. *Attention is paid*—whether from warranted respect or collective vanity or provincial narrowness, it hardly matters.

Such groups approach a fragile state of coherence only at the point where writers are coming together and the point where they are drifting apart. Especially does this seem true at the end, when there comes that tremor of self-awareness which no one would have troubled to feel during the years of energy and confidence. A tradition in process of being lost, a generation facing assault and ridicule from ambitious younger men—the rekindled sense of group solidarity is brought to a half-hour's flame by the hardness of dying. And it is at such moments that the mass media, never more than twenty years late, become aware of the problem: their publicity signals recognition and recognition a certificate of death.

The social roots of the New York writers are not hard to trace. With a few delightful exceptions—a tendril from Yale, a vine from Seattle—they stem from the world of the immigrant Jews, either workers or petty bourgeois.* They come at a moment in

* In placing this emphasis on the Jewish origins of the New York intellectuals, I am guilty of a certain—perhaps unavoidable—compression of the realities. Were I writing a book rather than an essay, I would have to describe in some detail the relationship between the intellectuals who came on the scene in the thirties and those of earlier periods. There were signifi-

the development of immigrant Jewish culture when there is a strong drive not only to break out of the ghetto but also to leave behind the bonds of Jewishness entirely. Earlier generations had known such feelings, and through many works of fiction, especially those by Henry Roth, Michael Gold, and Daniel Fuchs, one can return to the classic pattern of a fierce attachment to the provincialism of origins as it becomes entangled with a fierce eagerness to plunge into the Gentile world of success, manners, freedom. As early as the 1890's this pattern had already come into view, and with diminishing intensity it has continued to control Jewish life deep into the twentieth century; perhaps its last significant expression comes in Philip Roth's stories, where the sense of Jewish tradition is feeble but the urge to escape its suburban ruins extremely strong.

The New York intellectuals were the first group of Jewish writers to come out of the immigrant milieu who did not define themselves through a relationship, nostalgic or hostile, to memories of Jewishness. They were the first generation of Jewish writers for whom the recall of an immigrant childhood does not seem to have been completely overwhelming. (Is that perhaps one reason few of them tried to write fiction?) That this severance from Jewish roots and immigrant sources would later come to seem a little suspect, is another matter. All I wish to stress here is that, precisely at the point in the thirties when the New York intellectuals began to form themselves into a loose cultural-political tendency, Jewishness as idea and sentiment played no significant role in their expectations—apart, to be sure,

---

cant ties between *Partisan Review* and *The Dial, Politics* and the *Masses.* But I choose here to bypass this historical connection because I wish to stress what has been distinctive and perhaps unique.

A similar qualification has to be made concerning those intellectuals who have been associated with this milieu but have not been Jewish. I am working on the premise that in background and style there was something decidedly Jewish about the intellectuals who began to cohere as a group around *Partisan Review* in the late thirties—and one of the things that was "decidedly Jewish" was that most were of Jewish birth! Perhaps it ought to be said, then, that my use of the phrase "New York intellectuals" is simply a designation of convenience. I don't mean to suggest that there have been or will be no other intellectuals in New York. I am using the phrase as a shorthand for what might awkwardly be spelled out as "the intellectuals of New York who began to appear in the thirties, most of whom were Jewish."

from a bitter awareness that no matter what their political or cultural desires, the sheer fact of their recent emergence had still to be regarded, and not least of all by themselves, as an event within Jewish American life.

For decades the life of the East European Jews, both in the old country and the new, might be compared to a tightly gathered spring, trembling with unused force, which had been held in check until the climactic moment of settlement in America. Then the energies of generations came bursting out, with an ambition that would range from pure to coarse, disinterested to vulgar, and indeed would mix all these together, but finally—this ambition—would count for more as an absolute release than in any of its local manifestations. What made Sammy run was partly that his father and his father's father had been bound hand and foot. And in all the New York intellectuals there was and had to be a fraction of Sammy. All were driven by a sense of striving, a thrust of will, an unspoken conviction that time had now to be regained.

The youthful experiences described by Alfred Kazin in his autobiography are, apart from his distinctive outcroppings of temperament, more or less typical of the experiences of many New York intellectuals—except, at one or two points, for the handful that involved itself deeply in the radical movement. It is my impression, however, that Kazin's affectionate stress on the Jewish sources of his experience is mainly a feeling of retrospect, mainly a recognition in the fifties and sixties that no matter how you might try to shake off your past, it would still cling to your speech, gestures, skin, and nose; it would still shape, with a thousand subtle movements, the way you did your work and raised your children. In the thirties, however, it was precisely the idea of discarding the past, breaking away from families, traditions, and memories which excited intellectuals. They meant to declare themselves citizens of the world and, that succeeding, perhaps consider becoming writers of this country.

The Jewish immigrant world branded upon its sons and daughters marks of separateness even while encouraging them to dreams of universalism. This subculture may have been formed to preserve ethnic continuity, but it was the kind of continuity that would reach its triumph in self-disintegration. It taught its children both to conquer the Gentile world and to be conquered by it, both to leave an intellectual impress and to accept the dominant social norms. By the twenties and thirties the values dominating Jewish immigrant life were mostly secular, radical, and universalist, and if these were often conveyed through a parochial vocabulary, they nonetheless carried some remnants of European culture. Even as they were moving out of a constricted immigrant milieu, the New York intellectuals were being prepared by it for the tasks they would set themselves during the thirties. They were being prepared for the intellectual vocation as one of assertiveness, speculation, and free-wheeling; for the strategic maneuvers of a vanguard, at this point almost a vanguard in the abstract, with no ranks following in the rear; and for the union of politics and culture, with the politics radical and the culture cosmopolitan. What made this goal all the more attractive was that the best living American critic, Edmund Wilson, had triumphantly reached it: he was the author of both *The Triple Thinkers* and *To the Finland Station;* he served as a model for emulation, and he gave this view of the intellectual life a special authority in that he seemed to come out of the mainstream of American life.

That the literary avant-garde and the political left were not really comfortable partners would become clear with the passage of time; in Europe it already had. But during the years the New York intellectuals began to appear as writers and critics worthy of some attention, there was a feeling in the air that a union of *the advanced*—critical consciousness and political conscience— could be forged.

Throughout the thirties the New York intellectuals believed, somewhat naïvely, that this union was not only a desirable possibility but also a tie both natural and appropriate. Except, however, for the Surrealists in Paris, and it is not clear how seriously this instance should be taken, the paths of political radicalism and cultural modernism have seldom met. To use Poggioli's terms, the New York writers were more an "intelligentsia" than an "intellectual elite," and more inclined to an amorphous "proletarianizing" than to an austere partisanship for modernism.

The history of the West in the last century offers many instances in which Jewish intellectuals played an important role in the development of political radicalism; but almost always this occurred when there were sizable movements, with the intellectuals serving as spokesmen, propagandists, and functionaries of a party. In New York, by contrast, the intellectuals had no choice but to begin with a dissociation from the only significant radical movement in this country, the Communist Party. What for European writers like Koestler, Silone, and Malraux would be the end of the road was here a beginning. In a fairly short time, the New York writers found that the meeting of political and cultural ideas which had stirred them to excitement could also leave them stranded and distressed. Radicalism, in both its daily practice and ethical biases, proved inhospitable to certain aspects of modernism—and not always, I now think, mistakenly. Literary modernism often had a way of cavalierly dismissing the world of daily existence, a world that remained intensely absorbing to the New York writers. Literary modernism could sometimes align itself with reactionary movements, a fact that was intensely embarrassing and required either torturous explanations or complex dissociations. The New York writers discovered, as well, that their relationship to modernism as a purely literary phenomenon was less authoritative and more ambiguous than they had wished to feel. The great battles for Joyce and Eliot and Proust had been fought in the twenties and mostly won; and now, while clashes with entrenched philistinism might still take place, they were mostly skirmishes or mopping-up operations (as in the polemics against the transfigured Van Wyck Brooks). The New York writers came at the end of the modernist experience, just as they came at what may yet have to be judged the end of the radical experience, and as they certainly came at the end of the immigrant Jewish experience. One shorthand way of describing their situation, a cause of both their feverish brilliance and their recurrent instability, is to say that *they came late.*

During the thirties and forties their radicalism was anxious, problematic, and beginning to decay at the very moment it was adopted. They had no choice: the crisis of socialism was worldwide, profound, with no end in sight, and the only way to avoid that crisis was to bury oneself, as a few did, in the left-wing sects. Some of the New York writers had gone through the "political school" of Stalinism, a training in coarseness from which not all recovered; some had even spent a short time in the organizational coils of the Communist Party. By 1936, when the anti-Stalinist *Partisan Review* was conceived, the central figures of that moment—Philip Rahv, William Phillips, Sidney Hook—had shed whatever sympathies they once felt for Stalinism, but the hope that they could find another ideological system, some cleansed version of Marxism associated perhaps with Trotsky or Luxemburg, was doomed to failure. Some gravitated for a year or two toward the Trotskyist group, but apart from admiration for Trotsky's personal qualities and dialectical prowess, they found little satisfaction there; no version of orthodox Marxism could retain a hold on intellectuals who had gone through the trauma of abandoning the Leninist *Weltanschauung* and had experienced the depth to which the politics of this century, most notably the rise of totalitarianism, called into question the once-sacred Marxist categories. From now on, the comforts of system would have to be relinquished.

Though sometimes brilliant in expression and often a stimulus to the kind of cultural speculation at which they excelled, the radicalism of the New York intellectuals during the thirties was not a deeply grounded experience. It lacked roots in a popular movement which might bring intellectuals into relationship with the complexities of power and stringencies of organization. From a doctrine it became a style, and from a style a memory. It was symptomatic that the *Marxist Quarterly*, started in 1937 by a spectrum of left intellectuals and probably the most distinguished Marxist journal ever published in this country, could survive no more than a year. The differences among its founders, some like James Burnham holding to a revolutionary Marxist line and others like Sidney Hook and Lewis Corey moving toward versions of liberalism and social democracy, proved too severe for collaboration. And even the radicalism of the *Partisan Review* editors and writers during its vivid early years—how deeply did it cut, except as a tool enabling them to break away from Marxism? Which of those writers and readers who now look back nostalgically have troubled to examine the early files of this important magazine and read—with embarrassment? amusement? pleasure? —the political essays it printed?

Yet if the radicalism of the New York intellectuals seems to have been without much political foundation or ideological strength, it certainly played an important role in their own development. For the New York writers, and even, I suspect, those among them who would later turn sour on the whole idea of radicalism (including the few who in the mid-sixties would try to erase the memory of having turned sour), the thirties represented a time of intensity and fervor, a reality or illusion of engagement, a youth tensed with conviction and assurance: so that even Dwight Macdonald, who at each point in his life has made a specialty out of mocking his previous beliefs, could not help displaying tender feelings upon remembering his years, God help us, as a "revolutionist." The radicalism of the thirties gave the New York intellectuals their distinctive style: a flair for polemic, a taste for the grand generalization, an impatience with what they regarded (often parochially) as parochial scholarship, an internationalist perspective, and a tacit belief in the unity—even if a unity beyond immediate reach—of intellectual work.

By comparison with competing schools of thought, the radicalism of the anti-Stalinist left, as it was then being advanced in *Partisan Review,* seemed cogent, fertile, alive: it could stir good minds to argument, it could gain the attention of writers abroad, it seemed to offer a combination of system and independence. With time the anti-Stalinist intellectuals came to enjoy advantages somewhat like those which have enabled old radicals to flourish in the trade unions: they could talk faster than anyone else, they knew their way around better, they were quicker on their feet. Brief and superficial as their engagement with Marxism may have been, it gave the intellectuals the advantage of dialectic, sometimes dialectic as it lapsed into mere double-talk.

Yet in fairness I should add that this radicalism did achieve something of substantial value in the history of American culture. It helped destroy—once and for all, I would have said until recently—Stalinism as a force in our intellectual life, and with Stalinism those varieties of Populist sentimentality which the Communist movement of the late thirties exploited with notable skill. If certain sorts of manipulative soft-headedness have been all but banished from serious American writing, and the kinds of rhetoric once associated with Archibald MacLeish and Van Wyck Brooks cast into permanent disrepute, at least some credit for this ought to go to the New York writers.

◄§

It has recently become fashionable, especially in the pages of the *New York Review of Books,* to sneer at the achievements of anti-Stalinism by muttering darkly about "the Cold War." But we ought to have enough respect for the past to avoid telescoping several decades. The major battle against Stalinism as a force within intellectual life, and in truth a powerful force, occurred before anyone heard of the Cold War; it occurred in the late thirties and early forties. In our own moment we see "the old crap," as Marx once called it, rise to the surface with unnerving ease; there is something dizzying in an encounter with Stalin's theory of "social Fascism," particularly when it comes from the lips of young people who may not even be quite sure when Stalin lived. Still, I think there will not and probably cannot be repeated in our intellectual life the ghastly large-scale infatuation with a totalitarian regime which disgraced the thirties. Some achievements, a very few, seem beyond destruction.

A little credit is therefore due. Whatever judgments one may have about Sidney Hook's later political writings, and mine have been very critical, it is a matter of decency to recall the liberating role he played in the thirties as spokesman for a democratic radicalism and a fierce opponent of all the rationalizations for totalitarianism a good many intellectuals allowed themselves. One reason people have recently felt free to look down their noses at "anti-Communism" as if it were a mass voodoo infecting everyone from far right to democratic left, is precisely the toughness with which the New York intellectuals fought against Stalinism. Neither they nor anybody else could re-establish socialism as a viable politics in the United States; but for a time they did help to salvage the honor of the socialist idea—which meant primarily to place it in the sharpest opposition to all totalitarian states and systems. What many intellectuals now say they take for granted, had first to be won through bitter and exhausting struggle.

I should not like to give the impression that Stalinism was the beginning and end of whatever was detestable in American intellectual life during the thirties. Like the decades to come, perhaps like all decades, this was a "low dishonest" time. No one who grew up in, or lived through, these years should wish for a replay of their ideological melodramas. Nostalgia for the thirties is a sentiment possible only to the very young or the very old, those who have not known and those who no longer remember. Whatever distinction can be assigned to the New York intellectuals during those years lies mainly in their persistence as a small minority, in their readiness to defend unpopular positions against apologists for the Moscow trials and the vigilantism of Popular Front culture. Some historians, with the selectivity of retrospect, have recently begun to place the New York intellectuals at the center of cultural life in the thirties—but this is both a comic misapprehension and a soiling honor. On the contrary; their best hours were spent on the margin, in opposition.

Later, in the forties and fifties, most of the New York intellectuals would abandon the effort to find a renewed basis for a socialist politics—to their serious discredit, I believe. Some would vulgarize anti-Stalinism into a politics barely distinguishable from reaction. Yet for almost all New York intellectuals the radical years proved a decisive moment in their lives. And for a very few, the decisive moment.

I have been speaking here as if the New York intellectuals were mainly political people, but in reality this was true for only a few of them, writers like Hook, Macdonald, and perhaps Rahv. Most were literary men or journalists with no experience in any political movement; they had come to radical politics through the pressures of conscience and a flair for the dramatic; and even in later years, when they abandoned any direct political involvement, they would in some sense remain "political." They would maintain an alertness toward the public event. They would respond with eagerness to historical changes, even if these promised renewed favor for the very ideas they had largely discarded. They would continue to structure their cultural responses through a sharp, perhaps excessively sharp, kind of categorization, in itself a sign that political styles and habits persisted. But for the most part, the contributions of the New York intellectuals were not to political thought. Given the brief span of time during which they fancied themselves agents of a renewed Marxism, there was little they could have done. Sidney Hook wrote one or two excellent books on the sources of Marxism, Harold Rosenberg one or two penetrating essays on the dramatics of Marxism; and not much more. The real contribution of the New York writers was toward creating a new, and for this country almost exotic, style of work. They thought of themselves as cultural radicals even after they had begun to wonder whether there was much point in remaining political radicals. But what could this mean? Cultural radicalism was a notion extremely hard to define and perhaps impossible to defend, as Richard Chase would discover in the late fifties when against the main drift of New York opinion he put forward the idea of a radicalism without immediate political ends but oriented toward criticism of a meretricious culture. What Chase did not live long enough to see was that his idea, much derided at the time, would lend itself a decade later to caricature through success.

Chase was seriously trying to preserve a major impetus of New York intellectual life: the exploration and defense of literary modernism. He failed to see, however, that this was a task largely fulfilled and, in any case, taking on a far more ambiguous and less militant character in the fifties than it would have had twenty or thirty years earlier. The New York writers had done useful work in behalf of modernist literature. Without fully realizing it, they were continuing a cultural movement that had begun in the United States during the mid-nineteenth century: the return to Europe, not as provincials knocking humbly at the doors of the great, but as equals in an enterprise which by its very nature had to be international. We see this at work in Howells's reception of Ibsen and Tolstoy; in Van Wyck Brooks's use of European models to assault the timidities of American literature; in the responsiveness of *The Little Review* and *The Dial* to European experiments and, somewhat paradoxically, in the later fixation of the New Critics, despite an ideology of cultural provincialism, on modernist writing from abroad.

The New York critics, and most notably *Partisan Review*, helped complete this process of internationalizing American culture (also, by the way, Americanizing international culture). They gave a touch of glamour to that style which the Russians and Poles now call "cosmopolitan." *Partisan Review* was the first journal in which it was not merely respectable but a matter of pride to print one of Eliot's *Four Quartets* side by side with Marxist criticism. And not only did the magazine break down the polar rigidities of the hard-line Marxists and the hard-line nativists; it also sanctioned the idea, perhaps the most powerful cultural idea of the last half-century, that there existed an all but incomparable generation of modern masters, some of them still alive, who in this terrible age represented the highest possibilities of the human imagination. On a more restricted scale, *Partisan Review* helped win attention and respect for a generation of European writers—Silone, Orwell, Malraux, Koestler, Serge—who were not quite of the first rank as novelists but had suffered the failure of socialism.

If the *Partisan* critics came too late for a direct encounter with new work from the modern masters, they did serve the valuable end of placing that work in a cultural context more vital and urgent than could be provided by any other school of American criticism. For many young people up to and through World War II, the *Partisan* critics helped to mold a new sensibility, a mixture of rootless radicalism and a desanctified admiration for writers like Joyce, Eliot, and Kafka. I can recall that even in my orthodox Marxist phase I felt that the central literary expression of the time was a now half-forgotten poem by a St. Louis writer called "The Waste Land."

In truth, however, the New York critics were then performing no more than an auxiliary service. They were following upon the work of earlier, more fortunate critics. And even in the task of cultural consolidation, which soon had the unhappy result of overconsolidating the modern masters in the academy, the New York critics found important allies among their occasional opponents in the New Criticism. As it turned out, the commitment to literary modernism proved insufficient either as a binding literary purpose or as a theme that might inform the writings of the New York critics. By now modernism was entering its period of decline; the old excitements had paled and the old achievements been registered. Modernism had become successful; it was no longer a literature of opposition, and thereby had begun that metamorphosis signifying its ultimate death. The problem was no longer to fight for modernism; the problem was now to consider why the fight had so easily ended in triumph. And as time went on, modernism surfaced an increasing portion of its limitations and ambiguities, so that among some critics earlier passions of advocacy gave way to increasing anxieties of judgment. Yet the moment had certainly not come when a cool and objective reconsideration could be undertaken of works that had formed the sensibility of our time. The New York critics, like many others, were trapped in a dilemma from which no escape could be found, but which lent itself to brilliant improvisation: it was too late for unobstructed enthusiasm, it was too soon for unobstructed valuation, and meanwhile the literary work that was being published, though sometimes distinguished, was composed in the heavy shadows of the modernists. At almost every point this work betrayed the marks of *having come after.*

Except for Harold Rosenberg, who would make "the tradition of the new" a signature of his criticism, the New York writers slowly began to release those sentiments of uneasiness they had been harboring about the modernist poets and novelists. One instance was the notorious Pound case,* in which literary and moral values, if not jammed into a head-on collision, were certainly entangled beyond easy separation. Essays on writers like D. H. Lawrence—what to make of his call for "blood consciousness," what one's true response might be to his notions of the leader cult—began to appear. A recent book by John Harrison, *The Reactionaries*, which contains a full-scale attack on the politics of several modernist writers, is mostly a compilation of views that had been gathering force over the last few decades. And then, as modernism stumbled into its late period, those recent years in which its early energies have evidently reached a point of exhaustion, the New York critics became still more discomfited. There was a notable essay several years ago by Lionel Trilling in which he acknowledged mixed feelings toward the modernist writers he had long praised and taught. There was a cutting attack by Philip Rahv on Jean Genet, that perverse genius in whose fiction the compositional resources of modernism seem all but severed from its moral—one might even say, its human—interests.

For the New York intellectuals in the thirties and forties there was still another focus of interest, never quite as strong as radical politics or literary modernism but seeming, for a brief time, to promise a valuable new line of discussion. In the essays of

---

* In 1948 Ezra Pound, who had spent the war years as a propagandist for Mussolini and whose writings contained strongly anti-Semitic passages, was awarded the prestigious Bollingen Prize. The committee voting for this award contained a number of ranking American poets. After the award was announced, there occurred in the pages of *Partisan Review, Commentary,* and other journals a harsh dispute as to its appropriateness.

writers like Clement Greenberg and Dwight Macdonald, more or less influenced by the German neo-Marxist school of Adorno-Horkheimer, there were beginnings at a theory of "mass culture," that mass-produced pseudo-art characteristic of industrialized urban society, together with its paralyzed audiences, its inaccessible sources, its parasitic relation to high culture. More insight than system and more intuition than knowledge, this slender body of work was nevertheless a contribution to the study of that hazy area where culture and society meet. It was attacked by writers like Edward Shils as being haughtily elitist, on the ground that it assumed a condescension to the tastes and experiences of the masses. It was attacked by writers like Harold Rosenberg, who charged that only people taking a surreptitious pleasure in dipping their noses into trash would study the "content" (he had no objection to sociological investigations) of mass culture. Even at its most penetrating, the criticism of mass culture was beset by uncertainty and improvisation; perhaps all necessary for a beginning.

Then, almost as if by common decision, the whole subject was dropped. For years hardly a word could be found in the advanced journals about what a little earlier had been called a crucial problem of the modern era. One reason was that the theory advanced by Greenberg and Macdonald turned out to be static: it could be stated but apparently not developed. It suffered from weaknesses parallel to those of Hannah Arendt's theory of totalitarianism: by positing a *cul de sac*, a virtual end of days, for twentieth-century man and his culture, it proposed a suffocating relationship between high or minority culture and the ever-multiplying mass culture. From this relationship there seemed neither relief nor escape, and if one accepted this view, nothing remained but to refine the theory and keep adding grisly instances.

In the absence of more complex speculations, there was little point in continuing to write about mass culture. Besides, hostility toward the commercial pseudo-arts was hard to maintain with unyielding intensity, mostly because it was hard to remain all that *interested* in them—only in Macdonald's essays did both hostility and interest survive intact. Some felt that the whole matter had been inflated and that writers should stick to their business, which was literature, and intellectuals to theirs, which was ideas. Others felt that the movies and TV were beginning to show more ingenuity and resourcefulness than the severe notions advanced by Greenberg and Macdonald allowed for, though no one could have anticipated that glorious infatuation with trash which Marshall McLuhan would make acceptable. And still others felt that the multiplication of insights, even if pleasing as an exercise, failed to yield significant results: a critic who contributes a nuance to Dostoevsky criticism is working within a structured tradition, while one who throws off a clever observation about Little Orphan Annie is simply showing that he can do what he has done.

There was another and more political reason for the collapse of mass culture criticism. One incentive toward this kind of writing was the feeling that industrial society had reached a point of affluent stasis where major upheavals could now be registered much more vividly in culture than in economics. While aware of the dangers of reductionism here, I think the criticism of mass culture did serve, as some of *its* critics charged, conveniently to replace the criticism of bourgeois society. If you couldn't stir the proletariat to action, you could denounce Madison Avenue in comfort. Once, however, it began to be felt among intellectuals in the fifties that there was no longer so overwhelming a need for political criticism, and once it began to seem in the sixties that there were new openings for political criticism, the appetite for cultural surrogates became less keen.

Greenberg now said little more about mass culture; Macdonald made no serious effort to extend his theory or test it against new events; and in recent years, younger writers have seemed to feel that the whole approach of these men was heavy and humorless. Susan Sontag has proposed a cheerfully eclectic view which undercuts just about everything written from the Greenberg-Macdonald position. Now everyone is to do "his thing," high, middle, or low; the old puritan habit of interpretation and judgment, so inimical to sensuousness, gives way to a programmed receptivity; and we are enlightened by lengthy studies of the ethos of the Beatles.

By the end of World War II, the New York writers had reached a point of severe intellectual crisis, though as frequently happens at such moments, they themselves often felt they were entering a phase of enlarged influence and power. Perhaps indeed there was a relation between inner crisis and external influence. Everything that had kept them going—the idea of socialism, the advocacy of literary modernism, the assault on mass culture, a special brand of literary criticism—was judged to be irrelevant to the postwar years. But as a group, just at the time their internal disintegration had seriously begun, the New York writers could be readily identified. The leading critics were Rahv, Phillips, Trilling, Rosenberg, Abel, and Kazin. The main political theorist was Hook. Writers of poetry and fiction related to the New York milieu were Delmore Schwartz, Saul Bellow, Paul Goodman, and Isaac Rosenfeld. And the recognized scholar, and also inspiring moral force, was Meyer Schapiro.

A sharp turn occurs, or is completed, soon after World War II. The intellectuals now go racing or stumbling from idea to idea, notion to notion, hope to hope, fashion to fashion. This instability often derives from a genuine eagerness to capture all that seems new—or threatening—in experience, sometimes from a mere desire to capture a bitch goddess whose first name is Novelty. The abandonment of ideology can be liberating: a number of talents, thrown back on their own resources, begin to grow. The surrender of "commitment" can be damaging: some writers find themselves rattling about in a gray and chilly freedom. The culture opens up, with both temptation and generosity, and together with intellectual anxieties there are public rewards, often deserved. A period of dispersion; extreme oscillations in thought; and a turn in politics toward an increasingly conservative kind of liberalism—reflective, subtle, acquiescent.

The postwar years were marked by a sustained discussion of the new political and intellectual problems raised by the totalitarian state. Nothing in received political systems, neither Marxist nor liberal, adequately prepared one for the frightful mixture of terror and ideology, the capacity to sweep along the plebeian masses and organize a warfare state, and above all the readiness to destroy entire peoples, which characterized totalitarianism. Still less was anyone prepared—who had heeded the warning voices of the Russian socialist Martov or the English liberal Russell?—for the transformation of the revolutionary Bolshevik state, either through a "necessary" degeneration or an internal counterrevolution, into one of the major totalitarian powers. Marxist theories of Fascism—the "last stage" of capitalism, with the economy statified to organize a permanent war machine and mass terror employed to put down rebellious workers—came to seem, if not entirely mistaken, then certainly insufficient. The quasi- or pseudo-Leninist notion that "bourgeois democracy" was merely a veiled form of capitalist domination, no different in principle from its open dictatorship, proved to be a moral and political disaster. The assumption that socialism was an or-dained "next step," or that nationalization of industry constituted a sufficient basis for working-class rule, was as great a disaster. No wonder intellectual certainties were shattered and these years marked by frenetic improvisation! At every point, with the growth of Communist power in Europe and with the manu-facture of the Bomb at home, apocalypse seemed the face of to-morrow.

So much foolishness has been written about the New York intellectuals and their anti-Communism, either by those who have signed a separate peace with the authoritarian idea or those who lack the courage to defend what *is* defensible in their own past, that I want here to be both blunt and unyielding.

Given the enormous growth of Russian power after the war and the real possibility of a Communist take-over in Europe, the intellectuals—and not they alone—had to reconsider their political responses.* An old-style Marxist declaration of recti-tude, a plague repeated on both their houses? Or the difficult position of making foreign policy proposals for the United States, while maintaining criticism of its social order, so as to block to-

---

* Some recent historians, under New Left inspiration, have argued that in countries like France and Italy the possibility of a Communist seizure of power was really quite small. Perhaps; counterfactuals are hard to dispose of. What matters is the political consequences these historians would retro-spectively have us draw, if they were at all specific on this point. Was it erroneous, or reactionary, to believe that resistance had to be created in Europe against further Communist expansion? What attitude, for example, would they have had intellectuals, or anyone else, take during the Berlin crisis? Should the city, in the name of peace, have been yielded to the East Germans? Did the possibility of Communist victories in Western Europe require an extraordinary politics? And to what extent are present reconsiderations of Communist power in postwar Europe made possible by the fact that it was, in fact, successfully contained?

talitarian expansion without resort to war? Most intellectuals
decided they had to choose the second course, and they were
right.

Like anticapitalism, anti-Communism was a tricky politics, all
too open to easy distortion. Like anticapitalism, anti-Communism
could be put to the service of ideological racketeering and reaction. Just as ideologues of the fanatic right insisted that by
some ineluctable logic anticapitalism led to a Stalinist terror,
so ideologues of the authoritarian left, commandeering the same
logic, declared that anti-Communism led to the politics of
Dulles and Rusk. There is, of course, no "anticapitalism" or
"anti-Communism" in the abstract; these take on political flesh
only when linked with a larger body of programs and values, so
that it becomes clear what *kind* of "anticapitalism" or "anti-
Communism" we are dealing with. It is absurd, and indeed
disreputable, for intellectuals in the sixties to write as if there
were a unified "anti-Communism" which can be used to enclose
the views of everyone from William Buckley to Michael Harrington.

There were difficulties. A position could be worked out for
conditional support of the West when it defended Berlin or introduced the Marshall Plan or provided economic help to underdeveloped countries; but in the course of daily politics, in the
effort to influence the foreign policy of what remained a capitalist power, intellectuals could lose their independence and slip
into vulgarities of analysis and speech.

Painful choices had to be faced. When the Hungarian revolution broke out in 1956, most intellectuals sympathized strongly
with the rebels, yet feared that active intervention by the West
might provoke a world war. For a rational and humane mind,
anti-Communism could not be the sole motive, it could be only
one of several, in political behavior and policy; and even those
intellectuals who had by now swung a considerable distance to
the right did not advocate military intervention in Hungary.
There was simply no way out—as, more recently, there was none
in Czechoslovakia.

It became clear, furthermore, that United States military intervention in underdeveloped countries could help local reactionaries in the short run, and the Communists in the long run.
These difficulties were inherent in postwar politics, and they

ruled out—though for that very reason, also made tempting—a simplistic moralism. These difficulties were also exacerbated by the spread among intellectuals of a crude anti-Communism, often ready to justify whatever the United States might do at home and abroad. For a hard-line group within the American Committee for Cultural Freedom, all that seemed to matter in any strongly felt way was a sour hatred of the Stalinists, historically justifiable but more and more a political liability even in the fight against Stalinism. The dangers in such a politics now seem all too obvious, but I should note, for whatever we may mean by the record, that in the early fifties they were already being pointed out by a mostly unheeded minority of intellectuals around *Dissent.* Yet, with all these qualifications registered, the criticism to be launched against the New York intellectuals in the postwar years is not that they were strongly anti-Communist but, rather, that many of them, through disorientation or insensibility, allowed their anti-Communism to become something cheap and illiberal.

Nor is the main point of *moral* criticism that the intellectuals abandoned socialism. We have no reason to suppose that the declaration of a socialist opinion induces a greater humaneness than does acquiescence in liberalism. It could be argued (I would) that in the ease with which ideas of socialism were now brushed aside there was something shabby. It was undignified, at the very least, for people who had made so much of their Marxist credentials now to put to rest so impatiently the radicalism of their youth. Still, it might be said by some of the New York writers that reality itself had forced them to conclude socialism was no longer viable or had become irrelevant to the American scene, and that while this conclusion might be open to political argument, it was not to moral attack.

Let us grant that for a moment. What cannot be granted is that the shift in ideologies required or warranted the surrender of critical independence which was prevalent during the fifties. In the trauma—or relief—of ideological ricochet, all too many intellectuals joined the American celebration. It was possible, to cite but one of many instances, for Mary McCarthy to write: "Class barriers disappear or tend to become porous [in the U.S.]; the factory worker is an economic aristocrat in comparison with the middle-class clerk. . . . *The America* . . . *of vast inequalities and dramatic contrasts is rapidly ceasing to exist"* * (emphasis added). Because the New York writers all but surrendered their critical perspective on American society—*that* is why they were open to attack.** *

It was the growth of McCarthyism which brought most sharply into question the role of the intellectuals. Here, presumably, all men of good will could agree; here the interests of the intellectuals were beyond dispute and directly at stake. The record is not glorious. In New York circles it was often said that Bertrand Russell exaggerated wildly in describing the United States as "subject to a reign of terror" and that Simone de Beauvoir retailed Stalinist clichés in her reportage from America. Yet it should not be forgotten that, if not "a reign of terror," McCarthyism was frightful and disgusting, and that a number of Communists and fellow-travelers, not always carefully specified, suffered serious harm.

A magazine like *Partisan Review*, was, of course, opposed to McCarthy's campaign, but it failed to take the lead on the issue of freedom which might once again have imbued the intellectuals with fighting spirit. Unlike some of its New York counterparts, it did print sharp attacks on the drift toward conservatism, and it did not try to minimize the badness of the situation in the name of anti-Communism. But the magazine failed to speak out with enough force and persistence, or to break past the hedgings of those intellectuals who led the American Committee for Cultural Freedom.

---

* Fifteen years later, again swept along by the *Zeitgeist*, Miss McCarthy would write that the Communist societies, because of their concentration of ownership, made economic planning more feasible than did capitalist societies. She is perhaps the last intellectual in the world who seems not to have heard about the disasters of "planning" in totalitarian society (e.g., recent reports from Czechoslovakia).

** One such attack was an essay of mine, "This Age of Conformity," *Partisan Review*, 1954. Looking at it again I believe that, apart from some gratuitous polemical sentences, its main thrust still holds. No close, let alone sympathetic, analysis can be found in this essay as to why intellectuals now felt themselves so much more at home in capitalist society than they had in the thirties or why they felt themselves driven to an intransigent anti-Communism. I wrote as a polemicist, not as a historian or a sociologist of knowledge; and if that limited the scope it did not, I think, blunt the point of my attack.

Commentary, under Elliot Cohen's editorship, was still more inclined to minimize the threat of McCarthyism. In September 1952, at the very moment McCarthy became a central issue in the Presidential campaign, Cohen could write: "McCarthy remains in the popular mind an unreliable, second-string blowhard; his only support as a great national figure is from the fascinated fears of the intelligentsia"—a mode of argument all too close to that of the anti-anti-Communists who kept repeating that Communism was a serious problem only in the minds of anti-Communists.

In the American Committee for Cultural Freedom the increasingly conformist and conservative impulses of the New York intellectuals, or at least of a good number of them, found formal expression. I quote at length from Michael Harrington in a 1955 issue of *Dissent,* first because it says precisely what needs to be said and second because it has the value of contemporary evidence:

In practice the ACCF has fallen behind Sidney Hook's views on civil liberties. Without implying any "conspiracy" theory of history . . . one may safely say that it is Hook who has molded the decisive ACCF policies. His *Heresy Yes, Conspiracy No* articles were widely circulated by the Committee, which meant that in effect it endorsed his systematic, explicit efforts to minimize the threat to civil liberties and to attack those European intellectuals who, whatever their own political or intellectual deficiencies, took a dim view of American developments. Under the guidance of Hook and the leadership of Irving Kristol, who supported Hook's general outlook, the American Committee cast its weight not so much in defense of those civil liberties which were steadily being nibbled away, but rather against those few remaining fellow-travelers who tried to exploit the civil-liberties issue.

At times this had an almost comic aspect. When Irving Kristol was executive secretary of the ACCF, one learned to expect from him silence on those issues that were agitating the whole intellectual and academic world, and enraged communiqués on the outrages performed by people like Authur Miller and Bertrand Russell in exaggerating the dangers to civil liberties in the U.S.

Inevitably this led to more serious problems. In an article by Kristol, which first appeared in *Commentary* and was later circulated under the ACCF imprimatur, one could read such astonishing and appalling statements as "there is one thing the American people know about Senator McCarthy; he, like them, is unequivocally anti-Communist. About the spokesmen for American liberalism, they feel they know no such thing. And with some justification." This in the name of defending cultural freedom!

Harrington then proceeded to list several instances in which the ACCF had "acted within the United States in defense of freedom." But

these activities do not absorb the main attention or interest of the Committee; its leadership is too jaded, too imbued with the sourness of indiscriminate anti-Stalinism to give itself to an active struggle against the dominant trend of contemporary intellectual life in America. What it *really* cares about is a struggle against fellow-travelers and "neutralists"—that is, against many European intellectuals. . . .

One of the crippling assumptions of the Committee has been that it would not intervene in cases where Stalinists or accused Stalinists were involved. It has rested this position on the academic argument . . . that Stalinists, being enemies of democracy, have no "right" to democratic privileges. . . . But the actual problem is not the metaphysical one of whether enemies of democracy (as the Stalinists clearly are) have a "right" to democratic privileges. What matters is that the drive against cultural freedom and civil liberties takes on the guise of anti-Stalinism.

Years later came the revelations that the Congress for Cultural Freedom, which had its headquarters in Paris and with which the American Committee was for a time affiliated, had received secret funds from the CIA. Some of the people, it turned out, with whom one had sincerely disagreed were not free men at all; they were known accomplices of an intelligence service. What a sad denouement! And yet not the heart of the matter, as the malicious *Ramparts* journalists have tried to make out. Most of the intellectuals who belonged to the ACCF seem not to have had any knowledge of the CIA connection—on this, as on anything else, I would completely accept the word of Dwight Macdonald. It is also true, however, that these intellectuals seem not to have inquired very closely into the Congress's sources of support. That a few, deceiving their closest associates, established connections with the CIA was not nearly so important, however, as that a majority within the Committee acquiesced in a politics of acquiescence. We Americans have a strong taste for conspiracy theories, supposing that if you scratch a trouble you'll find a villain. But history is far more complicated; and squalid as the CIA tie was, it should not be used to smear honest people who had nothing to do with secret services even as they remain open to criticism for what they did say and do.

At the same time, the retrospective defenses offered by some New York intellectuals strike me as decidedly lame. Meetings and magazines sponsored by the Congress, Daniel Bell has said, kept their intellectual freedom and contained criticism of U.S. policy—true but hardly to the point, since the issue at stake is not the opinions the Congress tolerated but the larger problem of good faith in intellectual life. The leadership of the Congress did not give its own supporters the opportunity to choose whether they wished to belong to a CIA-financed group. Another defense, this one offered by Sidney Hook, is that private backing was hard to find during the years it was essential to publish journals like *Preuves* and *Encounter* in Europe. Simply as a matter of fact, I do not believe this. For the Congress to have raised its funds openly, from nongovernmental sources, would have meant discomfort, scrounging, penny-pinching: all the irksome things editors of little magazines have always had to do. By the postwar years, however, leading figures of both the Congress and the Committee no longer thought or behaved in that tradition.

Dwight Macdonald did. His magazine *Politics* was the one significant effort during the late forties to return to radicalism. Enlivened by Macdonald's ingratiating personality and his table-hopping mind, *Politics* brought together sophisticated muckraking with torturous revaluations of Marxist ideology. Macdonald could not long keep in balance the competing interests which finally tore apart his magazine: lively commentary on current affairs and unavoidable if depressing retrospects on the failure of the left. As always with Macdonald, honesty won out (one almost adds, alas) and the "inside" political discussion reached its climax with his essay "The Root Is Man," in which he arrived at a kind of anarcho-pacifism based on an absolutist morality. This essay was in many ways the most poignant and authentic expression of the plight of those few intellectuals—Nicola Chiaromonte, Paul Goodman, Macdonald—who wished to dissociate themselves from the postwar turn to *Realpolitik* but could not find ways of transforming sentiments of rectitude and visions of utopia into a workable politics. It was also a perfect leftist rationale for a kind of internal emigration of spirit and mind, with some odd shadings of similarity to the Salinger cult of the late fifties.*

The overwhelming intellectual drift, however, was toward the right. Arthur Schlesinger, Jr., with moony glances at Kierkegaard, wrote essays in which he maintained that American society had all but taken care of its economic problems and could now concentrate on raising its cultural level. The "end of ideology" became a favorite shield for intellectuals in retreat, though it was never entirely clear whether this phrase meant the end of "our" ideology (partly true) or that all ideologies were soon to disintegrate (not true) or that the time had come to abandon the nostalgia for ideology (at least debatable). And in the mid-fifties, as if to codify things, there appeared in *Partisan Review* a symposium, "Our Country and Our Culture," in which all but three or four of the thirty participants clearly moved away from their earlier radical views. The *rapprochement* with "America the Beautiful," as Mary McCarthy now called it in a tone not wholly ironic, seemed almost complete.

In these years there also began that series of gyrations in opinion, interest, and outlook—so frenetic, so unserious—which would mark our intellectual life. In place of the avant-garde idea we now had the *style of fashion,* though to suggest a mere replacement may be too simple, since as Poggioli remarks, fashion has often shadowed the avant-garde as a kind of dandified double. Some intellectuals turned to a weekend of religion, some to a semester of existentialism,** some to a holiday of Jewishness without faith or knowledge, some to a season of genteel conservatism.

---

* It is not clear whether Macdonald still adheres to "The Root Is Man." In a recent BBC broadcast he said about the student uprising at Columbia: "I don't approve of their methods, but Columbia will be a better place afterwards." Perhaps it will, perhaps it won't; but I don't see how the author of "The Root Is Man" could say this, since the one thing he kept insisting was that means could not be separated from ends, as the Marxists too readily separated them. He would surely have felt that if the means used by the students were objectionable, then their ends would be contaminated as well—and thereby the consequences of their action. But in the swinging sixties not many people troubled to remember their own lessons.

** The most lasting contribution this school of thought seems to have made to America is an adjective, as in "existential crisis," which communicates the sensation of depth without the burden of content.

Leslie Fiedler, no doubt by design, seemed to go through more of such episodes than anyone else: even his admirers could not always be certain whether he was *davenning* or doing a rain dance.

These twists and turns were lively, and they could all seem harmless if only one could learn to look upon intellectual life as a variety of play, like *potsie* or *king of the hill*. What struck one as troubling, however, was not this or that fashion (tomorrow morning would bring another), but the dynamic of fashion itself, the ruthlessness with which, to remain in fashion, fashion had to keep devouring itself.

It would be unfair to give the impression that the fifteen years after the war were without significant growth or achievement among the New York writers. The attempt of recent New Left ideologues to present the forties and fifties as if they were no more than a time of intellectual sterility and reaction is an oversimplification. Together with the turn toward conservative acquiescence, there were serious and valuable achievements. Hannah Arendt's book on totalitarianism may now seem open to many criticisms, but it certainly must rank as a major piece of work which, at the very least, made impossible—I mean, implausible—those theories of totalitarianism which, before and after she wrote, tended to reduce Fascism and Stalinism to a matter of class rule or economic interest. Daniel Bell's writing contributed to the rightward turn of these years, but some of it, such as his excellent little book *Work and Its Discontents*, constitutes a permanent contribution, and one that is valuable for radicals too. The stress upon complexity of thought which characterized intellectual life during these years could be used as a rationale for conservatism, and perhaps even arose from the turn toward conservatism; but in truth, the lapsed radicalism of earlier years *had* proved to be simplistic, the world of late capitalism *was* perplexing, and for serious people complexity *is* a positive value. Even the few intellectuals who resisted the dominant temper of the fifties underwent during these years significant changes in their political outlooks and styles of thought: e.g., those around *Dissent* who cut whatever ties of sentiment still held them to the Bolshevik tradition and made the indissoluble connection between democracy and socialism a crux of their thought. Much that happened during these years is to be deplored and dismissed, but not all was waste; the increasing sophistication and complication of mind was a genuine gain, and it would be absurd, at this late date, to forgo it.

In literary criticism there were equivalent achievements. The very instability that might make a shambles out of political thought could have the effect of magnifying the powers required for criticism. Floundering in life and uncertainty in thought could make for an increased responsiveness to art. In the criticism of men like Trilling, Rahv, Stuart Chase, and F. W. Dupee there was now a more authoritative relation to the literary text and a richer awareness of the cultural past than was likely to be found in their earlier work. And a useful tension was also set up between the New York critics, whose instinctive response to literature was through a social-moral contextualism, and the New Critics, whose formalism may have been too rigid yet proved of great value to those who opposed it.

Meanwhile, the world seemed to be opening up, with all its charms, seductions, and falsities. In the thirties the life of the New York writers had been confined: the little magazine as island, the radical sect as cave. Partly they were recapitulating the pattern of immigrant Jewish experience: an ingathering of the flock in order to break out into the world and taste the Gentile fruits of status and success. Once it became clear that waiting for the revolution might turn out to be steady work and that the United States would neither veer to Fascism nor sink into depression, the intellectuals had little choice but to live within (which didn't necessarily mean, become partisans of) the existing society.

There was money to be had from publishers, no great amounts, but more than in the past. There were jobs in the universities, even for those without degrees. Some writers began to discover that publishing a story in *The New Yorker* or *Esquire* was not a sure ticket to Satan; others to see that the academy, while perhaps less exciting than the Village, wasn't invariably a graveyard for intellect and might even provide the only harbor in which serious people could do their own writing and perform honorable work. This dispersion involved losses, but usually there was nothing sinister about it—unless one clung, past an appropriate age, to the fantasy of being a momentarily unemployed "profes-

sional revolutionist." Writers ought to know something about the
world; they ought to test their notions against the reality of the
country in which they live. Worldly involvements would, of
course, bring risks, and one of these was power, really a very
trifling kind of power, but still enough to raise the fear of corruption. That power corrupts everyone knows by now, but we
ought also to recognize that powerlessness, if not corrupting, can
be damaging—as in the case of Paul Goodman, a courageous
writer who stuck to his anarchist beliefs through years in which
he was mocked and all but excluded from the New York journals, yet who could also come to seem, in his very rectitude, an
example of asphyxiating righteousness.

What brought about these changes? Partly ideological adaptation, a feeling that capitalist society was here to stay and there
wasn't much point in maintaining a radical position or posture.
Partly the sly workings of prosperity. But also a loosening of the
society itself, the start of that process which only now is in full
swing—I mean the remarkable absorptiveness of modern society,
its readiness to abandon traditional precepts for a moment of
excitement, its growing permissiveness toward social criticism,
perhaps out of indifference, or security, or even tolerance.

In the sixties well-placed young professors and radical students would denounce the "success," sometimes the "sellout," of
the New York writers. Their attitude reminds one a little of
George Orwell's remark about wartime France: only a Pétain
could afford the luxury of asceticism, ordinary people had to live
by the necessities of materialism. But really, when you come to
think of it, what did this "success" of the intellectuals amount to?
A decent or a good job, a chance to earn extra money by working hard, and in the case of a few, like Trilling and Kazin, some
fame beyond New York—rewards most European intellectuals
would take for granted, so paltry would they seem. For the New
York writers who lived through the thirties expecting never to
have a job at all, a regular pay check might be remarkable; but
in the American scale of things it was very modest indeed. And
what the "leftist" prigs of the sixties, sons of psychiatrists and
manufacturers, failed to understand—or perhaps understood only
too well—was that the "success" with which they kept scaring
themselves was simply one of the possibilities of adult life, a
possibility, like failure, heavy with moral risks and disappoint-

ment. Could they imagine that they, too, might have to face the common lot? I mean the whole business: debts, overwork, varicose veins, alimony, drinking, quarrels, hemorrhoids, depletion, the recognition that one might prove not to be another T. S. Eliot, but also some good things, some lessons learned, some "rags of time" salvaged and precious.

Here and there you could find petty greed or huckstering, now and again a drop into opportunism; but to make much of this would be foolish. Common clay, the New York writers had their share of common ambition. What drove them, and sometimes drove them crazy, was not, however, the quest for money, nor even a chance to "mix" with White House residents; it was finally, when all the trivia of existence were brushed aside, a gnawing ambition to write something, even three pages, that might live.

The intellectuals should have regarded their entry into the outer world as utterly commonplace, at least if they kept faith with the warning of Stendhal and Balzac that one must always hold a portion of the self forever beyond the world's reach. Few of the New York intellectuals made much money on books and articles. Few reached audiences beyond the little magazines. Few approached any centers of power, and precisely the buzz of gossip attending the one or two sometimes invited to a party beyond the well-surveyed limits of the West Side showed how confined their life still was. What seems most remarkable in retrospect is the innocence behind the assumption, sometimes held by the New York writers themselves with a nervous mixture of guilt and glee, that whatever recognition they won was cause for either preening or embarrassment. For all their gloss of sophistication, they had not really moved very far into the world. The immigrant milk was still on their lips.

In their published work during these years, the New York intellectuals developed a characteristic style of exposition and polemic. With some admiration and a bit of irony, let us call it the style of brilliance. The kind of essay they wrote was likely to be wide-ranging in reference, melding notions about literature and politics, sometimes announcing itself as a study of a writer or literary group but usually taut with a pressure to "go beyond" its subject, toward some encompassing moral or social observation. It is a kind of writing highly self-conscious in mode, with an unashamed vibration of bravura and display. Nervous, strewn with knotty or flashy phrases, impatient with transitions and other concessions to dullness, willfully calling attention to itself as a form or at least an outcry, fond of rapid twists, taking pleasure in dispute, dialectic, dazzle—such, at its best or most noticeable, was the essay cultivated by the New York writers. Until recently its strategy of exposition was likely to be impersonal (the writer did not speak much as an "I") but its tone and bearing were likely to be intensely personal (the audience was to be made aware that the aim of the piece was not judiciousness but rather a strong impress of attitude, a blow of novelty, a wrenching of accepted opinion, sometimes a mere indulgence of vanity).

In most of these essays there was a sense of *tournament,* the writer as gymnast with one eye on other rings, or as skilled infighter juggling knives of dialectic. Polemics were harsh, often rude. And audiences nurtured, or spoiled, on this kind of performance, learned not to form settled judgments about a dispute until all sides had registered their blows: surprise was always a possible reward.

This style may have brought new life to the American essay, but in contemporary audiences it often evoked a strong distaste and even fear. "Ordinary" readers could be left with the fretful sense that they were not "in," the beauties of polemic racing past their sluggish eye. Old-line academics, quite as if they had just crawled out of *The Dunciad,* enjoyed dismissing the New York critics as "unsound." And for some younger souls, the cliffs of dialectic seemed too steep. Seymour Krim has left a poignant account of his disablement before "the overcerebral, Europeanish, sterilely citified, pretentiously alienated" New York intellectuals. Resentful at the fate which drove them to compare themselves with "the overcerebral, etc., etc.," Krim writes that he and his friends "were often tortured and unappeasably bitter about being the offspring of this unhappily unique-ingrown-screwed-up breed." Similar complaints could be heard from other writers and would-be writers who felt that New York intellectualism threatened their vital powers.

At its best the style of brilliance reflected a certain view of the intellectual life: free-lance dash, peacock strut, daring hypothesis, knockabout synthesis. For better or worse it was radically different from the accepted modes of scholarly publishing and middle-brow journalism. It celebrated the idea of the intellectual as antispecialist, or as a writer whose speciality was the lack of a speciality: the writer as dilettante-connoisseur, *Luftmensch* of the mind, roamer among theories. But it was a style which also lent itself with peculiar ease to a stifling mimicry and decadence. Sometimes it seemed—no doubt mistakenly—as if any sophomore, indeed any parrot, could learn to write one of those scintillating *Partisan* reviews, so thoroughly could manner consume matter. In the fifties the cult of brilliance became a sign that writers were offering not their work or ideas but their persona as content; and this was but a step or two away from the exhibitionism of the sixties. Brilliance could become a sign of intellect unmoored: the less assurance, the more pyrotechnics. In making this judgment I ought to register the view that serious writers may prove to be brilliant and take pleasure in the proving, but insofar as they are serious, their overriding aim must be absolute lucidity.

If to the minor genre of the essay the New York writers made a major contribution, to the major genres of fiction and poetry they made only a minor contribution. As a literary group and no more than a literary group, they will seem less important than, say, the new critics, who did set in motion a whole school of poetry. A few poets—John Berryman, Robert Lowell, Randall Jarrell, perhaps Stanley Kunitz—have been influenced by the New York intellectuals, though in ways hard to specify and hardly comprising a major pressure on their work: all were finished writers by the time they brushed against the New York milieu. For one or two poets, the influence of New York meant becoming aware of the cultural pathos resident in the idea of the Jew (not always distinguished from the idea of Delmore Schwartz). But the main literary contribution of the New York milieu has been to legitimate a subject and tone we must uneasily call American Jewish writing. The fiction of urban malaise, second-generation complaint, Talmudic dazzle, woeful alienation, and dialectical irony, all found its earliest expression in the pages of *Commentary* and *Partisan Review*—fiction in which the Jewish world is not merely regained in memory as a point of beginnings, an archetypal Lower East Side of spirit and place, but is also treated as a portentous metaphor of man's homelessness and wandering.

Such distinguished short fictions as Bellow's *Seize the Day,* Schwartz's "In Dreams Begin Responsibility," Mailer's "The Man Who Studied Yoga," and Malamud's "The Magic Barrel" seem likely to survive the cultural moment in which they were written. And even if one concludes that these and similar pieces are not enough to warrant speaking of a major literary group, they certainly form a notable addition—a new tone, a new sensibility—to American writing. In time, these writers may be regarded as the last "regional" group in American literature, parallel to recent Southern writers in both sophistication of craft and a thematic dissociation from the values of American society. Nor is it important that during the last few decades both of these literary tendencies, the Southern and the Jewish, have been overvalued. The distance of but a few years has already made it clear that except for Faulkner Southern writing consists of a scatter of talented minor poets and novelists; and in a decade or so a similar judgment may be commonly accepted about most of the Jewish writers—though in regard to Bellow and Mailer settled opinions are still risky.

What is clear from both Southern and Jewish writing is that in a society increasingly disturbed about its lack of self-definition, the recall of regional and traditional details can be intensely absorbing in its own right, as well as suggestive of larger themes transcending the region. (For the Jewish writers New York was not merely a place, it was a symbol, a burden, a stamp of history.) Yet the writers of neither school have thus far managed to move from their particular milieu to a grasp of the entire culture; the very strengths of their localism define their limitations; and especially is this true for the Jewish writers, in whose behalf critics have recently overreached themselves. The effort to transform a Jewishness without religious or ethnic content into an emblem of universal dismay can easily lapse into sentimentality.

Whatever the hopeful future of individual writers, the "school" of American Jewish writing is by now in an advanced state of decomposition: how else explain the attention it has lately enjoyed? Or the appearance of a generation of younger Jewish writers who, without authentic experience or memory to draw upon, manufacture fantasies about the lives of their grand-fathers? Or the popularity of Isaac Bashevis Singer who, coming to the American literary scene precisely at the moment when writers composing in English had begun to exhaust the Jewish subject, could, by dazzling contrast, extend it endlessly backward in time and deeper in historical imagination?

Just as there appear today young Jewish intellectuals who no longer know what it is that as Jews they do not know, so in fiction the fading immigrant world offers a thinner and thinner yield to writers of fiction. It no longer presses on memory, people can now *choose* whether to care about it. We are almost at the end of a historic experience, and it now seems unlikely that there will have arisen in New York a literary school comparable to the best this country has had. Insofar as the New York intellectual atmosphere has affected writers like Schwartz, Rosenfeld, Bellow, Malamud, Mailer, Goodman, and Roth (some of these would hotly deny that it has), it seems to have been too brittle, too contentious, too insecure for major creative work. What cannot yet be estimated is the extent to which the styles and values of the New York world may have left a mark on the work of American writers who never came directly under its influence or have been staunchly hostile to all of its ways.

Thinking back upon intellectual life in the forties and fifties, and especially the air of malaise that hung over it, I find myself turning to a theme as difficult to clarify as it is impossible to evade. And here, for a few paragraphs, let me drop the porous shield of impersonality and speak openly in the first person.

We were living directly after the holocaust of the European Jews. We might scorn our origins; we might crush America with discoveries of ardor; we might change our names. But we knew that but for an accident of geography we might also now be bars of soap. At least some of us could not help feeling that in our earlier claims to have shaken off all ethnic distinctiveness there had been something false, something shaming. Our Jewishness might have no clear religious or national content, it might be helpless before the criticism of believers; but Jews we were, like it or not, and liked or not.

To recognize that we were living after one of the greatest and least explicable catastrophes of human history, and one for which we could not claim to have adequately prepared ourselves either as intellectuals or as human beings, brought a new rush of feelings, mostly unarticulated and hidden behind the scrim of consciousness. It brought a low-charged but nagging guilt, a quiet remorse. Sartre's brilliant essay on authentic and inauthentic Jews left a strong mark. Hannah Arendt's book on totalitarianism had an equally strong impact, mostly because it offered a coherent theory, or at least a coherent picture of the concentration camp universe. We could no longer escape the conviction that, blessing or curse, Jewishness was an integral part of our life, even if—and perhaps just because—there was nothing we could do or say about it. Despite a few simulated seders and literary raids on Hasidism, we could not turn back to the synagogue; we could only express our irritation with "the community" which kept nagging us like disappointed mothers; and sometimes we tried, through imagination and recall, to put together a few bits and pieces of the world of our fathers. I cannot prove a connection between the holocaust and the turn to Jewish themes in American fiction, at first urgent and quizzical, later fashionable and manipulative. I cannot prove that my own turn to Yiddish literature during the fifties was due to the shock following the war years. But it would be foolish to scant the possibility.

The violent dispute which broke out among the New York intellectuals when Hannah Arendt published her book on Eichmann had as one of its causes a sense of guilt concerning the Jewish tragedy—a guilt pervasive, unmanageable, yet seldom declared at the surface of speech or act. In the quarrel between those attacking and those defending *Eichmann in Jerusalem* there were polemical excesses on both sides, insofar as both were acting out of unacknowledged passions. Yet even in the debris of this quarrel there was, I think, something good. At least everyone was acknowledging emotions that had long gone unused. Nowhere else in American academic and intellectual life was there such ferocity of concern with the problems raised by Hannah Arendt. If left to the rest of the American intellectual world, her book would have been praised as "stimulating" and "thoughtful," and then everyone would have gone back to sleep. Nowhere else in the country could there have been the kind of public forum sponsored on this subject by *Dissent*: a debate sometimes ugly and outrageous, yet also urgent and afire—evidence that in behalf of ideas we were still ready to risk personal relationships. After all, it had never been dignity that we could claim as our strong point.

Nothing about the New York writers is more remarkable than the sheer fact of their survival. In a country where tastes in culture change more rapidly than lengths of skirts, they have succeeded in maintaining a degree of influence, as well as a distinctive milieu, for more than thirty years. Apart from reasons intrinsic to the intellectual life, let me note a few that are somewhat more worldly in nature.

There is something, perhaps a quasi-religious dynamism, about an ideology, even a lapsed ideology that everyone says has reached its end, which yields force and coherence to those who have closely experienced it. A lapsed Catholic has tactical advantages in his apostasy which a lifelong skeptic does not have. And just as Christianity kept many nineteenth-century writers going long after they had discarded religion, so Marxism gave bite and edge to the work of twentieth-century writers long after they had turned from socialism.

The years in which the New York writers gained some prominence were those in which the style at which they had arrived—irony, ambiguity, complexity, the problematic as mode of knowledge—took on a magnified appeal for the American educated classes. After World War II the cultivation of private sensibility and personal responsibility were values enormously popular among reflective people, to whom the very thought of public life smacked of betrayal and vulgarity.

An intelligentsia flourishes in a capital: Paris, St. Petersburg, Berlin. The influence of the New York writers grew at the time New York itself, for better or worse, became the cultural center of the country. And thereby, to return to Poggioli's categories, the New York writers slowly shed the characteristics of an intelligentsia and transformed themselves into—

An Establishment?

Perhaps. But what precisely *is* an Establishment? Vaguely sinister in its overtones, the term is used these days with gay abandon on the American campus; but except as a spread-eagle put-down it has no discernible meaning, and if accepted as a put-down, the problem then becomes to discover who, if anyone, is not in the Establishment. In England the term has had a certain clarity of usage, referring to an intellectual elite which derives from the same upper and middle classes as the men who wield political power and which shares with these men Oxbridge education and Bloomsbury culture. But except in F. R. Leavis's angrier tirades, "Establishment" does not bear the conspiratorial overtones we are inclined to credit in this country. What it does in England is to locate the social-cultural stratum guiding the tastes of the classes in power and thereby crucially affecting the tastes of the country as a whole.

In this sense, neither the New York writers nor any other group can be said to comprise an American Establishment, simply because no one in this country has ever commanded an equivalent amount of cultural power. The New York writers have few, if any, connections with a stable class of upper-rank civil servants or with a significant segment of the rich. They are notably without connections in Washington. They do not shape official or dominant tastes. And they cannot exert the kind of control over cultural opinion that the London Establishment is said to have maintained until recently. Critics like Trilling and Kazin are listened to by people in publishing, Rosenberg and Greenberg by people in the art world; but this hardly constitutes anything so formidable as an Establishment. Indeed, at the very time mutterings have been heard about a New York literary Establishment, there has occurred a rapid disintegration of whatever group ties may still have remained among the New York writers. They lack—and it is just as well—the first requirement for an Establishment: that firm sense of internal discipline which enables it to impose its values and tastes on a large public.

During the last few years the talk about a New York Establishment has taken an extremely unpleasant turn. Whoever does a bit of lecturing about the country is likely to encounter, after a few drinks, literary academics who inquire enviously, sometimes spitefully, about "what's new in New York." Such people seem to feel that exile in outlying regions means they are missing something remarkable (and so they are: the Balanchine company). The cause of their cultural envy is, I think, a notion that has become prevalent in our English departments that scholarship is somehow unworthy and the "real" literary life is to be found in the periodical journalism of New York. Intrinsically this is a dubious notion and for the future of American education, a disastrous one; when directed against the New York writers it leads to some painful situations. As polite needling questions are asked about the cultural life of New York, a rise of sweat comes to one's brow, for everyone knows what no one says: New York means Jews.*

Whatever the duration or extent of the influence enjoyed by the New York intellectuals, it is now reaching an end. There are signs of internal disarray: unhealed wounds, a dispersal of interests, the damage of time. More important, however, is the appearance these last few years of a new and powerful challenge to the New York writers. And here I shall have to go off on what may appear to be a long digression, since one cannot understand the present situation of the New York writers without taking into detailed account the cultural-political scene of America in the late sixties.

There is a rising younger generation of intellectuals: ambitious, self-assured, at ease with prosperity while conspicuously alienated, unmarred by the traumas of the totalitarian age, bored with memories of defeat, and attracted to the idea of power. This generation matters, thus far, not so much for its leading figures and their meager accomplishments, but for the political-cultural style—what I shall call the new sensibility—it thrusts into absolute opposition both to the New York writers and to other groups. It claims not to seek penetration into, or accommodation with, our cultural and academic institutions; it fancies the prospect of a harsh generational fight; and given the premise with which it begins—that everything touched by older men reeks of betrayal—its claims and fancies have a sort of propriety. It proposes a revolution, I would call it a counterrevolution, in sensibility. Though linked to New Left politics, it goes beyond any politics, making itself felt, like a spreading blot of anti-intellectualism, in every area of intellectual life. Not yet fully cohered, this new cultural group cannot yet be fully defined, nor

---

* Not quite no one. In an attack on the New York writers (*Hudson Review,* Autumn 1965) Richard Kostelanetz speaks about "Jewish group-aggrandizement" and "the Jewish American push." One appreciates the delicacy of his phrasing.

is it possible fully to describe its projected sensibility, since it declares itself through a refusal of both coherence and definition.

There is no need to discuss once more the strengths and weaknesses of the New Left, its moral energies and intellectual muddles. Nor need we be concerned with the tactical issues separating New Left politics from that of older left-wing intellectuals. Were nothing else at stake than, say, "coalition politics," the differences would be both temporary and tolerable. But in reality a deeper divergence of outlook has begun to show itself. The new intellectual style, insofar as it approximates a politics, mixes sentiments of anarchism with apologies for authoritarianism; bubbling hopes for "participatory democracy" with manipulative elitism; unqualified Populist majoritarianism with the reign of the cadres.

A confrontation of intellectual outlooks is unavoidable. And a central issue is certain to be the problem of liberalism, not liberalism as one or another version of current politics, nor even as a theory of power, but liberalism as a cast of mind, a structure of norms by means of which to humanize public life. For those of us who have lived through the age of totalitarianism and experienced the debacle of socialism, this conflict over liberal values is extremely painful. We have paid heavily for the lesson that democracy, even "bourgeois democracy," is a precious human achievement, one that, far from being simply a mode of mass manipulation, has been wrested through decades of struggle by the labor, socialist, and liberal movements. To protect the values of liberal democracy, often against those who call themselves liberals, is an elementary task for the intellectuals as a social group.

Yet what I have just been saying, axiomatic as it may seem, has in the last few years aroused opposition, skepticism, open contempt among professors, students, and intellectuals. On the very crudest, though by no means unpopular, level, we find a vulgarization of an already vulgar Marxism. The notion that we live in a society that can be described as "liberal Fascism" (a theoretic contribution from certain leaders of the Students for a Democratic Society) isn't one that serious people can take seriously; but the fact that it is circulated in the academic community signifies a counterrevolution of the mind: a refusal of nuance and observation, a willed return to the kind of political primitivism which used to declare the distinctions of bourgeois rule—democratic, authoritarian, totalitarian—as slight in importance.

For the talk about "liberal Fascism" men like Norman Mailer must bear a heavy responsibility, insofar as they have recklessly employed the term "totalitarian" as a descriptive for present-day American society. Having lived through the ghastliness of the Stalinist theory of "Social Fascism" (the granddaddy of "liberal Fascism") I cannot suppose any literate person really accepts this kind of nonsense, yet I know that people can find it politically expedient to pretend that they do. It is, in Ernst Nolte's phrase, "a lie which the intellect sees for what it is but which is [felt to be] at one with the deeper motivations of life."

There are sophisticated equivalents. One of these points to the failings and crises of democracy, concluding that the content of decision has been increasingly separated from the forms of decision-making. Another emphasizes the manipulation of the masses by communication media and declares them brainwashed victims incapable of rational choice and acquiescing in their own subjugation. A third decries the bureaucratic entanglements of the political process and favors some version, usually more sentiment than scheme, for direct plebiscitary rule. With varying intelligence, all point to acknowledged problems of democratic society; and there could be no urgent objection were these criticisms not linked with the premise that the troubles of democracy can be overcome by undercutting or bypassing representative institutions. Thus, it is quite true that the masses are manipulated, but to make that the crux of a political analysis is to lead into the notion that elections are mere "formalities" and majorities mere tokens of the inauthentic; what is needed, instead, is Marcuse's "educational dictatorship" (in which, I hope, at least some of the New York intellectuals would require the most prolonged re-education). And in a similar vein, all proposals for obligatory or pressured "participation," apart from violating the democratic right not to participate, have a way of discounting those representative institutions and limitations upon power which can alone provide a degree of safeguard for liberal norms.

Perhaps the most sophisticated and currently popular of antidemocratic notions is that advanced by Herbert Marcuse: his

contempt for tolerance on the ground that it is a veil for sub-
jection, a rationale for maintaining the *status quo,* and his consequent readiness to suppress "regressive" elements of the population lest they impede social "liberation." About these theories,
which succeed in salvaging the worst of Leninism, Henry David
Aiken has neatly remarked: "Whether garden-variety liberties
can survive the ministrations of such 'liberating tolerance' is not
a question that greatly interests Marcuse." Indeed not.

Such theories are no mere academic indulgence or sectarian
irrelevance; they have been put to significant use on the American campus as rationalizations for breaking up meetings of political opponents and as the justification for imaginary *coups d'état*
by tiny minorities of enraged intellectuals. How depressing that
"men of the left," themselves so often victims of repression,
should attack the values of tolerance and freedom.*

These differences concerning liberal norms run very deep and
are certain to affect American intellectual life in the coming
years; yet they do not quite get to the core of the matter. In the
Kulturkampf now emerging there are issues more consequential
than the political ones, issues that have to do with basic views
concerning the nature of human life.

One of these has been with us for a long time, and trying now
to put it into simple language, I feel a measure of uneasiness, as
if it were bad form to violate the tradition of antinomianism in
which we have all been raised.

---

* That Marcuse chooses not to apply his theories to the area of society in
which he himself functions is a tribute to his personal realism, or perhaps
merely a sign of a lack of intellectual seriousness. In a recent public discussion, recorded by the *New York Times Magazine* (May 26, 1968),
there occurred the following exchange:

Hentoff: We've been talking about new institutions, new structures, as the
only way to get fundamental change. What would that mean to you, Mr.
Marcuse, in terms of the university, in terms of Columbia?

Marcuse: I was afraid of that because I now finally reveal myself as a fink.
I have never suggested or advocated or supported destroying the established universities and building new anti-institutions instead. I have always
said that no matter how radical the demands of the students and no matter
how justified, they should be pressed within the existing universities. . . .
I believe—and this is where the finkdom comes in—that American universities, at least quite a few of them, today are still enclaves of relatively
critical thought and relatively free thought.

What, for "emancipated" people, is the surviving role of moral imperatives, or at least moral recommendations? Do these retain for us a shred of sanctity or at least of coercive value? The question to which I am moving is not, of course, whether the moral life is desirable or men should try to live it; no, the question has to do with the provenance and defining conditions of the moral life. Do moral principles continue to signify insofar as and if they come into conflict with spontaneous impulses, and more urgently still, can we conceive of moral principles retaining some validity if they do come into conflict with spontaneous impulses? Are we still to give credit to the idea, one of the few meeting points between traditional Christianity and modern Freudianism, that there occurs and must occur a deep-seated clash between instinct and civilization, nature and nurture, or can we now, with a great sigh of collective relief, dismiss this as still another hangup, perhaps the supreme hangup, of Western civilization?

For more than one hundred and fifty years there has been a line of Western thought, as also of sentiment in modern literature, which calls into question not one or another moral commandment or regulation, but the very idea of commandment and regulation; which insists that the ethic of control, like the ethic of work, should be regarded as spurious, a token of a centuries-long heritage of repression. Sometimes this view comes to us as a faint residue of Christian heresy, more recently as the blare of Nietzschean prophecy, and in our own day as a psychoanalytic gift.

Now, even those of us raised on the premise of revolt against received values, against the whole system of bourgeois constriction and antipleasure, did not—I suppose it had better be said outright—imagine ourselves to be exempt from the irksome necessity of regulation, even if we had managed to escape the reach of the commandments. Neither primitive Christians nor romantic naïfs, we did not suppose that we could entrust ourselves entirely to the beneficence of nature, or the signals of our bodies, as a sufficient guide to conduct. (My very use of the word "conduct," freighted as it is with normative associations, puts the brand of time on what I am saying.)

By contrast, the emerging new sensibility rests on a vision of innocence: an innocence through lapse or will or recovery, an innocence through a refusal of our and perhaps any other culture, an innocence not even to be preceded by the withering away of the state, since in this view of things the state could wither away only if men learned so to be at ease with their desires, all need for regulation would fade. This is a vision of life beyond good and evil, not because these experiences or possibilities of experience have been confronted and transcended, but because the categories by which we try to designate them have been dismissed. There is no need to taste the apple: the apple brings health to those who know how to bite it: and look more closely, there is no apple at all, it exists only in your sickened imagination.

The new sensibility posits a theory that might be called *the psychology of unobstructed need*: men should satisfy those needs which are theirs, organic to their bodies and psyches, and to do this they now must learn to discard or destroy all those obstructions, mostly the result of cultural neurosis, which keep them from satisfying their needs. This does not mean that the moral life is denied; it only means that in the moral economy costs need not be entered as a significant item. In the current vocabulary, it becomes a matter of everyone doing "his own thing," and once all of us are allowed to do "his own thing," a prospect of easing harmony unfolds. Sexuality is the ground of being, and vital sexuality the assurance of the moral life.

Whether this outlook is compatible with a high order of culture or a complex civilization I shall not discuss here; Freud thought they were not compatible, though that does not foreclose the matter. More immediately, and on a less exalted plane, one is troubled by the following problem: what if the needs and impulses of human beings clash, as they seem to do, and what if the transfer of energies from sexuality to sociality does not proceed with the anticipated abundance and smoothness? The new sensibility, as displayed in the writings of Norman Brown and Norman Mailer, falls back upon a curious analogue to *laissez-faire* economics, Adam Smith's invisible hand, by means of which innumerable units in conflict with one another achieve a resultant of co-operation. Is there, however, much reason to suppose that this will prove more satisfactory in the economy of moral conduct than it has in the morality of economic relations?

Suppose that, after reading Mailer's "The White Negro," my

"thing" happens to be that, to "dare the unknown" (as Mailer puts it), I want to beat in the brains of an aging candy-store keeper; or after reading LeRoi Jones, I should like to cut up a few Jews, whether or not they keep stores—how is anyone going to argue against the outpouring of my need? Who will declare himself its barrier? Against me, against my ideas it is possible to argue, but how, according to this new dispensation, can anyone argue against my *need*? Acting through violence I will at least have realized myself, for I will have entered (to quote Mailer again) "a new relation with the police" and introduced "a dangerous element" into my life; thereby, too, I will have escaped the cell block of regulation which keeps me from the free air of self-determination. And if you now object that this very escape may lead to brutality, you reveal yourself as hopelessly linked to imperfection and original sin. For why should anyone truly heeding his nature wish to kill or wound or do anything but love and make love? That certain spokesmen of the new sensibility seem to be boiling over with fantasies of blood, or at least suppose that a verbal indulgence in such fantasies is a therapy for the boredom in their souls, is a problem for dialecticians. And as for skeptics, what have they to offer but evidence from history, that European contamination?

When it is transposed to a cultural setting, this psychology—in earlier times it would have been called a moral psychology—provokes a series of disputes over "complexity" in literature. Certain older critics find much recent writing distasteful and tiresome because it fails to reach or grasp for that complexity which they regard as intrinsic to the human enterprise. More indulgent critics, not always younger, find the same kind of writing forceful, healthy, untangled. At first this seems a mere problem in taste, a pardonable difference between those who like their poems and novels knotty and those who like them smooth; but soon it becomes clear that this clash arises from a meeting of incompatible world outlooks. For if the psychology of unobstructed need is taken as a sufficient guide to life, it all but eliminates any need for complexity—or rather, the need for complexity comes to be seen as a mode of false consciousness, an evasion of true feelings, a psychic bureaucratism in which to trap the pure and the strong. If good sex signifies good feeling; good feeling, good being; good being, good action; and good action, a healthy polity, then we have come the long way round, past the Reichian way or the Lawrentian way, to an Emersonian romanticism minus Emerson's complicatedness of vision. The world snaps back into a system of burgeoning potentialities, waiting for free spirits to attach themselves to the richness of natural object and symbol—except that now the orgasmic blackout is to replace the Oversoul as the current through which pure transcendent energies will flow.

We are confronting, then, a new phase in our culture, which in motive and spring represents a wish to shake off the bleeding heritage of modernism and reinstate one of those periods of the collective naïf which seem endemic to American experience. The new sensibility is impatient with ideas. It is impatient with literary structures of complexity and coherence, only yesterday the catchwords of our criticism. It wants instead works of literature —though literature may be the wrong word—that will be as absolute as the sun, as unarguable as orgasm, and as delicious as a lollipop. It schemes to throw off the weight of nuance and ambiguity, legacies of high consciousness and tired blood. It is weary of the habit of reflection, the making of distinctions, the squareness of dialectic, the tarnished gold of inherited wisdom. It cares nothing for the haunted memories of old Jews. It has no taste for the ethical nail-biting of those writers of the left who suffered defeat and could never again accept the narcotic of certainty. It is sick of those magnifications of irony that Mann gave us, sick of those visions of entrapment to which Kafka led us, sick of those shufflings of daily horror and grace that Joyce left us. It breathes contempt for rationality, impatience with mind, and a hostility to the artifices and decorums of high culture. It despises liberal values, liberal cautions, liberal virtues. It is bored with the past: for the past is a fink.

Where Marx and Freud were diggers of intellect, mining deeper and deeper into society and the psyche, and forever determined to strengthen the dominion of reason, today the favored direction of search is not inward but sideways, an "expansion of consciousness" through the kick of drugs. The new sensibility is drawn to images of sickness, but not, as with the modernist masters, out of dialectical canniness or religious blasphemy; it takes their denials literally and does not even know the complex desperations that led them to deny. It seeks to charge itself into dazzling sentience through chemicals and the rhetoric of violence. It gropes for sensations: the innocence of blue, the ejaculations of red. It *ordains* life's simplicity. It chooses surfaces as against relationships, the skim of texture rather than the weaving of pattern. Haunted by boredom, it transforms art into a sequence of shocks which, steadily magnified, yield fewer and fewer thrills, so that simply to maintain a modest *frisson* requires mounting exertions. It proposes an art as disposable as a paper dress, to which one need give nothing but a flicker of notice. Especially in the theater it resurrects tattered heresies, trying to collapse aesthetic distance in behalf of touch and frenzy. (But if illusion is now worn out, what remains but staging the realities of rape, fellatio, and murder?) Cutting itself off from a knowledge of what happened before the moment of its birth, it repeats with a delighted innocence most of what did in fact happen: expressionist drama reduced to skit, agit-prop tumbled to farce, Melvillean anguish slackened to black humor. It devalues the word, which is soaked up with too much past history, and favors monochromatic cartoons, companionate grunts, and glimpses of the ineffable in popular ditties. It has humor, but not much wit. Of the tragic it knows next to nothing. Where Dostoevsky made nihilism seem sinister by painting it in jolly colors, the new American sensibility does something no other culture could have aspired to: it makes nihilism seem casual, good-natured, even innocent. No longer burdened by the idea of the problematic, it arms itself with the paraphernalia of postindustrial technique and crash-dives into a Typee of neo-primitivism.

Its high priests are Norman Brown, Herbert Marcuse, and Marshall McLuhan,* all writers with a deeply conservative bias:

---

* John Simon has some cogent things to say about Brown and McLuhan, the pop poppas of the new: ". . . like McLuhan, Brown fulfills the four requirements for our prophets: (1) to span and reconcile, however grotesquely, various disciplines to the relief of a multitude of specialists; (2) to affirm something, even if it is something negative, retrogressive, mad; (3) to justify something vulgar or sick or indefensible in us, whether it be television-addiction (McLuhan) or schizophrenia (Brown); (4) to abolish the need for discrimination, difficult choices, balancing mind and appetite,

all committed to a stasis of the given: the stasis of unmoving instinct, the stasis of unmovable society, the stasis of endlessly moving technology. Classics of the latest thing, these three figures lend the new sensibility an aura of profundity. Their prestige can be employed to suggest an organic link between cultural modernism and the new sensibility, though in reality their relation to modernism is no more than biographical.

Perhaps because it is new, some of the new style has its charms—mainly along the margins of social life, in dress, music, and slang. In that it captures the yearnings of a younger generation, the new style has more than charm: a vibration of moral desire, a desire for goodness of heart. Still, we had better not deceive ourselves. Some of those shiny-cheeked darlings adorned with flowers and tokens of love can also be campus *enragés* screaming "Up Against the Wall, Motherfuckers, This Is a Stickup" (a slogan that does not strike one as a notable improvement over "Workers of the World, Unite").

That finally there should appear an impulse to shake off the burdens and entanglements of modernism need come as no surprise. After all the virtuosos of torment and enigma we have known, it would be fine to have a period in Western culture devoted to relaxed pleasures and surface hedonism. But so far this does not seem possible: the century forbids it. What strikes one most forcefully about a great deal of the new writing and theater is its grindingly ideological tone, even if now the claim is for an ideology of pleasure. And what strikes one even more is the air of pulsing *ressentiment* which pervades this work, an often unearned and seemingly inexplicable hostility. If one went by the cues of a critic like Susan Sontag, one might suppose that the ethical torments of Kamenetz Podolsk and the moral repressiveness of Salem, Massachusetts, had finally been put to rest, in favor of creamy delights in texture, color, and sensation. But nothing of the sort is true, at least not yet; it is only advertised.

Keen on tactics, the spokesmen for the new sensibility proclaim it to be still another turn in the endless gyrations of mod-

---

and so reduce the complex orchestration of life to the easy strumming of a monochord. Brown and McLuhan have nicely apportioned the world between them: the inward madness for the one, the outward manias for the other."

ernism, still another revolt in the permanent revolution of twentieth-century sensibility. This approach is very shrewd, since it
can disarm in advance those older New York (and other) critics
who still respond with enthusiasm to the battle cries of modernism. But several objections or qualifications need to be registered:

Modernism, by its very nature, is uncompromisingly a minority
culture, creating and defining itself through opposition to a dominant culture. Today, however, nothing of the sort is true. Flood-
lights glaring and tills overflowing, the new sensibility is a success from the very start. The middle-class public, eager for thrills
and humiliations, welcomes it; so do the mass media, always on
the alert for exploitable sensations; and naturally there appear
intellectuals with handy theories. The new sensibility is both
embodied and celebrated in the actions of Mailer, whose condition as a swinger in America is not quite comparable with that
of Joyce in Trieste or Kafka in Prague or Lawrence anywhere;
it is reinforced with critical exegesis by Susan Sontag, a pub-
licist able to make brilliant quilts from grandmother's patches;
it is housed and braced by Robert Brustein, who has been writing drama reviews as if thumbing one's nose on the stage were
a sufficient act of social criticism.* And on a far lower level, it

---

* Reviewing a theatrical grope-in called *Dionysus in 69* (*New Republic*,
August 10, 1968), Brustein pulls back a little from his enthusiasm for the
swinging new. He remarks that in *Dionysus* "the pelvis becomes the actor's
primary organ of expression" and that "only about a third of Euripides's
play" *The Bacchae* is used in this "adaptation." (Why even a third? Who
needs words at all?) And then says Brustein: "The off-off-Broadway movement, which began so promisingly with *America Hurrah, MacBird,* and
the experimental probes of the Open Theatre, is now cultivating its worst
faults, developing an anarchic Philistinism which virtually throws the
writer out of the theater."

But if what the Dean of the Yale Drama School counterpoises to
Dionysus in 69 is *America Hurrah* and *MacBird*—noisy, coarse, derivative,
and third-rate—how can he possibly bring to bear serious critical standards?

[It is only fair to add that a few months after this essay was written,
Robert Brustein published "The Third Theatre Revisited," *New York
Review of Books,* February 13, 1969, in which he sharply criticized not
merely the Living Theatre, an institution in which hysteria has been
elevated to the dignity of authoritarianism, but the whole cultural trend
of which the Living Theatre is but an instance. Brustein speaks of a
development in which "the American avant-garde, for the first time in its
history, became the glass of fashion and the mold of form. What was
once considered special and arcane—the exclusive concern of an alienated,

has even found its Smerdyakov in LeRoi Jones, that parodist of apocalypse who rallies enlightened Jewish audiences with calls for Jewish blood. Whatever one may think of this situation, it is surely very different from the classical picture of a besieged modernism.

By now the search for the "new," often reduced to a trivializing of form and matter, has become the predictable old. To suppose that we keep moving from cultural breakthrough to breakthrough requires a collective wish to forget what happened yesterday and even the day before: ignorance always being a great spur to claims for originality. Alienation has been transformed from a serious and revolutionary concept into a motif of mass culture, and the content of modernism into the decor of *kitsch*. As Harold Rosenberg has pungently remarked:

The sentiment of the diminution of personality is an historical hypothesis upon which writers have constructed a set of literary conventions by this time richly equipped with theatrical machinery and symbolic allusions. . . . The individual's emptiness and inability to act have become an irrefrangible cliché, untiringly supported by an immense, voluntary phalanx of latecomers to modernism. In this manifestation, the notion of the void has lost its critical edge and is thoroughly reactionary.

The effort to assimilate new cultural styles to the modernist tradition brushes aside problems of value, quality, judgment. It rests upon a Philistine version of the theory of progress in the arts: all must keep changing, and change signifies a realization of progress. Yet even if an illicit filiation can be shown, there is a vast difference in seriousness and accomplishment between the modernism of some decades ago and what we have now. The great literary modernists (to cite but one instance) put at the center of their work a confrontation and struggle with the demons of nihilism; the literary swingers of the sixties, facing a nihilist violation, cheerfully remove the threat by what Fielding once called "a timely compliance." Just as in the verse of Swinburne echoes of Romanticism sag through the stanzas, so in

argumentative, intensely serious elite—was now accessible, through television and the popular magazines; vogues in women's fashions followed hard upon, and sometimes even influenced, vogues in modern painting; underground movies became box office bonanzas, and Andy Warhol's factory was making him a millionaire."]

much current writing there is indeed a continuity with modernism, but a continuity of grotesque and parody, through the doubles of fashion.

Still, it would be foolish to deny that in this *Kulturkampf*, the New York intellectuals are at a severe disadvantage. Some have simply gone over to the other camp. A critic like Susan Sontag employs the dialectical skills and accumulated knowledge of intellectual life in order to bless the new sensibility as a dispensation of pleasure, beyond the grubby reach of interpretation and thereby, it would seem, beyond the tight voice of judgment. That her theories are skillfully rebuilt versions of aesthetic notions long familiar and discarded; that in her own critical writing she interprets like mad and casts an image anything but hedonistic, relaxed, or sensuous—none of this need bother her admirers, for a highly literate spokesman is very sustaining to those who have discarded or not acquired intellectual literacy. Second only to Miss Sontag in trumpeting the new sensibility is Leslie Fiedler, a critic with an amiable weakness for thrusting himself at the head of parades marching into sight.*

* Fiedler's essay "The New Mutants" (*Partisan Review*, Fall 1965) is a sympathetic charting of the new sensibility, with discussions of "porno-esthetics," the effort among young people to abandon habits and symbols of masculinity in favor of a feminized receptiveness, "the aspiration to take the final evolutionary leap and cast off adulthood completely," and above all, the role of drugs as "the crux of the futurist revolt."

With uncharacteristic forbearance, Fiedler denies himself any sustained or explicit judgments of this "futurist revolt," so that the rhetorical thrust of his essay is somewhere between acclaim and resignation. He cannot completely suppress his mind, perhaps because he has been using it too long, and so we find this acute passage concerning the responses of older writers to "the most obscene forays of the young":

. . . after a while, there will be no more Philip Rahvs and Stanley Edgar Hymans left to shock—antilanguage becoming mere language with repeated use and in the face of acceptance; so that all sense of exhilaration will be lost along with the possibility of offense. What to do then except to choose silence, since raising the ante of violence is ultimately self-defeating; and the way of obscenity in any case leads as naturally to silence as to further excess?

About drugs Fiedler betrays no equivalent skepticism, so that it is hard to disagree with Lionel Abel's judgment that, "while I do not want to charge Mr. Fiedler with recommending the taking of drugs, I think his

But for those New York (or any other) writers not quite enchanted with the current scene there are serious difficulties.

They cannot be quite *sure*. Having fought in the later battles for modernism, they must acknowledge to themselves the possibility that, now grown older, they have lost their capacity to appreciate innovation. Why, they ask themselves with some irony, should "their" cultural revolution have been the last one, or the last good one? From the publicists of the new sensibility they hear the very slogans, catchwords, and stirring appeals which a few decades ago they were hurling in behalf of modernism and against such diehards as Van Wyck Brooks and Bernard de Voto. And given the notorious difficulties in making judgments about contemporary works of art, how can they be certain that Kafka is a master of despair and Burroughs a symptom of disintegration, Pollack a pioneer of innovation and Warhol a triviality of pop? The capacity for self-doubt, the habit of self-irony, which is the reward of decades of experience, renders them susceptible to the simplistic cries of the new.

Well, the answer is that there can be no certainty: we should neither want nor need it. One must speak out of one's taste and conviction, and let history make whatever judgments it will care to. But this is not an easy stand to take, for it means that after all these years one may have to face intellectual isolation and perhaps dismissal, and there are moments when it must seem as if the best course is to be promiscuously "receptive," swinging along with a grin of resignation.

In the face of this challenge, surely the most serious of the last twenty-five years, the New York intellectuals have not been able to mount a coherent response, certainly not a judgment sufficiently inclusive and severe. There have been a few efforts, some intellectual polemics by Lionel Abel and literary pieces by Philip Rahv; but no more. Yet if ever there was a moment when our culture needed an austere and sharp criticism—the one talent the New York writers supposedly find it death to hide—it is today. One could imagine a journal with the standards, if hopefully not the parochialism, of *Scrutiny*. One could imagine a journal like *Partisan Review* stripping the pretensions of the

whole essay is a confession that he cannot call upon one value in whose name he could oppose it."

current scene with the vigor it showed in opposing the Popular Front and neoconservative cultures. But these are fantasies. In its often accomplished pages *Partisan Review* betrays a hopeless clash between its editors' capacity to apply serious standards and their yearnings to embrace the moment. Predictably, the result leaves everyone dissatisfied.

One example of the failure of the New York writers to engage in criticism is their relation to Mailer. He is not an easy man to come to grips with, for he is "our genius," probably the only one, and in more than a merely personal way he is a man of enormous charm. Yet Mailer has been the central and certainly most dramatic presence in the new sensibility, even if in reflective moments he makes clear his ability to brush aside its incantations.* Mailer as thaumaturgist of orgasm; as metaphysician of the gut; as psychic herb-doctor; as advance man for literary violence; * * as dialectician of unreason; and above all, as a novelist who has laid waste his own formidable talent—these masks of brilliant, nutty restlessness, these papery dikes against squalls of boredom —all require sharp analysis and criticism. Were Mailer to read these lines he would surely grin and exclaim that, whatever else, his books have suffered plenty of denunciation. My point, however, is not that he has failed to receive adverse reviews, including some from such New York critics as Norman Podhoretz, Elizabeth Hardwick, and Philip Rahv; perhaps he has even had

* Two examples:

"Tom Hayden began to discuss revolution with Mailer. 'I'm for Kennedy,' said Mailer, 'because I'm not so sure I want a revolution. Some of those kids are awfully dumb.' Hayden the Revolutionary said a vote for George Wallace would further his objective more than a vote for RFK." (*Village Voice,* May 30, 1968—and by the way, some Revolutionary!)

"If he still took a toke of marijuana from time to time for Auld Lang Syne, or in recognition of the probability that good sex had to be awfully good before it was better than on pot, yet, still!—Mailer was not in approval of any drug, he was virtually conservative about it, having demanded of his eighteen-year-old daughter . . . that she not take marijuana, and never LSD, until she completed her education, a mean promise to extract in these apocalyptic times." (*The Armies of the Night*).

* * In this regard the editor of *Dissent* bears a heavy responsibility. When he first received the manuscript of "The White Negro," he should have expressed in print his objections to the passage in which Mailer discusses the morality of beating up a fifty-year-old storekeeper. That he could not bring himself to risk loosing a scoop is no excuse whatever.

too many adverse reviews, given the scope and brightness of his talent. My point is that the New York writers have failed to confront Mailer seriously as an intellectual spokesman, a cultural agent, and instead have found it easier to regard him as a hostage to the temper of our times. What has not been forthcoming is a recognition, surely a painful one, that in his major public roles he has come to represent values in deep opposition to liberal humaneness and rational discourse. That the New York critics have refused him this confrontation is both a disservice to Mailer and a sign that, whatever it may once have been, the New York intellectual community no longer exists as a significant force.

An equally telling sign is the recent growth in popularity and influence of the *New York Review of Books*. Emerging at least in part from the New York intellectual milieu, this journal has steadily moved away from the styles and premises with which it began. Its early dependence on those New York writers who lent their names to it and helped establish it seems all but over. The Jewish imprint has been blotted out; the *New York Review*, for all its sharp attacks on current political policies, is thoroughly at home in the worlds of American culture, publishing, and society. It features a strong Anglophile slant in its literary pieces, perhaps in accord with the *New Statesman* formula of blending leftish (and at one time, fellow-traveling) politics with Bloomsbury culture, Kingsley Martin with tips on wine. More precisely, what the *New York Review* has managed to achieve— I find it quite fascinating as a portent of things to come—is a link between campus "leftism" and East Side stylishness, the worlds of Tom Hayden and George Plimpton. Opposition to Communist politics and ideology is frequently presented in the pages of the *New York Review* as if it were an obsolete, indeed a pathetic, hangover from a discredited past or, worse yet, a dark sign of the CIA. A snappish and crude anti-Americanism has swept over much of its political writing—and to avoid misunderstanding, let me say that by this I do not mean anything so necessary as attacks on the ghastly Vietnam war or on our failures in the cities. And in the hands of writers like Andrew Kopkind (author of the immortal phrase, "morality . . . starts at the barrel of a gun"), liberal values and norms are treated with something very close to contempt.

Though itself too sophisticated to indulge in the more pre-posterous New Left notions, such as "liberal Fascism" and "confrontationism," the *New York Review* has done the New Left the considerable service of providing it with a link of intellectual respectability to the academic world. In the materials it has published by Kopkind, Tom Hayden, Philip Rahv, Edgar Z. Friedenberg, Jason Epstein, and others, one finds not an acceptance of the fashionable talk about "revolution" which has become an indoor and outdoor sport on the American campus, but a kind of rhetorical violence, a verbal "radicalism," which gives moral and intellectual encouragement to precisely such fashionable (self-defeating) talk.

This is by no means the only kind of political material to have appeared in the *New York Review;* at least in my own experience I have found its editors prepared to print articles of a sharply different kind; and in recent years it has published serious political criticism by George Lichtheim, Theodore Draper, and Walter Laqueur.

And because it is concerned with maintaining a certain level of sophistication and accomplishment, the *New York Review* has not simply taken over the new sensibility. No, at stake here is the dominant tone of this skillfully edited paper, an editorial keenness in responding to the current academic and intellectual temper—as for instance in that memorable issue with a cover featuring, no doubt for the benefit of its university readers, a diagram explaining how to make a Molotov cocktail. The genius of the *New York Review,* and it has been a genius of sorts, is not, in either politics or culture, for swimming against the stream.

Perhaps it is too late. Perhaps there is no longer available among the New York writers enough energy and coherence to make possible a sustained confrontation with the new sensibility. Still, one would imagine that their undimmed sense of the *Zeitgeist* would prod them to sharp responses, precise statements, polemical assaults. What, after all, would be risked in saying that we have entered a period of overwhelming cultural sleaziness?

Having been formed by, and through opposition to, the New York intellectual experience, I cannot look with joy at the prospect of its ending. But neither with dismay. Such breakups are inevitable, and out of them come new voices and energies. Yet precisely at this moment of dispersion, might not some of the New York writers achieve renewed strength if they were to struggle once again for whatever has been salvaged from these last few decades? For the values of liberalism, for the politics of a democratic radicalism, for the norms of rationality and intelligence, for the standards of literary seriousness, for the life of the mind as a humane dedication—for all this it should again be worth finding themselves in a minority, even a beleaguered minority, and not with fantasies of martyrdom but with a quiet recognition that for the intellectual this is likely to be his usual condition.*

* Of the several responses there have been to this piece, an exchange with Irving Kristol (*Commentary*, January 1969, pp. 12–16) and "The New York Intellectual," a poem in the May sequence in Robert Lowell's *Notebook 1967–68*, are notable.

Part IV

George Orwell:
"As the
Bones Know"

George Orwell wrote with his bones. To read again his essays, together with previously uncollected journalism and unpublished letters, is to encounter the bone-weariness, and bone-courage, of a writer who lived through the Depression, Hitlerism, Franco's victory in Spain, Stalinism, the collapse of bourgeois England in the thirties. Even when he wanted to pull back to his novels and even when he lay sick with tuberculosis, Orwell kept summoning those energies of combat and resources of irritation which made him so powerful a fighter against the cant of his age. His bones would not let him rest.

For a whole generation—mine—Orwell was an intellectual hero. He stormed against those English writers who were ready to yield to Hitler; he fought almost single-handed against those who blinded themselves to the evils of Stalin. More than any other English intellectual of our age, he embodied the values of personal independence and a fiercely democratic radicalism. Yet, just because for years I have intensely admired him, I hesitated to return to him. One learns to fear the disappointment of lapsed enthusiasms.

I was wrong to hesitate. Reading through these four large volumes *—the sheer *pleasure* of it cannot be overstated—has convinced me that Orwell was an even better writer than I had

* The Collected Essays, Journalism and Letters of George Orwell (New York: Harcourt, Brace & World, 1968).

supposed. He was neither a first-rank literary critic nor a major novelist, and certainly not an original political thinker; but he was, I now believe, the best English essayist since Hazlitt, perhaps since Dr. Johnson. He was the greatest moral force in English letters during the last several decades: craggy, fiercely polemical, sometimes mistaken, but an utterly free man. In his readiness to stand alone and take on all comers, he was a model for every writer of our age. And when my students ask, "Whom shall I read in order to write better?" I answer, "Orwell, the master of the plain style, that style which seems so easy to copy but is almost impossible to reach."

If you look through them casually, the earliest of Orwell's essays seem to share that blunt clarity of speech and ruthless determination to see what looms in front of one's nose that everyone admires in his later work. The first important essay came out in 1931, when Orwell was still in his late twenties, and is called "The Spike." It describes his experience as an unemployed wanderer on the roads of England, finding shelter in a "spike," or hostel, where the poor were given a bed and two or three meals but then required to move along. The piece makes one quiver with anger at the inhumanity of good works, but it is absolutely free of sentimentalism, and almost miraculously untainted by the sticky *luving* condescension of thirties radicalism.

Any ordinary writer should be willing to give his right arm, or at least two fingers, to have written that piece. Yet a close inspection will show, I think, that it doesn't reach Orwell's highest level of social reportage. There is still an occasional clutter of unabsorbed detail, still a self-consciousness about his role as half-outsider barging in upon and thereby perhaps subtly betraying the lives of the men on the road. The discipline of the plain style—and that fierce control of self which forms its foundation—comes hard.

For Orwell, it also came quickly. In a piece called "Hop Picking," written a few months later but now published for the first time, Orwell describes some weeks spent as an agricultural worker in the hop fields. The prose is now keener:

Straw is rotten stuff to sleep in (it is much more draughty than hay) and Ginger and I had only a blanket each, so we suffered agonies of cold for the first week. . . .

Dick's Café in Billingsgate . . . was one of the very few places where you could get a cup of tea for 1d, and there were fires there, so that anyone who had a penny could warm himself for hours in the early morning. Only this last week the London County Council closed it on the ground that it was unhygienic.

In "Hop Picking" Orwell had already solved the problem of narrative distance: how to establish a simultaneous relationship with the men whose experience he shared and the readers to whom he makes the experience available. "Hop Picking" was a small effort in the kind of writing Orwell would undertake on a large scale a few years later, when he produced his classic report on the condition of English miners, *The Road to Wigan Pier.* What Orwell commanded, above all, was a natural respect for the workers. He saw and liked them as they were, not as he or a political party felt they should be. He didn't twist them into Marxist abstractions, nor did he cuddle them in the fashion of New Left Populism. He saw the workers neither as potential revolutionists nor savage innocents nor stupid clods. He saw them as ordinary suffering and confused human beings: rather like you and me, yet because of their circumstances radically different from you and me. When one thinks of the falseness that runs through so much current writing of this kind it becomes clear that Orwell was a master of the art of exposition.

Other sides of Orwell's talent soon begin to unfold. He develops quickly: the idea of *pressure* is decisive. His career can be understood only as a series of moral and intellectual crises, the painful confrontation of a man driven to plunge into every vortex of misery that he saw, yet a man with an obvious distaste for the corruptions of modern politics.

Even in casual bits of journalism, his voice begins to come through. As a literary critic he seldom had the patience to work his way deeply into a text, though he did have an oblique sort of literary penetration. He remarks, in an otherwise commonplace review, that George Moore enjoyed the advantage of "not having an over-developed sense of pity; hence he could resist the temptation to make his characters more sensitive than they would have been in real life." In "Bookshop Memories," never before printed in a book, Orwell shows the peculiar sandpapery humor that would emerge in his later writings:

Seen in the mass, five or ten thousand at a time, books were boring and even slightly sickening. . . . The sweet smell of decaying paper appeals to me no longer. It is too closely associated in my mind with paranoiac customers and dead bluebottles.

In another early piece, not otherwise notable, there suddenly leaps out a sentence carrying Orwell's deepest view of life, his faith in the value and strength of common existence: "The fact to which we have got to cling, as to a life-belt, is that it *is* possible to be a normal decent person and yet to be fully alive."

Orwell's affectionate sense of English life, its oddities, paradoxes, and even outrages, comes through in an anecdote he tells:

. . . the other day I saw a man—Communist, I suppose—selling the *Daily Worker*, & I went up to him & said, "Have you the DW?—He: "Yes, sir." Dear Old England!

There are even a few early poems, slightly this side of *Weltschmerz,* which I rather like:

I know, not as in barren thought,
But wordlessly, as the bones know,
What quenching of my brain, what numbness,
Wait in the dark grave where I go.

Orwell's first fully achieved piece of writing appears in 1936: "Shooting an Elephant," a mixture of reminiscence and reflection. The essay takes off from his experience as a minor British official in Burma who, in the half-jeering, half-respectful presence of a crowd of "natives," must destroy a maddened elephant; and then it moves on to larger issues of imperialism and the corruption of human nature by excessive power. For the first time, his characteristic fusion of personal and public themes is realized, and the essay as a form—vibrant, tight-packed, nervous—becomes a token of his meaning. The evocation of brutality is brought to climax through one of those symbolic moments he would employ brilliantly in his later pieces: "The elephant's mouth was wide and open—I could see far down into caverns of pale pink throat."

During these years, the late thirties, Orwell went through a rapid political development. He kept assaulting the deceits of Popular Frontism, and this brought him even more intellectual loneliness than it would have in America. He tried to find a tenable basis for his anti-Stalinist leftism, a task at which he encountered the same difficulties other intellectuals did—which, after all, were intrinsic to a world-wide crisis of socialist thought. For a while he fought in Spain with the militia of the POUM, a left-wing anti-Communist party, and suffered a throat wound; back in England he spoke some painful truths about the Stalinist terror launched against dissident leftists on the Loyalist side, and for this he was hated by the *New Statesman* and most of the Popular Front intellectuals. He published one of his most valuable and neglected books, *Homage to Catalonia,* the record of his experience in Spain. He went through a brief interval in which he put forward a semi-Trotskyist line, denying that the bourgeois West could successfully oppose Hitlerism and insisting that the prerequisite for destroying Fascism was a socialist revolution in England. But when the war broke out, he had the good sense—not all his co-thinkers did—to see that his earlier views on combating Fascism had been abstract, unreal, ultimatistic. He supported the war, yet remained a radical, steadily criticizing social privilege and snobbism. Here is a passage in his previously unpublished "War-Time Diary," breathing his ingrained plebeian distaste for the English upper classes:

From a letter from Lady Oxford to the *Daily Telegraph:*
"Since most London houses are deserted there is little entertaining . . . in any case, most people have to part with their cooks and live in hotels."
Apparently nothing will ever teach these people that the other 99% of the population exists.

The high plateau of Orwell's career as essayist—and it is as essayist he is likely to be remembered best—begins around 1940. He had by then perfected his gritty style; he had settled into his combative manner (sometimes the object of an unattractive kind of self-imitation); and he had found his subjects: the distinctive nature of English life and its relation to the hope for socialism, a number of close examinations of popular culture, a series of literary studies on writers ranging from Dickens to Henry Miller, and continued social reportage on the life of the poor. His productivity during the next five or six years is amazing. He works for the BBC, he writes a weekly column for the socialist *Tribune,* he sends regular London Letters to *Partisan Review* in New York, he keeps returning to his fiction, and he still manages to produce such extraordinary essays as the appreciation of Dickens, the piquant investigation of boys' magazines, the half-defense of and half-assault on Kipling, the brilliant "Raffles and Miss Blandish," the discussion of Tolstoy's hatred for Shakespeare—to say nothing of such unknown gems, rescued from little magazines, as his moving essays on writers so thoroughly out of fashion as Smollett and Gissing.

We see him now in his mature public role. There is something irascible about Orwell, even pugnacious, which both conventional liberals and literary aesthetes find unnerving. He is constantly getting into fights, and by no means always with good judgment. He is reckless, he is ferociously polemical, and when arguing for a "moderate" opinion he is harsh and intransigent in tone.

My sense of Orwell, as it emerges from reading him in bulk, is rather different from that which became prevalent in the conservative fifties: the "social saint" one of his biographers called him, the "conscience of his generation" V. S. Pritchett declared him to be, or the notably good man Lionel Trilling saw in him. The more I read of Orwell, the more I doubt that he was particularly virtuous or good. Neither the selflessness nor the patience of the saint, certainly not the indifference to temporal passion that would seem a goal of sainthood, can be found in Orwell. He himself wrote in his essay on Gandhi: "No doubt alcohol, tobacco and so forth are things a saint must avoid, but sainthood is a thing that human beings must avoid."

As a "saint" Orwell would not trouble us, for by now we have learned how to put up with saints: we canonize them and are rid of them. Orwell, however, stirs us by his all too human, his truculent example. He stood in basic opposition to the modes and assumptions that have dominated English cultural life. He rejected the rituals of Good Form which had been so deeply ingrained among the English and took on a brief popularity among us in the fifties; he knew how empty, and often how filled with immoderate aggression the praise of moderation could be; he turned away from the pretentiousness of the "literary." He wasn't a Marxist or even a political revolutionary. He was something better: a revolutionary personality. He turned his back on his own caste; he tried to discover what was happening beyond the provincial limits of high-brow life. If he was a good man, it was mainly in the sense that he had measured his desperation and come to accept it as a mode of honor. And he possessed an impulse essential to a serious writer: he was prepared to take chances, even while continuing to respect the heritage of the past.

Both as writer and thinker, Orwell had serious faults. He liked to indulge himself in a pseudo-tough anti-intellectualism, some of it pretty damned nasty, as in his sneers at "pansy-pinks"—though later he was man enough to apologize to those he had hurt. He was less than clear-sighted or generous on the subject of the Jews, sharing something of the English impatience with what he regarded—in the 1940's!—as their need for special claims. He could be mean in polemics. During the war he was quite outrageous in attacking English anarchists and pacifists like Alex Comfort, Julian Symons, and George Woodcock for lending "objective" comfort to the Nazis. Yet it speaks well for Orwell that in a short time at least two of these men became his friends, and it isn't at all clear to me that in his angry and overstated denunciation, Orwell wasn't making a point against them and all other pacifists which must be seriously considered.

Meanwhile, one suddenly comes to a stop and notices that those of Orwell's letters reprinted in the few volumes of his collected prose are not, as letters, particularly interesting or distinguished. At first, this comes as a surprise, for one might have expected the same pungency, the same verbal thrust, as in the public writing. There is, however, nothing to be found of the qualities that make for great letter writing: nothing of the brilliant rumination of Keats in his letters, or the profound self-involvement of Joyce in his, or the creation of a dramatic persona such as T. E. Lawrence began in his. He seems to have poured all his energies into his published work and used his letters simply as a convenience for making appointments, conveying information, rehearsing opinion. Perhaps it's just as well, for he had a horror of exposing his private life and asked that no biography be written about him. In these days of instant self-revelation, there is something attractive about a writer who throws up so thick a screen of reticence.

One reason these uninteresting letters do finally hold our attention is that they put to rest the notion that Orwell's prose was an achievement easily come by. The standard critical formula is that he wrote in a "conversational" style, and he himself is partly responsible for this simplification. I think, however, that Yvor Winters was right in saying that human conversation is a sloppy form of communication and seldom a good model for prose. What we call colloquial or conversational prose is the result of cultivation, and can be written only by a disciplined refusal of the looseness of both the colloquial and the conversational. If you compare the charged lucidity of Orwell's prose in his best essays with the merely adequate and often flat writing of his letters, you see at once that the style for which he became famous was the result of artistry and hard work. It always is.

In an essay called "Why I Write," Orwell ends with a passage at once revealing and misleading:

All writers are vain, selfish and lazy, and at the very bottom of their motives there lies a mystery. Writing a book is a horrible, exhausting struggle, like a long bout of some painful illness. . . . Good prose is like a window pane. I cannot say with certainty which of my motives are the strongest, but I know which of them deserve to be followed. And looking back through my work, I see that it is invariably where I lacked a *political* purpose that I wrote lifeless books and was betrayed into purple passages. . . .

Orwell is saying something of great importance here, but saying it in a perverse way. (After a time he relished a little too much his role of embattled iconoclast.) He does *not* mean what some literary people would gleefully suppose him to mean: that only tendentiousness, only propaganda, makes for good prose. He deliberately overstates the case, as a provocation to the literary people he liked to bait. But a loyal reader, prepared to brush aside his mannerisms, would take this passage to mean that, once a minimal craftsmanship has been reached, good writing is the result of being absorbed by an end greater than the mere production of good writing. A deliberate effort to achieve virtuosity or beauty or simplicity usually results in mannerism, which is often no more than a way of showing off.

In his best work Orwell seldom allowed himself to show off. He was driven by a passion to clarify ideas, correct errors, persuade readers, straighten things out in the world and in his mind. Hemingway speaks of "grace under pressure," and many of his critics have used this marvelous phrase to describe the excellence of his style. What I think you get in Orwell at his best is something different: "pressure under grace." He achieves a state of "grace" as a writer through having sloughed off the usual vanities of composition, and thereby he speaks not merely for himself but as a voice of moral urgency. His prose becomes a prose of pressure, the issue at stake being too important to allow him to slip into fancies or fanciness. Moral pressure makes for verbal compression, a search like Flaubert's for *le mot juste,* but not at all to achieve aesthetic nicety, rather to achieve a stripped speech. And the result turns out to be aesthetically pleasing: the Christians, with much more to be risked, understood all this when they spoke of "dying into life."

Good prose, says Orwell, should be "like a window pane." He is both right and wrong. Part of his limitation as a literary critic is that he shows little taste for the prose of virtuosity: one can't easily imagine him enjoying Sir Thomas Browne. If some windows should be clear and transparent, why may not others be stained and opaque? Like all critics who are also significant writers themselves, Orwell developed standards that were largely self-justifying: he liked the prose that's like a window pane because that's the kind of prose he wrote.

His style doesn't seem to change much from early essays to late, but closely watched it shows significant modulations. At the outset his effort to be clear at all costs does involve him in heavy costs: a certain affectation of bluntness, a tendency to make common sense into an absolute virtue. But by the end, as in the superb prose of "Such, Such Were the Joys," there has occurred a gradual increase of control and thereby suppleness.

"Pressure under grace" brings rewards. Orwell learns to mold the essay into a tense structure, learns to open with a strong thrust ("Dickens is one of those writers who are well worth stealing"), and above all, to end with an earned climax, a release of the tension that has been accumulating and can now be put to the service of lucidity. I think a useful critical study could be made of the way he ends his essays. Here is the last paragraph on Dickens:

When one reads any strongly individual piece of writing, one has the impression of seeing a face somewhere behind the page. It is not necessarily the actual face of the writer. . . . What one sees is the face that the writer *ought* to have. Well, in the case of Dickens I see a face that is not quite the face of Dickens' photographs, though it resembles it. It is the face of a man about forty, with a small beard and a high color. He is laughing, with a touch of anger in his laughter, but no triumph, no malignity. It is the face of a man who is always fighting against something, but who fights in the open and is not frightened, the face of a man who is *generously angry*—in other words, of a nineteenth-century liberal, a free intelligence, a type hated with equal hatred by all the smelly little orthodoxies which are now contending for our souls.

The passage is marvelous, but if a criticism is to be made, it is that Orwell has composed a set piece too easily lifted out of context and in the final sentence has allowed himself to turn away from his subject in order to take a smack at fanatics of left and right. Yet this self-indulgence, if it is one, works pretty well, mainly because Orwell has by now so thoroughly persuaded his readers that the qualities he admires in Dickens *are* indeed admirable.

Here is another Orwell ending, this time from the essay on Swift, "Politics vs. Literature," published some seven years after the one on Dickens. Orwell makes some important observations on the problem of "belief" in literature:

In so far as a writer is a propagandist, the most one can ask of him is that he shall genuinely believe in what he is saying, and that it shall not be something blazingly silly. Today . . . one can imagine a good book being written by a Catholic, a Communist, a Fascist, a Pacifist, an Anarchist, perhaps by an old-styled Liberal or an ordinary Conservative; one cannot imagine a good book being written by a spiritualist, a Buchmanite or a member of the Ku Klux Klan. The views that a writer holds must be compatible with sanity, in the medical sense, and with the power of continuous thought: beyond that what we ask of him is talent, which is probably another name for conviction. Swift did not possess ordinary wisdom, but he did possess a terrible intensity of vision. . . . The durability of *Gulliver's Travels* goes to show that, if the force of belief is behind it, a world-view which only just passes the test of sanity is sufficient to produce a great work of art.

What grips our attention here is the ferocity with which Orwell drives home his point—by reaction, we almost see old Tolstoy rising from his grave to thunder against this heresy. Rhetorically, the passage depends on the sudden drop of the last sentence, with its shocking reduction of the preceding argument —so that in the movement of his prose Orwell seems to be enacting the curve of his argument. It is a method he must have picked up from Swift himself.

And, finally, here is the ending of his great essay, "How the Poor Die":

The dread of hospitals probably still survives among the very poor and in all of us it has only recently disappeared. It is a dark patch not far beneath the surface of our minds. I have said earlier that, when I entered the ward at the Hospital X, I was conscious of a strange feeling of familiarity. What the scene reminded me of, of course, was the reeking, pain-filled hospitals of the nineteenth century, which I had never seen but of which I had a traditional knowledge. And something, perhaps the black-clad doctor with his frowsy black bag, or perhaps only the sickly smell, played the queer trick of unearthing from my memory that poem of Tennyson's, "The Children's Hour," which I had not thought of for twenty years. It happened that as a child I had had it read aloud to me by a sick-nurse. . . . Seemingly I had forgotten it. Even its name would probably have recalled nothing to me. But the first glimpse of the ill-lit, murmurous room, with the beds so close together, suddenly roused the train of thought to which it belonged, and in the night that followed I found myself remembering the whole story and atmosphere of the poem, with many of its lines complete.

This ending seems to me a triumph of composition. All that has been detailed with such gruesome care about the terribleness of a French hospital is brought to imaginative climax through the anecdote at the end. Proust could hardly have done better.

Orwell died, in 1950, at the age of forty-six, stricken by tuberculosis. It is depressing to think that if he had lived, he would today be no more than sixty-five years old. How much we have missed in these two decades! Imagine Orwell ripping into one of Harold Wilson's mealy speeches, imagine him examining the thought of Spiro Agnew, imagine him dissecting the ideology of Herbert Marcuse, imagine him casting a frosty eye on the current wave of irrationalism in Western culture!

The loss seems enormous. . . . He was one of the few heroes of our younger years who remains untarnished. Having to live in a rotten time was made just a little more bearable by his presence.

⁓ᴥ

Silone:
A Luminous
Example

With his very first novels, *Fontamara* and *Bread and Wine*,
Ignazio Silone won a following of readers who soon came to
feel they were his secret friends. Silone could go almost anywhere in the world and find men who, having like himself experienced the failure of socialism, would immediately know how
to register and value the muted slyness and sadness of his books,
quite as old companions can speak to one another through a
shrug or a smile.

For such readers, but surely for others, too, Silone's every
word seems to bear a special quality, a stamp of fraternal but
undeluded humaneness. It is really something of a mystery,
which literary criticism with all its solemnities seems unable to
penetrate: how a man who writes so simply and unpretentiously
can nevertheless make everything he publishes uniquely his own.
For almost four decades—the most terrible of our century, perhaps the most terrible in Western history—Silone has been a
transforming presence: the least bitter of ex-Communists, the
most reflective of radical democrats.

His work is wry, sometimes saturnine; sardonic, sometimes disillusioned. Brought up in the Abruzzi, he knows and loves the
Italian peasants, but knows and loves too well for even a trace
of sentimentalism. Educated in Italy, a nation cursed with the
gift of rhetoric, he seems immune to all the enticements of verbal
display. He can make small things (a casual gesture by a char-

acter, a quiet phrase of his own, a minor anecdote) into tokens of all the redemptive possibilities in this century of betrayal. He brings together in his writing the grit of the peasant and the fever of the intellectual, so that to read him is to encounter the oldness, the weariness of Europe: all those wise and tormented priests who keep moving through his stories, all those hunted and doubting revolutionists broken on the wheel of memory.

What makes his stories so distinctively his own, so peculiarly and endlessly moving? Surely not any special wisdom; he would be the first to laugh at such a claim. What moves us, I think, is the sense we gain that while no wiser or politically "more correct" than the rest of us, Silone is, both as writer and person, profoundly contemplative, with every problem, every doubt, every failure of this age of failed revolutions having become part of his inner being.

And there is something else: the miracle—for it *is* a miracle— of his relationship to the people about whom he writes, the peasants of Italy. Silone is entirely free of the false identifications and grandiloquent delusions of Populism; for while he comes from the people, he is no longer of them. The man who in 1927, together with Togliatti, represented the Italian Communists at a crucial conference of the Comintern; who later became deeply involved in Italian socialist politics; who wrote, in *The School for Dictators,* a subtle analysis of the dynamics of Fascism; who kept returning in his essays to the central intellectual problems of the age—this man could hardly claim that he was still at home in the Abruzzi. Yet in all his books he is utterly free of those sins of aristocratism which stain the work of so many twentieth-century European writers. The miracle of Silone's relation to the peasants lies neither in distance nor in immersion, but in a readiness to leave and return, to experience estrangement yet maintain affection, to know in himself both the relief of deracination and the steadiness of rootedness. In this balance of response there is at least as much desperation as affection. Silone cares neither to deceive himself nor others: he does not romanticize the peasant figures who, together with the heretical priests and dissident revolutionists, embody his notion of character as moral example. He knows these peasants too well; he knows their brutishness and ignorance as he knows the vanity and fanaticism of the priests and revolutionists. Yet he believes in the peasants, at least in those potentialities of which they themselves are seldom aware. For Silone has learned how to wait, even for that which may never come.

All the while he keeps telling and writing down stories, at times no more than anecdotes, which hold one with their compressed powers of revelation, as if in the crucial incident, the central moment, everything a man needs to know can be brought together. The critic R. W. B. Lewis has put this very well: "Silone's characters exchange anecdotes like gifts; it is all they have, but it is everything. If genuine life is communion, according to Silone, its seed is the anecdote. . . . The role of fiction, like the end of life, is [for Silone] to be companionable." I shall be saying more about Silone's anecdotes as they illuminate and structure his novels, but here let me cite—because it seems to present a moral signature—an anecdote from one of his essays. He recalls a childhood moment when he saw a "small, barefoot, ragged little man" being dragged through the streets of his village. "Look how funny he is," the boy says to his father. Silone continues:

My father looked severely at me, dragged me to my feet by the ear and led me to his room. I had never seen him so angry at me.
"What have I done wrong?" I asked him, rubbing my injured ear.
"Never make fun of a man who's been arrested! Never!"
"Why not?"
"Because he can't defend himself. And because he may be innocent. In any case because he is unhappy."

The father's command—"Never make fun of a man who's been arrested"—is remarkable, a germ of Silone's whole later outlook; but the last sentence is overwhelming, worthy of Tolstoy. Thinking about this anecdote, I was reminded of a remark made by the Yiddish poet H. Leivick, a writer whom Silone is unlikely ever to have heard of. Leivick was accused by some of his critics of deviating into a Christian celebration of suffering, and he answered them with a sentence about Jesus: "I saw in him simply the prisoner." It is a sentence Silone could have spoken.

In *Fontamara*, the image of worker and peasant, which had achieved a symbolic elevation in Trotsky's *History of the Russian Revolution*, appears in a state of decomposition, its two parts split into figures of hostility. One of the few modern novels that has the genuine quality of a folk tale, or perhaps better, a comic fable, *Fontamara* tells the story of a peasant village in the Abruzzi resisting in its pathetic way the onthrusts of the Mussolini regime. To the peasants, the political problem first presents itself as one of city against country, town against village—and they are not entirely wrong, for they, the peasants, are at the very bottom, suffering the whole weight of Italian society. Simple but not simple-minded, unable to generalize very well from their suffering, yet aware that they must learn to, they show a sharp insight, through their complicated jokes and sly stories, into the nature of the social hierarchy. When a minor government flunkey, the Hon. Pelino, comes to gather their signatures for a petition that, as it happens, has not yet been composed, one of the peasants tells him a marvelous little fable:

"At the head of everything is God, Lord of Heaven. After him comes Prince Torlonia, lord of the earth. Then comes Prince Torlonia's armed guards. Then comes Prince Torlonia's armed guards' dogs. Then nothing at all. Then nothing at all. Then nothing at all. Then comes the peasants. And that's all."
"And the authorities, where do they come in?" asks the Hon. Pelino. Ponzio Pilato interrupted to explain that the authorities were divided between the third and fourth categories, according to the pay. The fourth category (that of the dogs) was a very large one.

From their bloody experiences the peasants must learn that they need the help of the town, and one way of reading *Fontamara* is as a series of explorations into, or encounters with, the town where the peasants try to discover their true allies—not the priest who is corrupt and bloated; not the old landowners, who are being squeezed by Mussolini's agents, yet remain as much as ever the enemies of the peasants; not the liberal lawyer, Don Circostanza, who betrays them with his windy rhetoric. Only when the most violent of the peasants, Berardo—it is significant that he owns no land and is therefore free of the conservative inclinations of even those peasants who have nothing more than a strip of rock or sand—only when he goes to Rome does he meet, after a series of tragicomic blunders, the agent of the revolutionary underground. At the end of the novel, a union has been achieved—hesitant, not fully understood, and quickly broken—between peasant and worker. The underground revolutionary brings to the peasants a miniature printing press, a product of urban technology, and the peasants print one issue of a little paper called *What Is to Be Done?* As one of them explains with a truly masterful grasp of political method, the question must be asked again and again, after each statement of their plight: *They have taken away our water.* What is to be done? *The priests won't bury our dead.* What is to be done? *They rape our women in the name of the law.* What is to be done? *Don Circostanza is a bastard.* What is to be done?

The question echoes, not accidentally, the title of Lenin's famous pamphlet, in which he first outlined his plan for a disciplined revolutionary party; nor is it an accident that both Lenin's pamphlet and the paper of Silone's peasants are written in times of extreme reaction. For *Fontamara* is the one important work of modern fiction that fully absorbs the Marxist outlook on the level of myth or legend; one of the few works of modern fiction in which the Marxist categories seem organic and "natural," not in the sense that they are part of the peasant heritage or arise spontaneously in the peasant imagination, but in the sense that the whole weight of the peasant experience, at least as it takes form in this book, requires an acceptance of these categories. What makes *Fontamara* so poignant as a political legend—despite the apparent failures, upon occasion, of Silone's language to equal in richness his gift for anecdote—is that he is a *patient* writer, one who has the most acute sense of the difference between what is and what he wishes. The peasants are shown in their nonpolitical actuality and the political actuality is shown as it moves in upon them, threatening to starve and destroy them; Silone does not assume the desired relationship between the two, though he shows the possibilities for a movement into that relationship; the book is both concrete—wonderfully concrete—in its steady view of peasant life and abstract—a brilliant paradigm— in its placing of peasant life in the larger social scheme. The political theories behind the book resemble the lines signifying longitude and latitude on a map; they are not the reality, not the mountains and plains and oceans; but they are indispensable for locating oneself among the mountains and plains and oceans; they are what gives the geography of society meaning and perspective.

Fontamara ends in defeat yet it exudes revolutionary hope and *élan*. Silone's next novel, *Bread and Wine*, is entirely different in tone: defeat is now final, the period of underground struggle at an end, and all that remains is resignation, despair, and obeisance before authority. The novel's hero, Pietro Spina, who partly reflects the opinions of his creator, is a revolutionary leader who from exile has returned to the peasant areas of his native Abruzzi in order to re-establish ties with his people and see whether his Marxist theories will hold up in experience. As he wanders about the countryside, the sick and hunted Spina gradually abandons his Marxism, but not his social rebelliousness; the priest's frock that he has adopted as a disguise begins to be more than a disguise; he must fulfill the responsibilities of his public role or what appears to be his public role, and must adjust his private emotions to this necessity; he becomes or aspires to become, a revolutionary Christian saint. He asks—in the words of Albert Camus—"Is it possible to become a saint without believing in God? That is the sole concrete problem worth considering nowadays." But he sees even farther than Camus: he dimly envisages, and in *The Seed Beneath the Snow* tries to realize, a fraternity beyond sainthood and then beyond good and evil.

Soon after arriving in the Abruzzi, Spina decides that the usual kinds of political propaganda are irrelevant in a Fascist country. People have been misled by slogans too long and too often; they instinctively distrust all phrases. To refute the government propaganda is pointless since no one, least of all its authors, believes it. People understand the truth well enough; it is courage and energy that they lack, not understanding; they are not ready to sacrifice themselves. Spina feels that what is now needed is not programs, even the best Marxist programs, but examples, a pilgrimage of good deeds: men must be healed, they must be stirred to heroism rather than exhorted and converted. Something more drastic, more radical than any kind of political action is needed to cope with the demoralization and corruption Spina finds in Italy.

Before coming to these conclusions Spina had already been uneasy about his political allegiance: "Has not truth, for me, become party truth? . . . Have not party interests ended by deadening all my discrimination between moral values?" The political doubts prompting these questions, together with his feeling that the Marxists in exile have lost touch with the realities of Italian life, lead Spina to the ethical ideal, the love concept, of primitive Christianity, which for him becomes "a Christianity denuded of all religion and all church control." Spina believes not in the resurrection of Jesus, only in his agony: Jesus figures for him entirely in human terms; in fact, the significance of Jesus is that he is the first, and perhaps the last, fully human being. To live as a Christian without the church means, for Spina, to shoulder the greatest possible insecurity before man and God. Spina rejects that duality between means and ends which is common to all political movements; unwilling to stake anything on the future, he insists that the only way to realize the good life, no matter what the circumstances, is to live it. "No word and no gesture can be more persuasive than the life and, if necessary, the death of a man who strives to be free, loyal, just, sincere, disinterested. A man who shows what a man can be."

If we abstract this view from its context in the novel, as Silone virtually invites us to, we are likely to reach mixed conclusions about its value. Much of what Silone says is undoubtedly true; anyone trying to organize a political underground would have to demonstrate his worthiness not only as a leader but as friend. But here we come to a difficulty. Once Silone's militant and saintly rebels acquired followers, they would have to be organized into some sort of movement, even if it claimed to be nonideological and was not called a party; and then that movement would be open to bureaucratic perils similar to those of the Marxist party which Spina had rejected—bureaucratic perils that would be particularly great in an atmosphere of saintly, if not apocalyptic, Messianism. Has not something of the sort happened to Christianity itself, in its transition from primitive rebelliousness to a number of accredited institutions?

Silone has here come up against a central dilemma of all political action: the only certain way of preventing bureaucracy is to refrain from organization, but the refusal to organize with one's fellow men can lead only to acquiescence in detested power or to isolated and futile acts of martyrdom and terrorism. This is not, of course, to deny the validity of specific organizational rejections; it is merely to question Silone's belief, as it appears in *Bread and Wine*, that political goals can be reached without political organization.

It is, however, entirely to Silone's credit that he recognizes this dilemma and embodies it in the action of his book; he does not try to pry his way out of it with some rusty formula. One of his finest strokes in *Bread and Wine* is the scene in which Spina takes off his priestly frock—this occurs, significantly, *as soon as* a possibility for political action appears. He takes off his priestly frock but we are not to suppose that his experience as Paolo Spada the false priest has not left a profound mark upon him. The duality between Spina and Spada—between the necessity for action and the necessity for contemplation, between the urge to power and the urge to purity—is reflected in Silone's own experience as novelist and political leader. Even after he wrote *The Seed Beneath the Snow,* a novel in which he exemplifies a kind of Christian passivity and mute fraternity, he continued to participate in the quite worldly Italian socialist movement. In his own practice as an Italian socialist, he has been forced to recognize that the vexatious problems of means and ends involves a constant tension between morality and expediency which can be resolved, if resolved at all, only in practice.

Yet it is precisely from these scrupulous examinations of conscience and commitment that so much of the impact of *Bread and Wine* derives; no other twentieth-century novelist has so fully conveyed the pathos behind the failure of socialism. *Bread and Wine* is a book of misery and doubt; it moves slowly, painfully, in a weary spiral that traces the spiritual anguish of its hero. The characteristic turning of the political novelist to some apolitical temptation is, in Silone's case, a wistful search for the lost conditions of simple life where one may find the moral resources which politics can no longer yield. This pastoral theme, winding quietly through the book and reaching full development only in its sequel, *The Seed Beneath the Snow,* is not an easy one for the modern reader to take at face value: we are quick, and rightly so, to suspect programs for simplicity. But in Silone's work it acquires a unique validity: he knows peasant life intimately and, perhaps because he does not himself pretend to be a peasant, seldom stoops to pseudofolk romanticizing; he is aware that a return to simplicity by a man like Spina must have its painful and ironic aspects; his turn to pastoral does not imply social resignation but is, on the contrary, buttressed by a still active sense of social rebelliousness; and most important of all, he employs the pastoral theme not to make a literal recommendation but to suggest, as a tentative metaphor, the still available potentialities of man.

Bread and Wine is a work of humility, unmarred by the adventurism or occasional obsession with violence which disfigures the political novels of André Malraux and Arthur Koestler. Whatever the ideological hesitations of Silone's novels, they remain faithful to the essential experience of modern Europe; and to the harsh milieu of political struggle they bring a cleansing freshness, a warmth of fraternity.

When Silone brought his long exile to an end and returned to Italy after World War II, he found himself in a troubling situation. He had been honored in Europe and America as a writer who had measured the human damage done by Fascism, yet his work was little known to his countrymen. He had led a life of exemplary resistance to Mussolini's dictatorship, yet his very independence, now prompting him to an unpopular struggle against the Italian Communists, made the younger writers feel uneasy or even hostile toward him. The memory of his refusal to accommodate himself to the Fascist regime stirred feelings of bad conscience among literary men who had managed to be more flexible. He was a hard man to accept.

Alas, men of exemplary stature are often hard to accept. Returned exiles stir up feelings of guilt and irritation. And even when, like Silone, they are quite free from pretensions to moral superiority or mannerisms of bravado, they must seem a silent rebuke to those who had been less heroic or more cautious. But Silone was a man of gloomy and sardonic humor, who had suffered so much in his own life and absorbed so fully the terribleness of this century that the shakiness of his reputation in Italy, though it must have hurt him, did not long keep him from his proper work. That work was simply to keep retelling, in book after book, his one inevitable story: the story of a man who will not make his peace and thereby, at the very extreme of helplessness, comes to seem a reassertion of the human. Silone kept retelling this story to himself, almost as if to assure himself that it was still possible, and to his readers, that community of friends who also needed to hear that it is still possible.

For Silone the crisis of the middle years was especially harsh. The return to his homeland was difficult; his own political views were in flux, sometimes in disorder; and his efforts as a writer to go beyond his masterpiece, *Bread and Wine,* were not really successful. The novels he now wrote, such as *The Seed Beneath the Snow* and *A Handful of Blackberries,* still displayed patches of his special realism and humor, but they were victimized by his exhausting struggle with his own beliefs, the struggle of a socialist who has abandoned his dogmas yet wishes to preserve his animating values. These novels seem a little sluggish in their moralism, a little flaccid in their straining toward primitive Christian virtue. Silone's intentions seemed now, for the first time, to get the better of his imagination. To be sure, his characteristic irony breaks out in these novels, but not enough of it is directed toward his own predispositions of thought. It was as if he were surrendering too much of his power of sophistication and yielding too completely to that pastoral impulse which, while always present in his work, had been held in check by his essentially cosmopolitan and sardonic imagination.

After some years of silence, however, Silone managed a notable recovery. In the late fifties and early sixties he published two short novels, *The Secret of Luca* and *The Fox and the Camellias,* which seem to me—not many readers, I suppose, share this judgment—works that are both pleasing and fresh. Though never a literary modernist (Verga, not Joyce, is his master), Silone has always been an original writer, most notably in his use of anecdote as a major element in narration and in his readiness to employ the novel as a medium of conversation with the reader. These two novels show that in his quietly restless way he succeeded in breaking past the crisis of the middle years, not because he had solved his problems of belief but because he now wrote with the ease of a man who knows these problems will stay with him until the day of his death.

The form Silone developed in these books is peculiarly adapted to his intellectual condition. He now favors a brief, compact, and unadorned narrative, with very little of his earlier richness of anecdote or contemplation. The validating detail we associate with the novel as a genre is almost entirely absent. Silone drives his events forward with such a singleness of purpose that one soon realizes he has some commanding idea in sight; yet these

tales—for they are more tales than novels—do not succumb to
the abstractness or didacticism of allegory. They demand to be
read, at all but one crucial point, as accounts of ordinary human
experience. I would be inclined to call them realistic fables:
realistic in that they are clearly meant as imitations of "real" life,
and fables in that they are strictly pruned to the needs of Silone's
theme, composing themselves in the reader's mind as a kind of
quizzical *exemplum.*

At the crux of these tales there occurs, however, an incident
which breaks with the expectations of familiar realism and requires from the reader an act of faith. In *The Secret of Luca* it is
the possibility that an illiterate peasant would be ready to spend
twenty years in prison to protect the honor of a woman he loved;
in *The Fox and the Camellias* it is the possibility that a Fascist
spy would be so overcome with guilt at betraying political
enemies that he would commit suicide. Both of these events
place a certain strain upon our sense of credence, but in the
setting of Silone's books they come to represent his demand, at
once imperious and relaxed, that we share with him a belief in
the recurrent possibility of goodness. Just as the slightness of
form in these books signifies Silone's tacit awareness that he
now lives on an intellectual margin, so his own break from strict
verisimilitude signifies his consequent need to tax us with moral
expectations. And in both books there is also something that is
equally rare in modern literature: the effort to present a truly
honorable man, indeed the effort to retrieve the idea of a truly
honorable man. Modern literature is not exactly overwhelmed
with this impulse.

On the surface *The Secret of Luca* is unconcerned with those
political-moral themes that have occupied its predecessors. It is
a simple story, deliberately "old-fashioned" in style and leisurely in pace, for Silone is here trying to yoke together a traditional and long-abused notion—the "aristocratic" notion of honor
—with the character of a man at the bottom of social life.

Luca Sabbatino has suffered a lifetime of imprisonment, though
everyone in his village knows him to be innocent of the crime
with which he was charged; and now that he has come back,
still unwilling to explain why he refused to defend himself, the
mystery of his conduct is probed by Andrea Cipriano, the son
of his closest friend and now a prominent radical leader. Luca's

story is unfolded in a series of conversations—some of them wonderfully humorous *—in which Andrea discovers his secret: that he, a simple peasant, had accepted decades of prison in order to protect the honor of a woman whom he had come to worship with "a love that was totally absurd."

It is an improbable story, of course. But that, Silone seems to suggest with a smile, is precisely the point: without the improbability there could be no revelation. Every act of moral selflessness is by its nature improbable; it is beyond the calculus of social prediction and therefore contains enormous social possibilities. And it has these possibilities, as the discomfort of both Luca's village and Andrea Cipriano indicate, simply because it is intolerable. Andrea gradually drops his party affairs and becomes involved, as a kind of novice, in an improvised community centering about Luca and including Don Serafino, an old and neglected priest who represents the Christian remnant of the church, and a nameless boy who adopts Luca because he finds him "good at being friends."

I have said that on the surface *The Secret of Luca* seems different from Silone's earlier, political novels; yet anyone familiar with his work will quickly see that this novel continues in the line of its predecessors, and indeed constitutes a summary recapitulation of Silone's own development. For in part Andrea is the early Silone, the author of *Fontamara* committed to the Marxist belief in mass action, and Andrea's education in humaneness as he learns Luca's story also reflects Silone's intellectual history. At the end Luca and Andrea are pronounced by Don Serafino—with an intent ironically at variance from Silone's—to be "a couple of innocents" who endanger "law and order."

In *The Secret of Luca* there is little of the abstractness or vaporousness one usually finds in modern attempts at allegory; the schema of intention does not dam the flow of incident. Nor is there that multiplicity and fluidity of reference that characterize modern symbolism. Yet, as we are absorbed by the sequence of

---

* An old Italian peasant thinks back to a moment of his childhood:
I remember Don Serafino asking me at the catechism examination to explain the sign of the cross. "It reminds us of the Passion of our Lord," I told him, "and it's also the way unfortunates sign their names." The parish priest remarked that my answer wasn't wrong, but that I was hardly in a position to revise the answers in the catechism.

action, we become aware that Luca's story is controlled by a kind of allegorical meaning, indicated by the very names of the characters: Luca Sabbatino, the light of Sabbath; Don Serafino, the angelic; Andrea, man. There need be no objection to this method as such, but I would complain that Silone reined in too tightly his gifts for anecdote, that he overdisciplined himself in behalf of his motivating ideas.

In *The Fox and the Camellias* the central figure, Daniele, is a former skilled worker turned farmer, who lives in Switzerland and is active in the Italian anti-Fascist underground. He is entirely free of the sententiousness and saintly aspirations of Silone's earlier figures—indeed, the book contains a striking repudiation of asceticism. He is a beautifully realized character: a man of sharp wit, capable of risking his life for an idea yet hardheaded both in his work as farmer and in his role as head of a family; irascible and annoying in manner yet representing in himself that humane impulse which is the heritage of the best in European socialism.

Into the affectionate and tranquil circle of Daniele's home there comes a secret Fascist agent who pretends to, or perhaps does, fall in love with Daniele's daughter, Silvia, a girl of fine intelligence and feeling. The secret agent then manages to come upon Daniele's papers and thereby almost to disrupt the underground. For Silvia this is a terrible blow, both to her own burgeoning emotions and to her sense of loyalty to her father. It is here that Silone releases his surprise: the secret agent kills himself out of remorse—and so determined is Silone to stress the apparently gratuitous aspect of this event, to insist upon treating it as an act of faith between writer and reader, that he does not even trouble to represent it directly. Back at the home of Daniele, the family begins to reknit its life and Daniele himself, wearied and aged but still a man of good feeling, remarks to his younger daughter: "I'm sorry about the young man. . . . He wasn't a bad young man."

What gives this fable of remorse and forgiveness its special strength is the relaxed assurance with which Silone tells it. No one in the world knows these people as well as he, no one else can so thoroughly endow the paradigmatic scheme of his tale with so many shrewd touches of observation. Everything is drawn with a pungent wryness and clarity, everything told with that speed which comes to a writer who has gained a final mastery over his subject. If *The Fox and the Camellias* wins one's affection as a portrait of men in moments of trouble and solidarity, it engages our reflective interest as a plea for the idea of the *possible*, without which life must become unendurable. Perhaps the one complaint that can be ventured is that in the ripeness of his career Silone should content himself with a form inherently minor, but it is a complaint one dares murmur only out of the ingratitude of affection.

Silone's novels contain a profound vision of what heroism can be in the modern world. Like Malraux, he appreciates the value of action, but he also realizes that in the age of totalitarianism it is possible for a heroic action to consist of nothing but stillness, that for Spina and many others there may never be the possibility of an outward or public gesture. For Ernest Hemingway heroism is always a visible trial, a test limited in time and symbolized in dramatic confrontations. For Silone heroism is a condition of readiness, a talent for waiting, a gift for stubbornness; the heroism of tiredness. Silone's heroic virtues pertain to people who live, as Bertolt Brecht put it, in "the dark ages" of twentieth-century Europe.

T. E. Lawrence:
The Problem
of Heroism

I wanted only to try to live in obedience to the promptings which
came from my true self. Why was that so very difficult?
—DEMIAN

Time has mercifully dulled the image he despised yet courted:
T. E. Lawrence is no longer the idol of the twenties, no longer
"Lawrence of Arabia." But for the minority of men to whom
reflection upon human existence is both a need and a pleasure,
Lawrence seems still to matter. He is not yet a name to be put
away in history, a footnote in dust. He continues to arouse
sympathy, outrage, excitement. If we come to him admiring
whatever in his life was extraordinary, we remain with him out
of a sense that precisely the special, even the exotic in Lawrence
may illuminate whatever in our life is ordinary.

During the early twenties, after his return from Arabia, Lawrence became a national hero, the adventurer through whom
Englishmen could once more savor the sensations of war and
rescue emotions of sentimental grandeur. What he had done in
Arabia—more important, what he had experienced—was epic in
its proportions, and even a glance at his life prompts one to speculate about the nature of heroism in our century. But trans-
planted from the desert to the lantern slides of the Albert Hall,
where Lowell Thomas was conjuring for the English their stain-
less version of "Lawrence of Arabia," the whole wartime experi-

ence shrank to farce. Partly to salvage it from vulgarities he himself had condoned, Lawrence wrote *The Seven Pillars of Wisdom*, a bravura narrative packed with accounts of battle yet finally the record of his search for personal equilibrium and value. By then, however, his public image had acquired a being and momentum of its own. So the book, too, though in some ways esoteric, became popular—and helped sustain the image it was meant to subvert.

This sad comedy was to continue to the end. In *The Seven Pillars of Wisdom* the ideal of a forthright manly heroism, which Lawrence had supposedly rescued for an unheroic age, was soon transformed into the burden of self-consciousness, a burden he was never to escape. The dynamiter of railroads and bridges turned out to be an intellectual harassed by ambition and guilt. The literary man who had read Malory between desert raids and later worried over the shape and rhythm of the sentences in his book, made himself into a pseudonymous recruit tending the "shit-cart" of his camp. And these were but a few of his transfigurations.

Thomas Edward Lawrence was born in 1888, the second of five sons in a comfortable Victorian family. The father, a reserved gentleman who is said never to have written a check or read a book, devoted himself to the domestic needs of his family and a number of mild sports. The mother, clearly of lower rank, was a strong-spirited Scotch woman, ambitious for her sons, eager to share in their growth, the true psychic center of the family. Mrs. Lawrence raised her boys to be straightforward Christians—and the unambiguous piety with which two of them later met their death in the trenches of France must command respect even from those who might prefer a touch of rebellion.

In his youth Lawrence shared the family devoutness, serving briefly as a Sunday-school teacher; but whatever mark his religious training left upon him, he refused all formal belief during his adult years. Almost all his biographers have noted strong religious traits in Lawrence, straining toward some absolute of value by which to brace his conduct. Fewer have remarked on the tacit assumption he shared with many serious persons of our century: that the religious sensibility could be nurtured only in a culture of radical skepticism. (His friend, Eric Kennington, has recorded a conversation in which the adult Lawrence, asked about religion, spoke of a "process without aim or end, creation followed by dissolution, rebirth, and then decay to wonder at and to love. But not a hint of a god and certainly none of the Christian God.")

"Lessons," wrote Mrs. Lawrence, "were never any trouble to Ned [Lawrence's boyhood name], he won prizes every year . . . In the senior locals in 1906, he placed first in English language and literature . . . and thirteenth in the first class of some 10,000 entrants." Like a good many of the achievements that would later be dredged up from Lawrence's boyhood, this is impressive, but hardly as remarkable as his admirers have wished to suggest. Ned Lawrence was a bright, lively, inquiring boy; not a prodigy.

One trait merits special notice. In a family where all the sons were encouraged to a modest independence of bearing, Ned Lawrence stood out for his nervous boldness, a readiness to risk himself. His escapades and feats of physical endurance, both as a boy and then as a student at Oxford, were in part the proofs of strength that a small-bodied person feels obliged to thrust at the world, in part symptoms of a vanity which took the form of needing always to seem original. But these escapades and feats can also be seen as anticipations of his adult view that life is a test through which the human will, to assert its mastery over contingency and pain, denies the flesh not only its desires but its needs.

At some point before entering Oxford in 1907 Lawrence discovered that he and his brothers, apparently the sons of a respectable Oxford gentleman, were actually of illegitimate birth. His father, an Anglo-Irish baronet named Sir Thomas Chapman, had left a wife and four daughters in Ireland to run off with a former nurse, the woman who now figured both in public and at home as his wife. In letters written many years later to Mrs. Bernard Shaw—letters that may be read but not quoted—Lawrence would claim that he had known these facts before the age of ten. Like others of his stories about his past, this claim seems implausible.

How deep a shock the discovery of illegitimate birth caused Lawrence, we do not really know. To what extent it was the source of his sense of "homelessness" during the later years and

his need to keep asserting himself through a series of new iden-
tities—this question demands speculation but does not permit a
firm conclusion. One may see in the boy's discovery a matrix for
those predispositions to suffering which would mark the later
Lawrence. One may see it as a blow to his pride and self-esteem.
But it is surely a vast simplification to claim, as does Richard
Aldington in his venomous biography, that Lawrence received
a wound that would leave him crippled for life. The bare facts
—his gift for leadership, his success in winning the loyalty of
distinguished men, his ability to complete a major literary work
—all show that Lawrence was not permanently disabled by the
effects of this adolescent trauma, if trauma it was. I add this last
qualification because we must allow for the possibility that whatever pain the revelation caused him, Ned Lawrence, as an English boy raised on romantic notions and romantic books, might
have felt it *interesting* to have a father capable of such uncon-
ventionality in behalf of love.

Large parts of the boy's experience were intellectually vital
and traditionally wholesome. A fondness for history led him to
take bicycle trips through the south of England and make rub-
bings of monumental brasses. On his bedroom walls were pasted
life-size portraits of knights who had performed heroic deeds in
the Crusades. He devoured the medieval romances of William
Morris with a relish that—hard as it may be for us to grasp—he
would retain throughout his life. He attended lectures by Flind-
ers Petrie that helped spark his interest in antiquities. And he
began spending time at the Ashmolean Museum in Oxford,
where he met the archaeologist D. G. Hogarth, who would become his mentor, friend, protector—at critical moments, a kind
of father.

During the summers of 1906, 1907, 1908, on bicycle trips
through France, Ned Lawrence visited cathedrals and castles,
made careful notes, and wrote letters to his mother which, if a
trifle too "composed," are still notable for an exactness of observation and phrasing beyond the usual capacity of an eighteen
or nineteen-year-old boy. In the summer of 1909 he undertook
a more adventurous trip: a walking tour of Syria, the interior of
which was almost inaccessible to Europeans. His purpose was to
prepare an Oxford thesis on the Crusaders' castles. When he inquired about Syria from C. M. Doughty, whose *Arabia Deserta*

he knew and loved, the older man sent back a note advising that the journey would be risky if undertaken alone. "Long daily marches," warned Doughty, "a prudent man who knows the country would consider out of the question." But Lawrence went.

Suffering heat, fever, and a beating at the hands of a thief, Lawrence tramped eleven hundred miles through Syria, an average of twenty a day when on the move. He lived with Arab village families, ate *leben*, the Syrian yogurt, and bread "almost leathery when fresh." He photographed some fifty castles and established to his own satisfaction the main point of his thesis.

Perhaps for the first time we come upon qualities in Lawrence that may be considered remarkable: an intense fascination with the past, a ruthless insistence upon seeing things for himself, a readiness to submit to the customs of a strange, often hostile people, an eagerness to pursue an idea or action to its extreme limits. And something else, still more important. In Syria Lawrence came to feel the hypnotic pull of an alien style of life, one that was almost the antipode of Western civilization. Toward the Arabs he would now be drawn by ties both stronger and less tender—certainly more abstract—than love. As he wrote a few years later to a friend: "You guessed right that the Arab appealed to my imagination. It is the old, old civilization which has refined itself clear of household gods, and half the trappings which ours hasten to assume."

By his twenty-first year Lawrence was beginning to think seriously about a career in archaeology, though whether he thought seriously about the close work required by archaeological scholarship is another matter. Through the help of D. G. Hogarth, Lawrence became attached in 1910 to a British Museum expedition that was to dig at Carchemish on the banks of the Euphrates. For most of the next three years—the happiest of his life, he called them—Lawrence worked as an assistant, miscellaneous, nimble, and erratic, to the head of the expedition, first Hogarth and then Leonard Woolley.

At Carchemish Lawrence formed a close—and as it seems in retrospect, significant—friendship with Sheik Hamoudi, the foreman of the dig; and when he took another hike through Syria in the summer of 1911 which ended in bouts of fever and dysentary, it was Hamoudi who nursed him back to life. "He is our brother," the Arab would later say about Lawrence, "our friend and leader. He is one of us." *One of us:* a tribute that would have pleased Lawrence, amused him in its distance from truth, and finally disturbed him. For in stumbling upon Conrad's phrase, which for us evokes the whole tangle of fraternity and aloneness in human relationships, Hamoudi touched unwittingly upon the problem of bad faith that would torment Lawrence throughout his time in Arabia.

One fact more about the early Lawrence: In January 1914, as the world hurried toward war, he and Woolley went off on a trip through the area that runs south of Gaza and Beersheba and east of Akaba, ostensibly to retrace the routes of Biblical journeys for the Palestine Expeditionary Fund, actually to provide the British army with maps of a zone under Turkish sovereignty. For once there is justice in a complaint by Richard Aldington: "None of the intellectuals writing on Lawrence has expressed the faintest regret or indignation at this official abuse of science and religion to screen politico-military activities. . . ." Had Lawrence been anything but a man of austere moral sensibilities, this "official abuse," not the worst deed of our century, would hardly be worth noticing. Had he justified it in the name of military need, criticism might be given pause. But what disturbs one is that there was a side of Lawrence—the eternal British undergraduate with his sneaking admiration for "public school" pranks—that would regard such an incident as a lark. If the essential Lawrence was a man whose ordeal in Arabia burned every bit of pomp out of him, there was another Lawrence, a Kiplingesque schoolboy susceptible to romantic vanities about the mission of England, who was never quite to disappear. During the war years this other Lawrence would break out in a giggling superciliousness toward those military men he found dense and an equally callow adulation of those, like Allenby, he found enlightened. And who knows? Perhaps without this lesser Lawrence we should not have had the man who wrote *The Seven Pillars of Wisdom.*

In the spring of 1916 Sherif Hussein of the Hejaz, descendent of the Prophet, and protector of the faith, launched a revolt against the Turks. For some time the British had been tempting him with promises of postwar independence; but this shrewd fanatic had played a cautious game, rightly enough from his point of view, since he neither trusted the infidel British nor cared to risk the vengeance of the Turks.

At first the Arabs gained a few local victories, hardly decisive and, in their very success, exposing a poverty of purpose and leadership. But having lost the advantage of surprise and unable, with their irregular bands, to do more than harass entrenched Turkish posts, they now faced the danger of being wiped out by counterattack. The Arabs were ignorant of modern warfare; they had no master plan and barely an idea of why one might be needed; their main advantage lay not in any capacities of their own but in the sluggishness of the Turks. To provide help and soothe Hussein, British headquarters in Cairo sent an experienced official, Ronald Storrs, as envoy to the Hejaz. With him went T. E. Lawrence, who until then had spent the war months as an impudent and quite undistinguished staff captain in Military Intelligence.

In *The Seven Pillars of Wisdom* Lawrence has left a brilliant description of his first exploratory visit from one Arab camp to another, studying Hussein's three elder sons, each of whom led a body of troops. Ali, Abdullah, Feisal: which of these princes could become the focal point of rebellion, the embodiment of Arab desire? The picture of Lawrence plunging into the chaos of the Arab world, measuring the worth of its leaders and quickly bringing order to its ranks—this picture is surely overdrawn if one considers the limited powers Lawrence actually enjoyed at the moment. Not until after his return to Cairo and his assignment as British liaison officer to the Arab troops in the winter of 1917 did he even begin to command such authority. Yet the picture is essentially faithful if one grants Lawrence the right—he won it in the desert and then through his book—to treat his own experience as a fable of heroism: the right, that is, to assign a scheme of purpose to hesitant improvisations which in the end did come to bear such a purpose.

It was Hussein's third son, Feisal, decided Lawrence, who could serve as the "armed prophet" of revolt: Feisal, "very tall and pillar-like," who displayed a posture of assurance and a patience for mediating tribal feuds. And, it had better be added, Feisal responsive to the cues of this darting little Englishman with his "kitchen Arabic," his love for flamboyant dress, his curious pleasure in bending to the ritual and guile of Arab politics.

The speed with which Lawrence now became a leader of the revolt is astonishing, yet not difficult to explain. Between the xenophobic suspicions of the Arabs, who saw infidels descending upon them, and the routine military outlook of the British, who saw inefficiency all about them—which is to say, between two kinds of narrow-mindedness, each reflecting a different century—there arose in the Hejaz a vacuum of leadership. For the revolt to survive, the vacuum had to be filled. And it could be filled only by a man able to endow it with a coherent idea such as would appeal both to the predatory caution and reckless fanaticism of the Arabs.

The idea Lawrence first brought to the Arab revolt was not primarily a military one; nor did it yet have in his private reflections those metaphysical bearings that would later absorb him. Lawrence began by approaching the revolt not as a partisan but as a strategist. He approached it as a problem in dynamics: what was needed to move these people into action and, given their notorious inconstancy, to keep them in action? what kind of an enterprise could they reasonably be expected to assume and complete? To ask such questions was to enter the realm of politics, not as a system of ideas but as a makeshift theory of national psychology.

The tribal Arabs with whom Lawrence had now to deal, unlike the city intelligentsia and middle class of Syria, had almost no tradition of nationalism; they knew at best glimmers and anticipations of national feeling. The Arabs were not a nation at all; they were remnants and shards of what might once have been a nation; they contained perhaps the elements from which a nation might be forged. But Lawrence could not wait (nor could the Arabs) until they became one; he could only think of a course of action which, if they were enabled to pursue it with some freedom, would stir the Arabs into behaving *as if* they were a nation.

What might bring this about? Primarily the belief that they could or should be a nation; a burgeoning sense of their possibilities, such as they themselves could barely express; and a strategy of conflict that pressed them into momentary coherence without risking the full-scale warfare for which they were not prepared, since they were as quick to drop into discouragement as to flare into passion. Lawrence had to improvise a strategy of national politics for a cluster of tribes that neither was a nation nor had a politics. He had to find symbols and tactics for transforming their primitive antagonism to the Turks into a facsimile of a modern purpose: but a modern purpose that could retain its thrust only by drawing upon the sources of the primitive antagonism.

Such considerations were obviously beyond the reach of most British officers, who saw only the noisy surface of Arab chaos and felt, therefore, that the best policy would be to bring in a sizable body of disciplined European troops. The French mission in the Hejaz, understanding Lawrence better, feared him more. It knew that any mobilization of Arab consciousness, no matter how useful at the moment, would threaten the structure of Allied power in the Middle East. No wonder that Lawrence complained in *The Seven Pillars of Wisdom* about the "blindness of European advisors, who would not see that rebellion was not war: indeed, was more of the nature of peace—a national strike perhaps." The moment Lawrence understood this, he was ready for his task.

In so reconstructing his situation, I do not mean to imply that Lawrence fully grasped the workings of Arab society and religion, or the role of colonial rivalries among the great powers, or the general problem of nationalism in our century. Far from it. But what he grasped with absolute mastery was that the revolt could succeed only if it wore the face of freedom, only if it used the language of autonomy, only if it became a cause. To become a cause, it would have to be fought mainly by the Arabs themselves and appear to be led mainly by the Arabs themselves. If they could not be trained to positional warfare in the style of the period, they would have to be directed to other varieties of combat in which the more experienced Turkish army could not decimate them. British troops, except for a few technical advisors, would have to be kept away from the desert, at least until the Arabs gained some sense of their own powers. Good light weapons and a steady flow of gold were indispensable. Upon the tribal rivalries, the greed, the religious particularism of the Arabs there would have to be grafted a façade of unity: from which, if skillful enough, there might yet come the reality of national existence.

Lawrence was not deluded. He understood that the nationalism of the colonial countries was often devious and venal; that today's oppressed might be tomorrow's oppressors; that once freedom was won there might follow a moral relapse which would make the whole effort seem a waste. But he also sensed that meanwhile there lay imbedded in this nationalism an unformed yearning for dignity. If, for a time, the Arabs could be brought to act by this yearning, the revolt might succeed. If not, it would fail.

Lawrence saw the revolt in its political wholeness and moral dynamism: not merely as it was, fouled by intrigue, cupidity and narrowness of spirit, but as it might become, an ideal possibility. He possessed the vision which, historically, was the Arabs' privilege: that was cause for elation. He knew they could not sustain his vision: that was cause for despair. Balancing elation and despair Lawrence, while still under thirty, reached full knowledge of the burdens of leadership.

Am I here endowing Lawrence with a coherence he would later claim but never really possess? Or assigning to him perceptions he would reach, if at all, only after the event? The record of his work and writings must stand as answer, but consider at least this sequence of passages, written before, during, and immediately after the revolt:

1915

I want to pull them all [the "little powers" of Arabia] together, & to roll up Syria by way of the Hejaz in the name of the Sherif. You know how big his repute is in Syria . . . we can rush right up to Damascus, & biff the French out of all hope of Syria. It's a big game. . . . (From a letter to D. G. Hogarth)

1916

A difference in character between the Turkish and Arab armies is that the more you distribute the former the weaker they become, and the more you distribute the latter the stronger they become. (From *The Arab Bulletin*)

1917

The Arab movement is a curious thing. It is really very small and weak in its beginning, and anybody who had command of the sea

could put an end to it in three or four days. It has capacity for expansion however—in the same degree—over a very wide area. It is as
though you imagine a nation or agitation that may be very wide, but
never very deep, since all the Arab countries are agricultural or
pastoral, and all poor today. . . .

On the other hand the Arab movement is shallow, not because the
Arabs do not care, but because they are few—and in their smallness
of numbers (which is imposed by their poverty of country) lies a
good deal of their strength, for they are perhaps the most elusive
enemy an army ever had. . . . It is indiscreet only to ask what Arabia
is. It has an East and a West and a South Border—but where or
what it is on the top no man knoweth. I fancy it is up to the Arabs
to find out! (From a letter to his parents)

1920

. . . but suppose we were an influence (as we might be), an idea, a
thing invulnerable, intangible, without front or back, drifting about
like a gas? Armies were like plants, immobile as a whole, firm-rooted,
nourished through long stems to the head. We might be a vapour,
blowing where we listed. Our kingdoms lay in each man's mind, and
as we wanted nothing material to live on, so perhaps we offered
nothing material to the killing.

. . . The Turk . . . would believe that rebellion was absolute, like
war, and deal with it on the analogy of absolute warfare. Analogy is
fudge, anyway, and to make war upon rebellion is slow and messy,
like eating soup with a knife.

. . . We had seldom to concern ourselves with what our men did,
but much with what they thought. . . . We had won a province when
we had taught the civilians in it to die for our ideal of freedom; the
presence or absence of the enemy was a secondary matter. (From
"The Evolution of a Revolt")

These passages chart Lawrence's growing mastery of statement, but far more important, a development of thought and
value almost to the point of establishing him as a new person.
First, the simple-minded scheme for "biffing" the French. In
1917 the notation of a newly seen complexity: a notation somewhat distant, neutral, but not unsympathetic. And finally the
last statement, which Lawrence would work into *The Seven
Pillars of Wisdom,* rising to an earned and measured eloquence:
the revolt as idea, as undefiled conception. Yet this pattern is
surely too neat, for Lawrence did not shed his earlier views, he
buried them beneath his later ones. And the further qualification must be added that if the last passage gives us the essence

of what the revolt could still mean to Lawrence—for by 1920 it often turned to ashes in his mouth—the earlier passages provide evidence as to its less exalted realities.

In regard to so elusive a mind as Lawrence's, no simple distinction can be enforced between action and response, what "really" happened and what he made of it in memory. Lawrence neither was nor could be a detached observer; he was leader, follower, victim, all in one. He tells us that his first commanding view of the revolt came to him in March 1917 when, for ten days, he lay sick in the camp of Abdullah. Perhaps, in writing *The Seven Pillars of Wisdom*, Lawrence gave dramatic form to his memories by condensing a long experience of discovery into a moment of sudden realization. But this possibility should not be allowed to blur the fact that there was discovery. Even in Arabia history is not all muddle or chance; even in Arabia there is intelligence, plan, purpose. And to the extent that these were present in the revolt, they were significantly Lawrence's: not his alone, but his most forcefully.

It is possible that the innovations in military tactics claimed for Lawrence were neither so revolutionary nor so calculated as has been supposed—though by now only specialists and old friends will have strong opinions about Lawrence as commander. It is possible that a good many of his glamorous desert raids were of uncertain value—though in guerrilla warfare bold acts can have consequences beyond their immediate military effects. It is possible that without British gold Lawrence could not have held together the Arab chieftains, though one may wonder whether anyone else could have done it with twice as much gold. But one thing seems certain: it was Lawrence who grasped the inner logic of the revolt as a moral-political act and it was Lawrence who breathed into it a vibrancy of intention it had not previously known.

What his plunge into the desert meant to Lawrence he never fully said, perhaps because the main concern in his writings was to present his relations to the Arabs as a problem—a problem that could not be reduced to his private needs or desires.* From

---

* Some private desires there surely were. *The Seven Pillars of Wisdom* bears a fervid dedication in verse to "S.A.," who is generally taken to be an Arab Lawrence knew before the war. It has also been surmised, from

fragments of evidence left by Lawrence and those who were close to him, one may cautiously reconstruct some of his responses.

Lawrence, the cocky young officer who had been disliked so fiercely by the military regulars in Cairo, saw the Arabian campaign as an adventure in the simplest, most *English* sense of the word. This Lawrence took eagerly to the whole ritual-pageant of the Arab camps and Arab ceremonies and Arab powwows, though he knew that half the time they were mere displays veiling weakness. This Lawrence suddenly found himself cast in a role such as might satisfy the wildest fantasies of a middle-class English youth raised on romantic literature. With a sharp eye for stylized effects, he continued in his own way the tradition of those English visitors to the Middle East who have managed to penetrate native life without ceasing to be immaculately English.

He loved to ride with Feisal at the head of a racing camel army. He loved to dress in spotless white robes, sometimes scarlet and white. He loved to sit in Feisal's tent, gravely listening and dropping an occasional word during negotiations with tribal chiefs who were edging toward the Arab cause. He loved to compete with Auda Abu Tayi, leading sheik of the Howeitat, a warrior out of the barbaric past. And he took a special delight in acquiring for himself a bodyguard of dark-skinned Ageyl fighters, who formed a legion obedient to his command. An English officer, meeting Lawrence at Akaba in 1918, found him

. . . a small man dressed in extremely good and expensive Bedouin clothes, a richly braided and decorated goat's hair cloak over all, and on his head a wonderful silk kufaiyeh held in position by a gold agal. His feet were bare, and he had a gold Hejazi dagger in his belt. . . .

But even to act out this operatic role, Lawrence had to pay so terrible a price that one comes to disregard the flash and histrionics. From his return to the Hejaz until the day the British and Arabs entered Damascus, Lawrence accepted an appalling quantity of hardship. He learned to walk barefoot on hot sands

---

teasing hints dropped by Lawrence to his biographers, that one motive for wishing to undertake the campaign in the desert was to reach "S.A." But whether this person was, as Robert Graves insists, a woman Lawrence had met in Syria or whether it was the Arab boy Sheik Ahmoud whom he had befriended at Carchemish, we do not know. There are other possibilities, but they are little more than guesses.

with the aplomb of an Arab; to ride camels on lacerating marches; to go for days without food and then plunge his fingers into fatty stews; to show a contempt for pain which would win the respect of the most savage tribesman; to yield his body to exhaustion and then force it once again into war; to be on guard against those who might betray him for gold or wish him out of the way so they might pillage without check; to witness, often in necessary silence, repeated outbursts of cruelty (for the Arab's "sterile experience robbed him of compassion and perverted his human kindness to the image of the waste in which he hid"). And there were other, more intimate causes of suffering.

Lawrence never wished to persuade the Arabs that he had become one of them. Not only would that have been ludicrous, it would have threatened his mode of leadership. He did something more subtle and, in their eyes, impressive: he convinced the Arabs that in basic stoicism, outer bearing, and daily practice he could become remarkably like them. The dream of "going back," of stripping to a more primitive self, which has so often fascinated Western man, was an authentic motive in his Arabian experience; but it was also consciously used by Lawrence to further his public role.

For a man who was so deeply drawn to the idea and the experience of *overcoming*—particularly a self-overcoming in the sense foreshadowed by Nietzsche—the war in Arabia came to be a test through radical humiliation and pain.

As he immersed himself in the life of the desert, repeating again and again the cycle of exertion—a moment of high excitement, a plunge into activity, then sickness, self-scrutiny, the wild desire to escape, and finally a clenched return—Lawrence saw his experience as more than a romantic escapade or fearful discipline. Since in the bareness of the desert he had to remold his existence in order to meet a historical demand, he also found there the possibility of an action through which to carve out a chosen meaning for his life. From the trivia, the ugliness, the absurdity, the assured betrayal of events he would snatch a trophy of freedom.

In themselves courage and pain meant very little; men were being killed in France who also knew pain and showed courage. But they were mere dumb bodies led to slaughter. Lawrence, however, found himself in a situation where he might determine the character of his experience—or so it seemed to him in occasional moments of lucidity. To help make the Arabs into a free people was a task worthy of an ambitious man. To help steer the revolt past an enemy that would destroy it and allies that would disarm it, was a challenge worthy of a serious man. The fighting, to be sure, brought moments when such visions seemed utterly fatuous. There were wretched little raids where he had to use all his strength just to keep his forces from disintegrating, since the Arabs, indifferent to consequences, took pillage as the natural fruit of victory. There was the despair following a discovery that Zeid, Feisal's younger brother, had stupidly squandered a large sum of money and imperiled the revolt. There was the shock of learning that Auda, disgruntled in his greed, had entered into secret negotiations with the Turks. But through it all Lawrence kept hoping that he might do something fine in the desert, perhaps something extraordinary.

He seized upon the Arabian campaign as an occasion for heroism not merely or primarily as it meant courage and recklessness, but as it meant the possibility for stamping intelligence and value upon a segment of history. To leave behind the settled life of middle-class England, which seemed to offer little but comfort and destruction; to abandon the clutter of routine by which a man can fill his days, never knowing his capacity for sacrifice or courage; to break with the assumption that life consists merely of waiting for things to happen; to carve out an experience which, in the words of Georg Simmel, would "determine its beginning and end according to its own formative power"—these were the yearnings that Lawrence discovered in the revolt. And these are the motifs of his conduct that have made him so attractive to an age in which the capacities for heroism seem constantly to diminish.

Put aside the posturing and play-acting, put aside the embroidered robes and gold daggers, and there still remains the possibility of that rare action by which a man, rising above the limitations of moment and place, reaches the heart of excellence— a possibility, as Lawrence knew, that comes but rarely and must be seized with total desire, if seized at all. In the words of the hero of Malraux's *The Royal Way*, he wished to "put a scar on the map."

It is also in this sense, so utterly unlike the one I noticed a page or two back, that Lawrence undertook the Arabian campaign as an adventure: the sense, in Simmel's words, that an adventure is like a work of art, "for the essence of the work of art is . . . that it cuts out a piece of endlessly continuous sequence of perceived experience, giving it a self-sufficient form as though defined and held together by an inner core. . . . Indeed, it is an attribute of this form to make us feel that, in both the work of art and the adventure, the whole of life is somehow comprehended and consummated." Exactly what Lawrence came to hope for in the desert: that somehow, through an unimaginable exertion, the whole of his life would be comprehended and consummated.

At one decisive point, however, Lawrence's career turns sharply from the pattern suggested by Simmel. "The adventurer of genius," writes Simmel, "lives, as if by mystic instinct, at the point where the course of the world and the individual fate have, so to speak, not yet been differentiated from one another." About Lawrence this was not true, and everything that led him to think of his experience in Arabia as an imposture shows it could not be true. Consider the qualities implied by Simmel when he evokes the hero or, as he prefers to call him, "the adventurer of genius." The hero is a man with a belief in his inner powers, a confidence that he moves in rhythm with natural and historic forces, a conviction that he has been chosen for his part and thereby lifted above personal circumstances. At moments Lawrence felt one or another of these, but surely not with classic fulfillment or ease. Though his "individual fate" was indeed yoked to "the course of the world," in the end the two moved in profound opposition to each other.

Lawrence found it hard to believe in the very deeds he drove himself to perform. His fulfillment of the hero's traditional tasks was undercut at every point by a distrust and mockery of the idea of heroism. He could not yield himself to his own *charisma;* he was never certain of those secret gifts which for the hero ought to be an assured possession; he lived on the nerve's edge of consciousness, forever tyrannized by questions. At the end he abandoned his adventure with a feeling that inaction might be the most enviable of states and a desire to transform heroism into a discipline for the purging of self.

Is it fanciful to think that we have here a distinctly "modern"

mode of heroism? So it seemed to Herbert Read when he re-
viewed *The Seven Pillars of Wisdom* in 1928. "About the hero,"
wrote Read, "there is an essential undoubting directness . . .
essentially he is self-possessed, self-reliant, arrogant, unintelli-
gent. Colonel Lawrence was none of these. . . . He was a lame
duck in an age of lame ducks; a soldier spoilt by introspection
and self-analysis; a man with a load on his mind. . . . [Lawrence's
mind was] not great with thought, but tortured with some restless spirit that drives it out into the desert, to physical folly and
self-immolation, a spirit that never triumphs over the body and
never attains peace." Except for the ungenerous phrase about
"physical folly," Read was here both accurate and perceptive.
Read meant his remarks as a partial depreciation, but they point,
I think, to the very ground for our continued interest in Lawrence. By now it is almost impossible to accept as a model of the
heroic the sort of divine ox that Read claimed to admire. For
better or worse, the hero as he appears in the tangle of modern
life is a man struggling with a vision he can neither realize nor
abandon, "a man with a load on his mind."

As Lawrence assumed greater burdens of responsibility in the
desert campaign, his feeling that he had become a creature
apart, isolated from both the Arabs and English, kept steadily
growing. So, too, did his need to subject himself to the cruelest
accusations. Some of Lawrence's difficulties were of a personal
character and would have troubled him, though perhaps less
violently, even if he had never come to Arabia; others followed
from the very nature of warfare.

In the fall of 1917, during a scouting expedition into enemy
territory, Lawrence was captured by the Turks at Deraa. Fortunately not recognized, he was taken to be a deserter and
brought before the local commandant, "a bulky man [who] sat
on the bed in a night gown, trembling and sweating as though
with fever. . . ." There followed a scene in which physical torture
and sexual violation merged in a blur of pain. Later, in *The
Seven Pillars of Wisdom*, Lawrence would describe it with a
cold, almost clinical hysteria:

I remembered the corporal kicking with his nailed boot to get me
up . . . I remembered smiling at him, for a delicious warmth, prob-

ably sexual, was swelling through me: and then that he flung up his arm and hacked the full length of his whip into my groin. This doubled me half-over, screaming, or rather, trying impotently to scream, only shuddering through my open mouth. One giggled with amusement. A voice cried, "Shame, you killed him." Another slash followed. A roaring, and my eyes went black: while within me the core of life seemed to heave slowly up through the rending nerves. . . .

The two or three pages which recapture Lawrence's ordeal at Deraa anticipate a library of recollections by the victims of twentieth-century totalitarianism. Few are more terrible than Lawrence's, though even in this extreme self-exposure, so honest about that side of himself which sought after pain, he could not quite succeed in being candid about the extent of his violation. From it he never fully recovered; for years he would impress people as a man battling his nerves to maintain the appearance of control.

The incident at Deraa would have been enough to break stronger and more secure men, but one reason it so tortured Lawrence in memory has to do with his sexual life. That Lawrence did not have what today we call a normal relationship with a woman, seems an incontrovertible fact. He shied away from women unless they were notably maternal, and his repeated expressions of disgust concerning the sexual act go far beyond the bounds of timidity or fastidiousness. Whether Lawrence was a practicing homosexual it is not possible to say with any authority: the evidence of his friends ranges from genuine bewilderment to special pleading. There are passages in *The Seven Pillars of Wisdom* which show that Lawrence was drawn to the idea or image of homosexuality as it occurred with apparent simplicity and purity among his young Arab warriors. But if, as one suspects, his sexual impulses were usually passive and suppressed, that would have been all the more reason for suffering a poignant sense of isolation in the desert, where he was thrown into an exclusively male society and the habits of the Bedouins were accepted without fuss or judgment.

There were other, more public reasons for his despair. By the summer of 1917 he knew about the Sykes-Picot treaty, a secret arrangement among Britain, France, and Russia for perpetuating imperialism in the Middle East. This agreement made a farce of the promises of independence that had been given by Lawrence —though not by him alone—to the Arabs. Lawrence smarted under the knowledge that no matter what he would now say or do, he had no choice but to further this deceit. He had hoped, as he flamboyantly wrote in the suppressed preface for *The Seven Pillars of Wisdom*, "to restore a lost influence, to give 20 millions of Semites the foundations on which to build an inspired dream-palace of their national thoughts." The reality, which made him all the sicker as he became a legendary figure among the Arabs, was "a homesickness [which] came over me stressing vividly my outcast life among the Arabs, while I exploited their highest ideals, and made their love of freedom one more tool to make England win." And when, at a moment of climax in the Arabian campaign, Lawrence delivered a "halting, half-coherent speech" to the Serahin tribe—

There could be no rest-houses for revolt, no dividend of joy paid out. Its style was accretive, to endure as far as the senses would endure, and to use each such advance as base for further adventure, deeper privation, sharper pain. . . . To be of the desert was, as they knew, to wage unending battle with an enemy who was not of the world, nor life, nor anything but hope itself; and failure seemed God's freedom to mankind. . . . Death would seem best of all our works, the last free loyalty within our grasp, our final leisure. . . .

—he was speaking from the center of his new beliefs, assaulting his listeners at the point where he could make "their worldliness fade," but also, as he felt, enticing them into a net of deception.

Lawrence knew the Arabs had been selfish, narrow, treacherous all through the campaign but wondered whether, in the light of self-interest, they had not been justified. He knew Doughty had been right in saying the Arabs had "a presumptuous opinion of themselves, yet [also] a high indolent fantasy distempered with melancholy. . . ." Victory, wrote Lawrence, "always undid an Arab force." And in a fine sentence in *The Seven Pillars of Wisdom* he brought together his complex feelings about the Arabs: "The Arab respected force a little: he respected craft more, and often had it in an enviable degree: but most of all he respected blunt sincerity of utterance, nearly the sole weapon God had excluded from his armament."

Had Lawrence been a principled anti-imperialist for whom

sentiments of national pride were irrelevant, his problem might
have been easier to bear. But he was not a principled anti-
imperialist and he did retain sentiments of national pride. In
fact, his shame and guilt derived precisely from a lingering
belief in the British claim to fairness. Despite superb intuitions,
he never reached a coherent view of the world political struggle
in which finally he, too, was a pawn. There were moments when
he saw, but he could not long bear the vision, that his whole
adventure had been absorbed by a mere struggle for power.
Lawrence was a man—hopeless, old-fashioned romantic!—who believed in excellence and honor; he came at the wrong time, in
the wrong place.

On his thirtieth birthday, during a peaceful day shortly before
the entry into Damascus, Lawrence tried to examine himself
honestly, without delusion:

Four years ago I had meant to be a general and knighted when thirty.
Such temporal dignities (if I survived the next four weeks) were now
in my grasp. . . . There was a craving to be famous; and a horror of
being known to like being known. . . . The hearing other people
praised made me despair jealously of myself. . . . I began to wonder
if all established reputations were founded, like mine, on fraud. . . . I
must have had some tendency, some aptitude, for deceit. Without that
I should not have deceived men so well, and persisted two years in
bringing to success a deceit which others had framed and set afoot. . . .

As it now seemed to him, almost everything he had done was
negligible in scale and value, a triviality of success. This judg-
ment he would later express most forcibly in the preface to *The
Seven Pillars of Wisdom,* and the summary of this preface that
André Malraux has provided might almost have been written by
Lawrence himself:

. . . he was carried away at first by the appeal of liberty and was so
completely committed to its service that he ceased to exist; he lived
under the constant threat of torture; his life was ceaselessly crossed by
strange longings fanned by privations and dangers; he was incapable
of subscribing to the doctrines he preached for the good of his country at war . . . he ceased to believe in his civilization or in any other,
until he was aware of nothing but an intense solitude on the border-
line of madness; and what he chiefly recalled were *the agony, the
terrors and the mistakes.*

When the British and Arabs marched into Damascus, the war came to an end for Lawrence. "In the black light of victory, we could scarcely identify ourselves."

Lawrence returned to England in November 1918, hoping, as he had written to his friend Vyvyan Richards, for "a long quiet like a purge and then a contemplation and decision of future roads." Nothing of the sort proved to be possible. The Versailles peace conference was a few months away; Feisal would be coming, ill-prepared and vulnerable; the Arab cause required pleading. Time and again Lawrence found himself wishing to shake off his responsibilities to the Arabs, who seemed far less admirable in peace than in war. It was not hard to surmise by now the order of civilization they would be bringing to the Middle East: a mixture of the worst of several possible worlds. But having yielded himself to a historical action, Lawrence felt that as a matter of honor he had to see it through.

He remained, to all appearances, a figure coiled with energy and purpose. His mind was never more supple than during these months in which he prepared to sabotage French and then British ambitions. But in his writings of the period—the impression is strengthened by memoirs of his friends—one gains a sense of teeth clenched, hands tightened, a weariness beyond measure: as if he were trying to complete a necessary task and then lapse into silence.

In England Lawrence sent a memorandum to the Cabinet proposing the creation of several independent Arab states, with Hussein's sons as limited monarchs and with moderate guidance and help to come from the West. That the Arabs were not ready for independence Lawrence knew quite well; no long-suppressed people ever is, except as it breaks past the limits of its suppression. Lawrence reached the core of the problem in an article he published in 1920: "We have to be prepared to see [the Arabs] doing things by methods quite unlike our own, and less well; but on principle it is better that they half-do it than that we do it perfectly for them."

Lawrence realized that his proposal would be bitterly fought by the French, if only because it allowed independence to the Syrian coastal area which the Sykes-Picot treaty had reserved for France. He understood that the British, to gain any peace at all, would have to compromise with their main ally. What he did not foresee—and here one may charge him with political naïveté—was that strong voices in England would be eager to work out an arrangement giving Syria to the French and allowing Britain to dominate Iraq.

At the peace conference his status was ambiguous. Formally, he acted as advisor to the British delegation; actually, in the words of the Swedish writer Erik Lönnroth, he "functioned as representative of several Arab states which did not yet exist, and whose still vague contours he himself had greatly helped to form." The French, by now well briefed on his opinions and temper, treated him with frigid correctness. "If he comes as a British colonel, in an English uniform," read the instructions of the French foreign minister, "we will welcome him. But we will not accept him as an Arab. . . ." Yet it was precisely "as an Arab" that Lawrence did come, to badger and court Lloyd George, Arthur Balfour, Colonel Edward House, and even Clemenceau.

As negotiations dragged into the summer of 1919, it became clear that the British had decided to let France take Syria; in the labyrinth of cynicism and interest that would comprise the Versailles treaty, this was a small part of the bargain. The Arabs, sensing defeat, began to put up a show of truculence, notably in a popular congress held in Syria which proclaimed Feisal its head and independence its goal. The French, determined on a stern policy, were itching to drive Feisal's troops out of Damascus. And Lawrence, alone and powerless, grew increasingly estranged from his countrymen.

In the spring he had taken an airplane flight to Cairo with the intention of collecting his notes for *The Seven Pillars of Wisdom,* and when the plane crashed near Rome, had suffered a broken collarbone and rib fractures. The painful accident, together with the recent death of his father and the crumbling of his hopes at Versailles, brought him close to nervous exhaustion. As his reputation grew, his capacities declined. When the French heard of the flight to Cairo, they set up a panicky cry that he was returning to the Middle East to lead an Arab resistance; in reality, Lawrence was in no condition to lead anything. As he returned to Paris, all he could do was persist in a quixotic loyalty to the Arabs, a loyalty resting more on principle than affection. And this stubbornness—let us call it by its true name: this absolute unwill-ingness to sell out—began to strike his British colleagues as *un-reasonable*, an embarrassment to their diplomacy.

On July 17 Lord Curzon telegraphed Balfour that Lawrence should not be allowed to work with Feisal any longer, since this would "cause us serious embarrassment with the French." An official of the British Foreign Office attached to the Paris delega-tion wrote in confidence: "While fully appreciating the value of Lawrence as a technical advisor on Arab affairs, we regard the prospect of his return to Paris in any capacity with grave mis-givings. We and the War Office feel strongly that he is to a large extent responsible for our troubles with the French. . . ." At a peace conference, a man of principle can become a nuisance.

Lawrence kept searching for possibilities to maneuver. He appealed to the Americans in the name of self-determination; wrote pleading notes to the English leaders; sent a letter to the London *Times* arguing the Arab case and declaring—though this the editor did not print—that he regretted his wartime actions since the British government clearly had no intention of living up to the promises it had authorized him to make the Arabs. But it was hopeless, a lost cause. "By the mandate swindle," as Law-rence later said, "England and France got the lot." What Lawrence now felt came to far more than personal disappoint-ment; it was a rupture of those bonds of faith that had made him a good and, in some respects, characteristic Englishman of his day. Now he "looked at the West and its conventions with new eyes: they destroyed it all for me."

By the end of 1919 the strain had become too great. Lawrence told himself that he had failed, perhaps betrayed, the Arabs. He harassed himself mercilessly in the writing of *The Seven Pillars of Wisdom*. And then, at the very moment of failure, he was thrust into public notoriety through Lowell Thomas's illustrated lecture, "With Allenby in Palestine and Lawrence in Arabia," a spectacle that in London alone drew over a million adoring spectators. Lawrence became a popular legend—cheap and vul-gar—through the devices of a skillful journalist.

But also, one must add, through his own connivance: a con-nivance in which vanity and masochism joined to betray him. "I'm a sublimated Aladdin, the thousand and second Knight, a Strand-Magazine strummer," moaned Lawrence in early 1920, for he was far too intelligent not to see what Thomas was doing to him. Yet he failed to correct the numerous distortions, even after Hubert Young, his wartime companion, protested Thomas's statement that the British officers in Arabia had not accompanied Lawrence to the front. And he went to hear Thomas's lecture at least five times, apparently relishing his transformation into "a Strand-Magazine strummer." When "spotted," reports Thomas, "he would turn crimson, laugh in confusion, and hurry away with a stammered word of apology."

How was this possible? Why did Lawrence permit and even encourage Thomas to continue? There is no single answer, only a complex of possible reasons. The vaudeville in which Lawrence was cast as prince of the desert, served as a balm to feelings that had been hurt at Versailles: there was pleasure of a kind in being recognized at the Albert Hall and stared at in the streets. His new public role appealed to his sense of the sardonic, his sense of the distance between hidden truth and outer parody. It stimulated a kind of self-mortification, a twisting of the knife of public shame into the wounds of his ego. But at best these are explanations, and neither justify nor excuse. The truth is that it is hard to understand this episode, and harder still to accept it, unless of course we are prepared to show a little kindness toward a stricken man.

Yet not a hopelessly stricken man, for on one side of him Lawrence continued to behave like a tough and bouncy Irishman. Precisely during this period of failure, heartsickness, and notoriety Lawrence kept working away with an insatiable ambition, often for whole days and nights, at *The Seven Pillars of Wisdom*. Largely written in 1919, the manuscript was lost, completely and painfully redone, and in 1922 set up in proof at the Oxford *Times*. How ambitious he was Lawrence revealed in a letter to Edward Garnett:

Do you remember my telling you once that I collected a shelf of "Titanic" books (those distinguished by greatness of spirit, "sublimity," as Longinus would call it): and that they were *The Karamazovs*, *Zarathustra* and *Moby Dick*. Well, my ambition was to make an English fourth. You will observe that modesty comes out more in the performance than the aim.

"An English fourth" Lawrence did not quite make. Still, the book is one of the few original works of English prose in our century, and if Lawrence's name lives past the next half-century it may well be for the book rather than the experience behind it. The book is subtitled "a triumph," and in regard to the Arabian campaign, formally its central action, this must surely be read as irony. In another sense, however, it *is* a triumph: a vindication of consciousness through form.

As autobiography *The Seven Pillars of Wisdom* is veiled, ambiguous, misleading; less a direct revelation than a performance from which the truth can be wrenched. Nor can it be taken as formal history, since it focuses too subjectively, too obsessively, perhaps too passionately on its theme: which is the felt burden of history rather than history itself. Yet the book *as an act* has become part of the history of our politics, and is as necessary for comprehending the twentieth century as Brecht's poems or Kafka's novels or Pirandello's plays.

Primarily the book is a work of art, the model for a genre that would become all too characteristic of the age: a personal narrative through which a terrible experience is relived, burned out, perhaps transcended. This genre, to be perfected by the victims of totalitarianism, is a perilous one, succumbing too easily to verbal mannerism and tending to wash away the distinction between history and fable.

The Seven Pillars of Wisdom is a work of purgation and disgorgement. It is also, in order to resist the pressures of memory, a work of the most artful self-consciousness in which Lawrence is constantly "arranging words, so that the one I care for most is either repeated, or syllable-echoed, or put in a startling position." Robert Graves has said that "the nervous strain of its ideal of faultlessness is oppressive," and Lawrence himself found that the book is "written too hard. There are no flat places where a man can stand still for a moment. All ups and downs, engine full on or brakes hard on." The feverish state in which Lawrence composed the book, especially the early drafts—

I tie myself into knots trying to reenact everything, as I write it out. It's like writing in front of a looking-glass, and never looking at the paper, but always at the imaginary scene.

—may help to explain why the book is "written too hard."

Its power depends upon a doubleness of perspective. It can be read as a narrative of high excitements and descriptive flourish.

The scene is rendered with fierce, exotic particularity, as if to force the reader into a sensuous participation in Lawrence's experience. Details are thrust out with brutal, even shocking intent; for in this kind of narrative the reader must not be allowed to settle into any comfort of expectation. The bleakness of the desert, the sudden killing of an Arab soldier, the horror of an assault upon helpless Turkish prisoners, the nomadic grandeur of a man like Auda, the nightmare detachment of the Deraa incident and then, at increasingly frequent intervals, the turnings toward aloneness, the merciless guerrilla raids Lawrence conducted against his self—these and a thousand other bits comprise the agitated surface of the book.

Yet at every crucial point the writing, through wrenchings of metaphor and perspective, pulls attention away from the surface. It turns toward something else, at first a mere scattering of sentiments and then the growing and molding "I" of the book: an "I" that is not at all the conventional first-person narrator but an approximation of a figure who comes into being, like Melville's Ishmael, through the writer's struggle to write his book. It is the emergence of this self which keeps *The Seven Pillars of Wisdom* from being a mere recital of excitements and horrors.

Because he tries to maintain an almost intolerable pitch of intensity, Lawrence seems repeatedly to fall into a state of exhaustion, and the book to crumble into a series of set pieces, sections detailing a more or less complete incident. By the nature of the set piece, these sections are detachable and can be read as self-contained accounts of human exhaustion. Being detachable, they are so packed with nervous bravado and ambitious phrasing as to call attention to their life *as a form,* a series of compositional feats matching the feats of Lawrence's adventure. Yet through this accumulation of set pieces there recurs the struggle of a self in formation; and therein the book gains a kind of unity.

To an age that usually takes its prose plain, Lawrence's style is likely to seem mannered. Unquestionably there are passages that fail through a surplus of effort; passages that betray the hot breath of hysteria; passages that contain more sensibility than Lawrence could handle or justify. But it is dangerous to dismiss such writing simply because we have been trained to suspect the grand. Lawrence was deliberately trying to achieve large-scale effects, a rhetoric of action and passion that may almost be called baroque: the style pursuing the thought. And while the reader has every reason to discriminate among these effects, it would be dull to condemn Lawrence merely for their presence.

Lawrence strives for a style of thrust and shock, and then, by way of balance, for passages of extreme sensibility. He often uses words with a deliberate obliqueness or off-meaning, so as to charge them with strangeness and potential life. The common meaning of these key words is neither fully respected nor wholly violated; but twisted, sometimes into freshness, sometimes into mere oddity. All of this followed from conscious planning: "I find that my fifth writing . . . of a sentence makes it more shapely, pithier, stranger than it was. Without that twist of strangeness no one would feel an individuality, a differentness, behind the phrase."

It is a coercive prose, as it is a coercive book, meant to shake the reader into a recognition of what is possible on this earth. No one can end it with emotions of repose or resolution; there is no pretense at conciliatory sublimation. The result, throughout, is a tensing of nerves and sensibility, a series of broken reflections upon human incompleteness. It is a modern book.

For Lawrence there was now to be one more significant entry into public life. Within a few months after the signing of the Versailles treaty, it became clear that he had been entirely right about the Middle East, and the massed heads of the French and British governments entirely wrong. By 1920 the British were pouring millions of pounds into Iraq in order to suppress Arab insurgents; the French were bombarding Damascus and spreading hatred with each discharge of their cannon. Soon the British decided they would have to modify their policy, which had been neither effective nor economical, and when Winston Churchill took over the Colonial Office in 1921 he offered Lawrence a post as advisor on Middle East affairs.

Lawrence now joined in political conferences in Cairo and for a brief time returned to the desert, where he helped work out a *modus vivendi* between the British and Arabs. A greater measure of autonomy was granted the Arabs in Iraq; the British army but not the RAF withdrawn; Feisal allowed to assume the throne; and peace momentarily restored. Lawrence said that justice had finally been done, but the Arabs, wishing complete independence, took a less sanguine view.

His labor in composing *The Seven Pillars of Wisdom* and then the interval of service under Churchill had distracted Lawrence from himself. Now that both were done and nothing appeared to absorb or consume him, there could be no evading the central fact of his postwar years: *that, in his freedom, he no longer knew how or why to live.* It was the problem faced by many sensitive men of his generation, and Lawrence, who more than most had earned the right to speak of it, could find no solution, no way out.

He was physically wearied, morally depleted, a man without the strength of true conviction. He had run through life too fast, and now had to face the cruel problem of how to continue living though his life was done. The ordinary ways of middle-class England he could not settle into; the literary world, which he admired to excess, made him wildly uncomfortable; and politics seemed dirty, mean, a mug's game. Religion as dogma or institution left him as cold as in the past, yet there burned in him a desire for some enlarging selfless purpose he could neither find nor name. Lord Halifax was surely right when he said that "some deep religious impulse moved him . . . some craving for the perfect synthesis of thought and action which alone could satisfy his test of ultimate truth and his conception of life's purpose."

Perhaps Lawrence's trouble was simply that of a man who, at the end of a great adventure, returns home and finds it impossible to slide into quiet and routine. (Some years later he would choose to translate the *Odyssey,* a book about a hero whose return is endlessly delayed.) Whatever the reason, his life was painfully distraught. He would walk the streets of London for nights on end, lost in moodiness and self-examination. He ate poorly, carelessly. His home in Oxford, palled by the death of two brothers in the war, was unbearable. A mist of affection separated him from his mother. After his return from Paris, she has remembered, he would sit motionless as stone for entire mornings. In London he found new friends, many of them famous men, to whom he could occasionally burst out in oblique confession; but good will and understanding were not enough.

"The worst thing about the war generation of introspects," he wrote several years later to the novelist Henry Williamson, "is that they can't keep off their blooming selves." Caught up as he was with his "blooming self," Lawrence would lapse into bouts of self-pity and puerile shows of vanity. It is easy enough to dislike and judge the Lawrence of these days. But there were times when he expressed with a rare clarity and poignance, the sense of drift he shared with so many of his contemporaries.

"What more?" he wrote to Eric Kennington in 1922. "Nothing. I'm bored stiff: and very tired, and a little ill, and sorry to see how mean some people I wanted to respect have grown." A year later, after he had joined the RAF, he wrote to Lionel Curtis: "It's terrible to hold myself voluntarily here: and yet I want to stay here till it no longer hurts me. . . . Do you think there have been many lay monks of my persuasion? One used to think that such frames of mind would have perished with the age of religion: and yet here they rise up, purely secular."

Somewhat later Lawrence wrote in a letter to Robert Graves: "You see, I know how false the praise is: how little the reality compared with the legend: how much luck: how little merit. Praise makes a man sick, if it is ignorant praise." And when Graves remarked that there were two selves in Lawrence, a Bedouin self "longing for the bareness, simplicity, harshness of the desert—that state of mind of which the desert is a symbol—and the over-civilized European self," Lawrence answered: "The two selves, you see, are mutually destructive. So I fall between them into the nihilism which cannot find, in being, even a false god in which to believe." Later still, in a note to an unknown correspondent, probably in 1929, Lawrence wrote:

I have done with politics, I have done with the Orient, and I have done with intellectuality. O, Lord, I am so tired! I want so much to lie down and sleep and die. Die is best because there is no reveille. I want to forget my sins and the world's weariness.

And in the early thirties Lawrence told a friend that he felt himself to be "an extinct volcano, a closed oyster, and I must discourage treasure-hunters from the use of tin-openers. . . ."

Taken from over a decade of Lawrence's life and grouped together in isolation, such passages unavoidably form a melodramatic picture. They omit the plateaus of ordinariness which fill the bulk of any life. They omit the moments of commonplace satisfaction. But that they are faithful to what Lawrence felt most deeply, that they show the most important side of his postwar life, seems beyond doubt. Through these years Lawrence suffered from a loss of *élan*, a sense of the void, the terror of purposelessness. He suffered from a nihilism which revealed itself as a draining of those tacit impulsions, those root desires and values which make men continue to live.

This condition was by no means unique to Lawrence. When Hemingway wrote his stories, with their variations on the theme of *nada;* when Pirandello drove skepticism to intolerable extremes in his plays; when so somber a figure as Max Weber could speak of the "disenchantment of the world" and the likelihood that "not summer's bloom lies ahead of us, but rather a polar night of icy darkness and hardness"—they, too, were confronting the sense of the void, the sense that human life had entered a phase of prolonged crisis in which all of its sustaining norms had lost their authority. Lawrence reached these feelings in a unique way, through the desert of Arabia rather than the trenches of France. But once this strain of the exotic is put aside, there remains a common lot, a shared dilemma.

It is this Lawrence—the hero who turns into a bewildered man suffering the aftermath of heroism—who now seems closest to us. Had Lawrence simply returned to the wholesome life of an English gentleman, writing neither *The Seven Pillars of Wisdom* nor the remarkable letters to Lionel Curtis, he would still have been noteworthy. Such a man, however, could hardly have captured the imagination of reflective people as the actual Lawrence did. His wartime record was remarkable, the basis for all that was to come; without it he might have been just another young man afflicted with postwar malaise. But what finally draws one to Lawrence, making him seem not merely an exceptional figure but a representative man of our century, is his courage and vulnerability in bearing the burden of consciousness. "One used to think that such frames of mind would have perished with the age of religion: and yet here they rise up, purely secular."

Tensions of the kind Lawrence suffered during the years after the war cannot be borne indefinitely. In August 1922, as if to wipe out all he had once been, Lawrence joined the Royal Air

Force as an ordinary recruit under the name of John Hume Ross. Six months later, when his identity became known, he was forced to leave but allowed to join the regular army. There he remained until 1925, when his pleas and the intervention of powerful friends persuaded Air Marshal Trenchard to accept him again, this time under the name of T. E. Shaw. Until his death in 1935 Lawrence served the RAF as clerk and mechanic, in England and India.

For a man to whom power, fame, and money were within reach, Lawrence's decision to bury himself in the ranks was an extraordinary one; for a man who had fought all his life against the force of his own ambition, it was a climax of self-mortification, an act of symbolic suicide. No single explanation can account for thirteen years spent in a military whose spirit was at war with his passion for freedom, whose discipline chafed and humiliated him. All the explanations together are also unsatisfactory, except perhaps as they come to an absolute need to break from his old self, the heroic Lawrence and the helpless Lawrence both.

"Honestly," he wrote to Robert Graves,

it was a necessary step, forced on me by an inclination toward ground-level: by a despairing hope that I'd find myself on common ground with men . . . by an itch to make myself ordinary in a mob of likes: also I'm broke. . . . It's going to be a brain-sleep, and I'll come out of it less odd than I went in: or at least less odd in other men's eyes.

And in a preface that he wrote for the catalogue to Eric Kennington's exhibit of Arab portraits, there is a brief but perhaps deeper statement of motive: "Sometimes we wish for chains as a variety."

There were other, slightly different explanations. "Partly, I came here to eat dirt till its taste is normal to me. . . ." Less candidly, he told some people he had joined the RAF to insure himself a regular income. To Lionel Curtis, who brought out his metaphysical side, he wrote:

Free-will I've tried, and rejected: authority I've rejected (not obedience, for that is my present effort, to find equality only in subordination. It is domination whose taste I have been cloyed with): action I've rejected: and the intellectual life: and the receptive senses: and the battle of wits. . . .

Somehow he managed to live through the torments of basic training, for which he was ten years and one war too old. He learned to claw his way past the obscenities that filled the barracks where he slept. He found odd sensations of pleasure and pain in breaking himself to obey men he knew to be unworthy of his obedience. And at times there was a rough companionship, a peace of sorts. Today we would call it an "adjustment."

But again: why did he do it? To stamp forever upon his conscience the need for refusing power; to put himself beyond the possibility of taking power; to find some version of the monasticism he craved; to make up for the guilts that lingered from the war; to return to the commonest of common life; to punish himself and test again his capacity for accepting pain; to distinguish himself in suffering—truth lies in all these but in none alone. We should not sentimentalize. Except for the months of basic training, Lawrence did not feel himself to be suffering acutely. He was happy or, if not happy, then peaceful for long stretches of time. Whether he was stationed in England or Karachi did not seem to matter much: he was the same in one place as another. Still, it would also be sentimental to forget that he had surrendered, had accepted his dispossession:

I was an Irish nobody. I did something. It was a failure. And I became an Irish nobody.

Throughout the years in service there were small pleasures, bits of compensation. Like a character in Conrad, he achieved a severe responsibility in his daily work, the "job-sense" that sees one through. ("One had but to watch him scrubbing a barrack-room table," recalled a corporal from the tank corps, "to realize that no table had been scrubbed just in that way before.") He found physical pleasure and a sense of freedom in racing his motorcycle across the narrow English roads. He made lasting friends in both the army and RAF, with whom he lived on terms of intermittent ease. He made friends, as well, with some of the greatest writers of the day: Bernard Shaw, E. M. Forster, Thomas Hardy. (Hardy he venerated with a filial emotion which is one of the most simply "human" of his qualities.) He tried his hand at critical essays, which are neither quite first-rate nor merely commonplace: a fine one on Landor, a respectable one on H. G. Wells. He turned the *Odyssey* into firm, often pungent